*In the Shadow
of the Giant:
Thomas Wolfe*

Edited by
Mary Aswell Doll
and Clara Stites

OHIO

UNIVERSITY

PRESS

ATHENS

*In the Shadow
of the Giant:*
Thomas Wolfe

CORRESPONDENCE OF

EDWARD C. ASWELL AND

ELIZABETH NOWELL

1949–1958

*

Ohio University Press books are printed on acid-free paper ∞

The letters of Edward C. Aswell and Elizabeth Nowell are printed by permission
of the Estate of Thomas Wolfe, Paul Gitlin, Administrator, C. T. A.
and by permission of the Houghton Library, Harvard University.

The quotations from *Sophie's Choice,* copyright © 1979 by William Styron,
reprinted by permission of Random House, Inc.

Designed by Laury A. Egan

Library of Congress Cataloging-in-Publication Data

Aswell, Edward C. (Edward Campbell), 1900 – 1958.
In the shadow of the giant, Thomas Wolfe : correspondence of
Edward C. Aswell and Elizabeth Nowell, 1949 – 1958 /
edited by Mary Aswell Doll and Clara Stites.

Includes bibliographical references and index.
ISBN 0-8214-0904-2 (alk. paper)
1. Wolfe, Thomas, 1900 – 1938 — Friends and associates.
2. Wolfe, Thomas, 1900 – 1938 — Correspondence.
3. Aswell, Edward C. (Edward Campbell), 1900 – 1958 — Correspondence.
4. Nowell, Elizabeth — Correspondence.
5. Novelists, American — 20th century — Friends and associates.
6. Editors — United States — Correspondence.
7. Literary agents — United States — Correspondence.

I. Nowell, Elizabeth. II. Doll, Mary Aswell. III. Stites, Clara.
IV. Title. V. Title: In the shadow of the giant.

PS3545.O337Z616   1988   813'.52 – dc19   88 – 12486

"But who only has seen a giant on
the earth has never known him."

Notebooks 1, p. 263, from Wolfe's
pocket notebook 6
Wednesday, November 28, 1928

Contents

Acknowledgments   ix

Introduction   xi

Chapter One
"Between us, we'll do our best . . . ."
ASWELL, APRIL 7, 1949   3

Chapter Two
"I dont think devotion to *any*body is worth
killing yourself over."
NOWELL, FEBRUARY, 1950   31

Chapter Three
"You are not free to reveal my confidences."
ASWELL, APRIL 14, 1951   55

Chapter Four
"Wheels within wheels. But maybe it will
all get us and Tom somewhere some day."
NOWELL, SEPTEMBER 11, 1952   97

Chapter Five
"The Terry business becomes more shocking
and more complicated all the time."
ASWELL, SEPTEMBER 29, 1953   129

Chapter Six
"So maybe I should walk right up to
the lion's jaws and say my say."
NOWELL, FEBRUARY 22, 1954   169

Chapter Seven
"If I had the command of all Tom's adjectives,
I still could not praise you enough . . . ."
ASWELL, MARCH 23, 1955   187

Chapter Eight
"I trust you more than any living editor
and want to 'string along with you',
as Tom used to say."
NOWELL, JUNE 26, 1956   205

Chapter Nine
"You can count on us completely . . . ."
ASWELL, APRIL 11, 1957   221

Chapter Ten
"I'm working against time and death more
unmistakably than anyone ever did."
NOWELL, JUNE 20, 1958   229

Epilogue   249

Index   251

Plates   *follow page* 170

Acknowledgments

IT is with gratitude that we acknowledge the many people who helped us during the four years we worked on this book. For information about Aswell's career and life: Elizabeth Alson, the late Mary Louise Aswell, David Donald, Helen Pell, and Gray Williams. Special thanks go to Bill Cutler, for his recollections about Aswell and for his editorial suggestions along the way. For information about Nowell's career and life: the Bryn Mawr College Alumni Office, William Bond, Nancy Hale Bowers, James Boyer, Gwen Jassinoff Campbell, Annie Laurie Crawford, Daniel Fuchs, the late Albert Halper and his wife Lorna, Frances Lanza, Maxim Lieber, Joanne Marshall Mauldin and the many childhood and college friends of Nowell who shared their memories of her with the editors. Thanks, too, to Pearl and Dan Bell, for providing bed and board, to Nancy Wardwell for her friendship and to our families for helping in so many ways.

We also wish to acknowledge the following: Leslie Field, whose idea it was in the first place; Paul Gitlin, administrator of the Wolfe Estate and helpful throughout; the staff of the Houghton Library Reading Room; Richard Kennedy, for his advice and loving friendship to Nowell and to us; Aldo Magi, who meant it when he said, "Call on me for anything at anytime"; Louis Rubin, for his insightful critique; and Duane Schneider, for his steadfast encouragement.

Finally, we wish to thank the anonymous reviewers of our manuscript in its draft and final stages for their constructive and thorough comments.

Introduction

In the Shadow of the Giant

*

EDWARD C. ASWELL, Thomas Wolfe's last editor, and Elizabeth Nowell, Wolfe's literary agent and first biographer, met Wolfe early in their careers and were in one way or another involved with his life for the remainder of theirs. Although Wolfe died in 1938, Aswell and Nowell continued to think about him, talk about him, and write about him for the next twenty years, until their own deaths in 1958. They wrote to each other sometimes twice a day, sometimes in the middle of the night, often to excess. Their ostensible topic was business: how to produce more Wolfe publications out of the posthumous material in the estate, how to generate income for Wolfe's family through the estate, how to "get Wolfe right." Their letters to each other reflect a commitment — call it an obsession — to keep the memory of Wolfe's greatness alive. But through their work together they recaptured some of the vitality of a past shared with Wolfe. The correspondence between Aswell and Nowell thus offers a fascinating look at a relationship between two people living in the shadow of a giant.

Aswell's letters at first do not reveal the extent of Wolfe's influence on his life. Signing his letters "Cordially" or "Best as always," he appears distanced both from Nowell and from the subject he shared with Nowell — Wolfe. Nevertheless, Aswell's personality unfolds over the years to reveal a man of surprising contradictions. Devoted to Wolfe's work, almost sanctifying it, he yet had dared to tamper with the posthumous material, making extensive changes in phrasing and structuring of the original text. Rather than keeping the postcards Wolfe had sent him from the West, Aswell had given them away, forgetting to whom or for what reason. Reputed to be a forbidding man, with strong and often stubborn convictions, Aswell could be persuaded to reverse opinions which he had expressed earlier in absolute terms. Still, when outside forces challenged his control of the Wolfe Estate, Aswell would hold firm, often in the belief that academic scholarship (which he abhorred) would distort the Wolfe he knew. These and other contradictions form a dynamic in Aswell's correspondence with Nowell.

Edward McCoy Aswell, son of Carrie Campbell and McCoy Campbell Aswell, was born in Nashville, Tennessee, on October 9, 1900, six days after Thomas Wolfe's birth in Asheville, North Carolina. Although he did not meet Wolfe until 1937 and could not have read his work until the late twenties, Aswell felt a deep kinship with him. Both men were from the South, both attended Harvard during the early twenties, and by the thirties Aswell considered Wolfe America's greatest living writer.

Like Wolfe, the young Aswell was something of a prodigy. When he was three years old, he gave the welcome address at his church's Christmas service; at seven, he delivered a speech called "Roosevelt on the Bible" for President Roosevelt's visit to Nashville. At twelve, he graduated from grade school with a 98 average. Four years later in 1916 — the same year Wolfe entered the University of North Carolina at Chapel Hill — Aswell graduated from Hume-Fogg High School. As the son of a draftsman who earned only $2,600 a year, Aswell delayed college for five years until he could pay for his own education. He went to work as a salesman for Carter Shoe Company in Nashville, then for its allied company, Goding Shoe, in Chicago. There he attended night school at Northwestern University for two years. But his heart was set on Harvard, "whose prestige," he wrote in his admissions application, "will in some degree attach itself to me as a graduate of the institution."

In 1922, Aswell was accepted to Harvard on partial scholarship, intending to major in business. Instead, he majored in history and literature and, as a four-year scholarship student, graduated magna cum laude in 1926, three years after Wolfe left Cambridge for a teaching position at New York University. During his senior year, Aswell devised a house plan which reorganized undergraduate living. He also changed his middle name from McCoy to Campbell and chaired the editorial board of the *Harvard Crimson*. According to a letter in his dossier, Aswell's *Crimson* editorials were "the best that paper has ever produced in the opinion of the older members of the Faculty." The letter also said of Aswell, "He is better — I should say — in positions where his success is not dependent on the personal impression he makes on first interviews as his manner is rather stiff — that is, he is not an easy 'mixer'."

After graduation from Harvard, Aswell married Anna Vera Vaughn in 1927 and spent four years as assistant editor of *Forum* magazine. In 1931 he joined the staff of the *Atlantic Monthly,* where he met Mary Louise White, to whom he became engaged after his divorce from Vaughn. When Aswell announced his engagement, both he and Mary Lou were fired by their boss, Ellery Sedgwick. Married for the second time January 1, 1935,

Aswell became assistant editor at Harper and Brothers. Mary Lou was offered a position with *Harper's Bazaar,* but when she became pregnant, she gave up full-time editing to assume the duties of wife and mother; Edward Duncan was born in 1936, and Mary Elizabeth in 1940. Through Mary Lou, Aswell came to know Elizabeth Nowell, who had been an undergraduate with Mary Lou at Bryn Mawr.

Unlike Aswell, Nowell reveals her personality immediately in the correspondence. Her style, chatty and informal, sets up a perfect foil to Aswell's style. She signed her letters "Goombye" or "Love." References to her children's chicken pox or the neighbor's dogs punctuate her insightful and often impudent comments about the publishing world in general or Wolfe in particular. Her letters were written rapidly, usually late at night, sometimes with little reverence for accepted punctuation and spelling. She relished debating the past with Aswell and revealed a skill for argumentation and interpretation. She knew how to tell a good story; she wanted desperately to get the facts right. She also cared deeply about her work, sometimes to the point of extreme anxiety. While Aswell's interest in Wolfe was legendary, almost mythical, Nowell's was historical and personal. Because their perspectives ran counter to each other and because each was strong willed, sparks often flew on the pages. But throughout the years, both expressed extraordinary warmth and admiration — for each other and for Thomas Wolfe.

Elizabeth Howland Nowell was born on June 10, 1904, in South Dartmouth, Massachusetts, the second child and first daughter of Clara Earle Howland and Joseph Cornell Nowell. From 1911 to 1920 she attended Friends Academy in New Bedford, Massachusetts, establishing an early literary reputation with her essay "Advantages of Enlistment," for which she won four prizes. According to the local newspaper, Nowell had only a few days to write the essay. Hastily she wrote 550 words, "then came the task of boiling down what was already a concise handling of the subject, and which Miss Nowell accomplished in 399 words,"[1] one word under the 400-word limit.

From 1920 to 1922, Nowell attended the Ethel Walker School in Simsbury, Connecticut, then went on to Bryn Mawr College as a New England States Matriculation Scholar. Her Bryn Mawr transcript includes a note: "Honorable, reliable — unusually intelligent and lithe spirited — not essentially a leader — Very pleasant disposition — 4th in class of 24."

Graduating from Bryn Mawr in 1926, Nowell moved to New York,

---

[1] *New Bedford* [Massachusetts] *Standard,* 1919.

took classes at Columbia University, and in 1928 applied unsuccessfully for an editorial position at Charles Scribner's Sons on Fifth Avenue. "No women," they told her, so she went immediately downstairs to the bookstore and got a sales job in the juvenile department. By that spring, Nowell was assistant to Miss S. Elizabeth DeVoy, associate editor for the Scribner's art department. There, Nowell met Thomas Wolfe, who had come to see the first printed sample of *Look Homeward, Angel*.[2]

Nowell stayed at Scribner's until 1933, working chiefly on the editorial staff of *Scribner's Magazine* and reading occasional book manuscripts for Maxwell Perkins. During this time, Perkins selected a number of shorter pieces from Wolfe's manuscripts to be edited for *Scribner's Magazine*. Nowell did not edit these stories, but she apparently typed some of the edited manuscripts and learned to read Wolfe's handwriting. Her work for Perkins and her ability to decipher Wolfe stood her in good stead when she left Scribner's to join the literary agency of Maxim Lieber.[3]

Wolfe, concerned because his stories had been published only in *Scribner's Magazine,* wanted to find other magazines interested in his work. When Perkins suggested Nowell, Wolfe took several sections of manuscript to her at the Lieber agency. From *K 19*, Nowell and Lieber selected the "Boom Town" chapter, which was eventually sold to the *American Mercury* and selected for the *O. Henry Memorial Award Prize Stories of 1934*. Although Wolfe complained about the $192 paid by the *American Mercury,* the publication of "Boom Town" marked the real beginning of his relationship with Elizabeth Nowell.

In 1934, Nowell left Lieber to start her own agency at 114 East 56th Street.[4] Wolfe, Nancy Hale, Eugene Joffee, and several other Lieber writers went with her. From 1934 to 1938, Nowell spent much of her time editing and selling Wolfe's short fiction. According to Richard S. Kennedy and to Nowell's own accounts, she began reading through Wolfe's manuscripts selecting pieces that could stand on their own as stories, until "by mid-1935 about half of the items that now make up *From Death to*

[2] Elizabeth Nowell, "Wolfe and Perkins As I Knew Them," an unfinished, unpublished manuscript, the Nowell files, Houghton Library.

[3] Nowell said she did not actually "decipher" Wolfe's handwriting so much as she "intuited" what the undulations and lines on a page might mean (Elizabeth Nowell, ed., *The Letters of Thomas Wolfe* [New York: Scribner, 1956], p. xv; hereafter cited as *Letters*).

[4] In several of her letters, Nowell said she left Lieber to start her own agency with Edith Howard Walton. Although no further record of their partnership seems to exist, Walton was also a Bryn Mawr graduate (1925) and, like Aswell, had been an editor for the *Forum* (1928–33). Walton died in 1975.

Morning had been sold to periodicals" by Nowell.[5] She helped prepare *The Story of a Novel* for publication in the *Saturday Review of Literature* and later in book form by Scribner's. She worked with Wolfe to whittle down and sell "The Bell Remembered," "I Have a Thing to Tell You," "Mr. Malone," "The Child by Tiger," "The Lost Boy," and other stories. As Wolfe scholars Kennedy, David H. Donald, and James D. Boyer have all pointed out, Wolfe learned from her editing and gradually began to shape his own writing more carefully.

*

BY THE TIME Wolfe made his break with Scribner's in 1937, he and Nowell were close friends. As Wolfe turned away from Perkins, he relied more and more on Nowell, using her office address for his business and personal mail, seeking her assistance with a myriad of personal matters, and turning to her for encouragement about his work.

Wolfe mailed his final letter about leaving Scribner's to Perkins in January 1937, then spent the summer near Asheville, North Carolina. In August he made a series of phone calls in search of a new publisher but met with no success. After his return to New York in early September, Wolfe kept almost entirely to himself. According to Nowell, he would approach no other publishers, nor would he let her do it for him. As a result, it was not until November that Edward Aswell learned from Bernard De Voto, one of Wolfe's severest critics, that Wolfe had left Scribner's. Skeptical, he called Nowell for confirmation, which she gave. She also arranged for Aswell and Wolfe to meet on November 11, 1937.

By all accounts, Aswell and Wolfe liked each other immediately. Aswell expressed his admiration for Wolfe's work — he had read everything Wolfe had ever published — and impulsively offered a generous advance on Wolfe's next novel, sight unseen. In December, Wolfe accepted Aswell's offer, then spent Christmas at the Aswell home in Chappaqua, New York. In honor of the occasion, Mary Lou arranged a Christmas feast to correspond with Wolfe's literary account of festive holidays. It was, Wolfe wrote to Nowell, "a swell Christmas . . . the best one I have had since I was a kid."[6]

Wolfe finally signed the Harper contract on December 31, 1937. The following spring was "one of the happiest and most productive periods

[5] Richard S. Kennedy, *Beyond Love and Loyalty: The Letters of Thomas Wolfe and Elizabeth Nowell* (Chapel Hill: University of North Carolina Press, 1983), p. xiv.
[6] *Letters,* p. 696.

of Wolfe's entire life."[7] Wolfe was working hard on his next book, preparing a prospectus for Aswell, and gradually adding more and more material to it from his piles of manuscript. Generally, Wolfe wrote for most of the day, then spent his evenings with Nowell or Aswell. Wolfe's secretary, Gwen Jassinoff, usually worked until about 6 p.m. at Wolfe's apartment and remembers the visits by Nowell or Aswell. Nowell would come in and stretch out on the day bed with her feet up and pillows behind her. Then she and Wolfe would talk, always about business, while Wolfe paced up and down the room. When Aswell came, it was most often to go out to dinner with Wolfe. The two men would then spend an evening in good talk, mostly about Wolfe's work.

In May, Wolfe was invited to speak at Purdue University and used the invitation as an occasion to plan a two- to three-week vacation in the West. Intending to store his manuscript at Harper while he was away, Wolfe began organizing the chapters of *The Web and the Rock* and preparing a thirteen-page outline of the book. On May 6, he wrote Aswell about the manuscript, saying that it would require at least "a good year of steady uninterrupted work, to complete the job" and adding, "I do not believe that I am in need of just the same kind of editorial help at this moment as Mr. Perkins so generously and unselfishly gave me in 1933, 1934. . . . It is, of course, comforting and of immense value to me to know that when I do need help it will be generously and patiently given. At any rate, I hope that is the program for the present, and that you can take care of the manuscript for me until I get back."[8]

Wolfe never did get back to New York. After a successful visit to Purdue, he continued westward to Portland, spent two weeks touring the national parks, then traveled to Seattle and Victoria and Vancouver, B.C., and back to Seattle. On July 11, Wolfe was hospitalized with pneumonia at Firlawns, a private sanatorium just north of Seattle. In early August, he was moved to Providence Hospital in Seattle so that x-rays of his lungs could be taken. By early September, he was suffering violent headaches and periods of irrationality. On the advice of the doctors, Wolfe's sister Mabel, who had come to Seattle to be with Wolfe during his illness, took him by train to Johns Hopkins Hospital in Baltimore. Wolfe died there on September 15, 1938, of tuberculosis of the brain.

Both Nowell and Aswell saw Wolfe in Baltimore. Nowell went to Wolfe's funeral in Asheville, then returned to New York, profoundly depressed. She continued her loyalty to Wolfe, overseeing magazine publication of

[7] Elizabeth Nowell, *Thomas Wolfe: A Biography* (New York: Doubleday, 1960), p. 407.
[8] *Letters,* pp. 757ff.

A Western Journal and "The Party at Jack's" and attempting to sell "No More Rivers" for magazine publication. At Aswell's request she also annotated Wolfe's outline of his manuscript, identifying chapters and noting which sections were in rough or final form.

Aswell continued to struggle with the "mess" of Wolfe's manuscript. For the next three years he buried himself in the task of bringing Wolfe back to life through the posthumous works: *The Web and the Rock* (1939), *You Can't Go Home Again* (1940), and *The Hills Beyond* (1941). In a thirty-five page "Note" appended to *The Hills Beyond,* Aswell explained his editing problems and procedures. However, further study by Richard S. Kennedy and David H. Donald shows that Aswell underplayed the extent to which he edited and added to Wolfe's text.

In June 1941, Nowell married Naval Commander Charles Brush Perkins, and spent the war years following his ship up and down the East Coast. She and Charles Perkins had two daughters: Clara Howland, born in 1942, and Edna Brush, in 1944. She also did some writing of her own, publishing several short stories under the pen names Joseph Penniman and Sarah Grinnell.[9] After the war, Nowell helped her husband raise sheep on his farm in Wakefield, Rhode Island, and stayed in touch with her New York friends, including Perkins and Aswell.

Even with Wolfe dead and his final three books published, Nowell and Aswell continued their interest in him. In 1945, when Maxwell Perkins began collecting Wolfe's letters for publication, Nowell sent him all of the letters Wolfe had written to her. When Maxwell Perkins died in 1947, she wrote to Wolfe's family, urging them to appoint Aswell as administrator of the estate.[10] Nowell was divorced in 1948 and returned with her daughters to her mother's home in Massachusetts. There, she resumed her work as literary agent for Nancy Hale and later for Vardis Fisher and,

[9] At least two Penniman stories, "I Wish I Was Back in Sugar Loaf" and "In the Minute before It Would Strike," were sold to McCall's for *Redbook Magazine.* The first Grinnell story was published in *Harper's Bazaar* in 1938. Other stories appeared in *Yankee Magazine* and the *Toronto Star. The O. Henry Memorial Award Prize Stories of 1943* (Garden City, New York: The Country Life Press, 1943) included the Grinnell story "Standby," which also appeared in the January 1943 issue of *Harper's Bazaar.*

[10] Nowell had been instrumental in Aswell's selection as the administrator of Wolfe's estate after Perkins. But interestingly, when considering who might take Perkins's place at Scribner's, Nowell thought of Mary Louise Aswell before she thought of Ed Aswell. Mary Lou became fiction editor of *Harper's Bazaar* in 1944, one of the early editors to recognize and publish (among others) Eudora Welty, Carson McCullers, Jean Stafford, and Truman Capote. Nowell dismissed the idea of Mary Lou as a Scribner's editor, however, on the grounds that a woman would not be taken seriously in the book publishing world.

during the period covered by these letters, corresponded with Aswell and many others, collected and edited Wolfe's letters (Scribner, 1956), and wrote his biography (Doubleday, 1960).

Aswell, in the interim before this correspondence began, also changed jobs and divorced. An offer in 1947 from McGraw-Hill to head up Whittlesey House, their trade book division, enticed him away from Harper. He became a vice president at McGraw-Hill, where he was expected to inaugurate a fiction list for a company known primarily for textbooks. That year also brought his third marriage, to Knyvett Lee Albertson, and his appointment as administrator to the Wolfe Estate. Despite Aswell's work at Harper (with authors Richard Wright, Kay Boyle, and Fannie Hurst) and at McGraw-Hill (with authors Catherine Marshall and Taylor Caldwell) and despite his involvement with the Yale Committee in publishing Boswell's journals, Thomas Wolfe was never far from Aswell's mind. "The greatest man I have had the good fortune to know," he wrote, "the most singularly honest intellectually, and the most lovable, was one whose whole life was a continuous process of self-education. All his books eloquently proclaim the fact. Of course he was a genius, too. His name was Thomas Wolfe." [11]

*

By 1955, Nowell's collection of Wolfe's letters was nearly ready for publication, and the biography was well under way. But in July of 1955, Nowell found that she must undergo an operation for breast cancer. Meanwhile Aswell was having his own troubles at McGraw-Hill. In June of 1956, he was fired from his position there and spent the next two months searching for another job, finally becoming an editor at Doubleday. The following May, Aswell's wife died tragically in a fall. During the next year, Aswell described himself as exhausted and under terrible pressure. Nowell, her health rapidly failing in spite of a series of operations in Chicago and New York, continued working on the biography, explaining to Aswell that she was "working against time and death." Nowell was in the hospital for much of the summer of 1958, and it was there that she finished the biography, mailing home revisions and sections of the final chapter for her fifteen-year-old daughter Clara to type and mail to Aswell.

Nowell died at New York Memorial Hospital on August 24, 1958. Aswell received the completed manuscript soon after that and wrote to tell Clara that "the original manuscript of your mother's biography of

[11] *The Quindecennial Report,* (Boston: Merrymount Press, 1941), p. 12.

Thomas Wolfe is here, so you can rest easy in your mind knowing that it is safe. . . . whatever needs to be done I shall do, with complete devotion to your mother's purposes, and with the expectation of publishing the book next year."[12] But on November 5, 1958, Aswell died suddenly of a heart attack, bringing to a close his twenty-year commitment to Thomas Wolfe.

Between 1949 and her death in 1958, Nowell filed all her correspondence in orange-backed cardboard boxes that she kept on a shelf in her bedroom closet. Those files, from which this manuscript evolved, were sent to Houghton Library at Harvard just before Nowell's death. Today the files, bMS Am 1883.3 (157), remain very much as they were, many of them still in their original boxes, each box dated by Nowell on its spine. Within each file, the letters Nowell received and carbons of her own letters are divided alphabetically, but they have never been individually catalogued.

We, the daughters of Aswell and Nowell, never knew Wolfe, nor were we aware of the full extent of his influence upon our parents. Only now, in preparing this selection, can either of us begin to understand. For twenty years after Wolfe's death, our parents lived as if Wolfe lived inside their heads, so devotedly did they keep at their task. Aswell revealed things to Nowell no one else knew; yet he did not reveal all that he knew about the editing of the posthumous novels. Nowell depended on Aswell as on no one else; yet she worried about the constraints he might place on what she said about Wolfe.

In editing this book, we agreed that we could not present the complete correspondence. There are, quite simply, too many letters, many of them covering material either of little general interest or already well known. Instead, we have selected those letters which illumine four major themes of the correspondence: promotion of Wolfe, protection of Wolfe's reputation and stature, untold stories or gossip surrounding Wolfe and portraying an era, and the relationship between Aswell and Nowell. In handling the actual text of the letters we have made no corrections in grammar, punctuation, or spelling except when required for clarity, and, where possible, identifying in brackets the people they mention. In Nowell's letters, stylistic inconsistencies such as the lack of apostrophes in contractions often reflect the speed or emotion with which she was writing. Because of this and because Nowell's style contrasts so tellingly with Aswell's, we have retained her original punctuation and spelling.

We have, however, deleted sections of letters when these were repetitious

---

[12] Letter in collection of Clara Stites.

or when they strayed from the major themes of our focus. We also have not included every answer to every letter, sometimes because the replying letter is not in the file, sometimes because it adds little that is new to the correspondence. In other cases Aswell and Nowell phoned each other, leaving no written record. We have organized the letters chronologically, one year per chapter except in chapters 4 and 5 where a huge amount of material on John S. Terry led us to combine 1952 with the first seven months of 1953.

Mary Aswell Doll
Clara Stites

In the Shadow
of the Giant:
Thomas Wolfe

Chapter One

"Between us, we'll do our best . . . ."

ASWELL, APRIL 7, 1949

*

Wʜɪʟᴇ he was administrator of the Wolfe Estate, Maxwell E. Perkins had begun collecting Wolfe's letters in preparation for publication by Scribner's. After Perkins's death in 1947, Scribner's editor John Hall Wheelock needed a new editor for the letters. Elizabeth Nowell was the logical choice. She had been both friend and agent for Wolfe, and now, recently divorced and living with her two small children and her mother, she was looking for work. Edward C. Aswell, administrator of the estate since 1947 and Wolfe's last editor, would oversee the project. Scribner's would publish the book.[1]

As with all matters connected with Wolfe — even a decade after his death — what seemed simple soon became complicated. Nowell began her research at Harvard University's Houghton Library, repository of the huge William B. Wisdom Collection of Thomas Wolfe papers. She also researched the University of North Carolina Collection and the Scribner's

[1] John Hall Wheelock of Charles Scribner's Sons had initially written Nowell, asking her to edit a collection of Wolfe's letters. Aswell, editor in chief at McGraw-Hill and administrator for the Wolfe Estate since 1947, agreed to Scribner's suggestion that royalties be split fifty-fifty between Nowell and the Wolfe Estate and that Scribner's be the publisher. Scribner's also would pay Nowell an advance, part of which would cover photostating expenses at Houghton Library.

In March, when initial negotiations with Aswell and Scribner's were over, Nowell wrote her friend Kyle Crichton of Scribner's, telling him she was divorced and "working on Wolfe: editing his letters, about 500,000 words of them for his estate and Scribbiners. They wrote me and told me how they loved me and what a good job they were sure I'd do, and stuff like that, and back and forth it went for a month, but still no mention of set terms or money. So finally I wrote back and said, 'Look boys, I know publishing is a gentleman's profession and I hate to be so crass, but grit your teeth, boys, grit your teeth, take a deep breath and mention ᴍᴏɴᴇʏ', so they did" (March 10, 1949, Nowell files, Houghton Library).

files and wrote to anyone and everyone who might have corresponded with Wolfe. For Nowell, the job was fascinating if frustrating. She had to sort the Wisdom material — then largely uncataloged — decipher Wolfe's handwriting, track down names, obtain permissions, worry about libel. Her energy, knowledge, and irreverent humor quickly made friends for her among Houghton staff members. Clearly, she enjoyed the project and enjoyed being in contact again with the world she had left when she married.

Characteristically, Nowell threw herself into her work, usually commuting by train three days a week from New Bedford to Cambridge and working at home most other days and every night after her children were in bed. As she wrote to Jack Wheelock of Scribner's, she was eager to do the work but wanted no deadline because of her children. "Anyway," she wrote, "you know me: when I start a job I go practically crazy in my anxiety to get it done."[2]

Nowell also began to think of additional projects beyond the collection of letters — in particular a biography of Wolfe and an edition of his notebooks — and she raised questions to Aswell about the order of material and the origin of several characters in Wolfe's posthumous novels. As she worked, she found that the amount of Wolfe material and its disorganization made her task far greater than Aswell, Wheelock, or Scribner's had envisioned. In a six-page letter to Charles Scribner III, she described the Houghton material and ended her letter, "I think it'll take a lot of work, more than I realized till I actually read the stuff, but I think we can get a damn good book out of it: juicy, funny, tragic, valuable in revealing Tom as a writer in the different stages of his development. . . . Well, hell, Tom himself. Which is how it ought to be. Amen."[3]

Aswell had his own difficulties with the Scribner's arrangement. As a senior editor and vice president at McGraw-Hill, he felt a certain prerogative over the other Wolfe projects suggested by Nowell. Who would publish these? Scribner's and Wheelock, to whom Nowell owed her loyalty of nearly twenty years? Or McGraw-Hill and Aswell? And the job of administrator demanded evening and weekend time that often left him exhausted.

But Aswell's eagerness to see Wolfe's letters published overrode other

---

[2] Letter to John H. Wheelock, January 4, 1949, Nowell files, Houghton Library.

[3] Letter to Charles Scribner III, January 22, 1949, Nowell files, Houghton Library. Charles Scribner III was the third Charles Scribner of Charles Scribner's Sons, taking over from his father in 1932. Nowell had met him when she first applied for a job at Scribner's in 1928.

concerns. With Wolfe, Aswell had felt a psychic bond in the brief time — less than a year — that he had worked with him. According to his second wife, Mary Lou, Aswell had never known such excitement as he had known with Wolfe. His superstitious soul had been aroused by coincidences of time and place that seemed to weave his fate with Wolfe's. Together, Aswell with his great powers of organization, and Wolfe, with his genius, would form the Great Collaboration. After Wolfe died in 1938, Aswell had spent three years working on the posthumous novels and *The Hills Beyond*. But a part of him had died along with Wolfe, and for a decade he had lived a diminished life, calling himself "a sheep in Wolfe's clothing." With the chance to collaborate with Nowell, Aswell's mourning ended, and he could exercise a control over scholarship that would allow Wolfe's reputation to endure.

Meanwhile, practical considerations arose. When Maxwell Perkins had been Wolfe Estate administrator, he had given oral permission to John S. Terry of the New York University English department to write Wolfe's biography. Terry wrote to Nowell, asking for information about Wolfe. Neither Nowell nor Aswell trusted Terry: Nowell because she feared Terry would coast on her painstaking research, Aswell because he disliked Terry's indolent work habits. The situation revealed the differing styles of Nowell and Aswell as both tried to protect their own interests and the interests of the estate.

Of the twenty letters selected to represent the first year of the Aswell-Nowell correspondence, twelve are from Aswell and eight are from Nowell. Aswell replied to Nowell's questions about Wolfe's last novels. Yet as Nowell possibly suspected and as later scholars have confirmed, some of Aswell's statements about what Wolfe wrote were really about what Aswell himself had written in the name of posthumous editing. It seems that Aswell saw himself *as* Wolfe, the two as one — even so many years after Wolfe's death.

Perhaps because she had known Wolfe better than Aswell had, or perhaps because she had less personal stake in Wolfe's work, Nowell was more objective. In her search for letters to, from, or about Wolfe, she found discrepancies between Wolfe's account of his last manuscript and Aswell's. She tried to piece together past events so that her edition of Wolfe's letters would be accurate. The differences between her approach and Aswell's — differences which became an issue later in the correspondence — establish a vigorous dynamic. Nowell wanted to work and was eager to juggle many different projects at once. She also wanted fairness, for herself and for Wolfe. She wanted Wolfe to emerge whole cloth out of the fabric of his correspondence. Aswell wanted to preserve and magnify Wolfe. Nowell wanted issues faced squarely and immediately. Aswell hedged. Nowell's letters reflect a life in touch with home and heart and pocketbook. Aswell's reflect the office. Month by month, they established the pushes and pulls of a relationship that would last until they died.

Dear Liddy,

. . . Yes, you are right about where the idea came from. And I am more delighted than I can tell you that you are interested in taking on the job and that your personal situation is such that you can take it on. . . .

I really would like very much to have a talk with you and we must arrange to do that sooner or later. I don't know that it is necessary to do it immediately. The first job will be to collect as many of Tom's letters as you can. I gather that Mr. Perkins [Maxwell E. Perkins] had collected a great many before he died, so maybe you ought to begin by finding out just what Scribner's has. Then, the next step probably will be for you to go to Cambridge and see what letters exist in the Wisdom Collection at Harvard. That Collection, incidentally, is housed in the Houghton Library, a fairly new Georgian-type building alongside the monstrous Widener. The man to see there will be Mr. William A. Jackson. By an agreement between the Estate and Mr. Jackson, most of the Wolfe Collection is still being kept out of circulation. What I mean is, a person just can't walk in and ask to examine it and have his request granted. I insisted on this restriction and Jackson acceded to it just to keep a lot of people and curiosity seekers from getting at it and skimming the cream off before publishing projects like this one about the letters could be worked out. . . .

So far as I know, there is only one large group of Wolfe letters which, for reasons you can guess at and which I can explain in full later, cannot be included in this contemplated volume, or rather volumes, since Jack Wheelock [John Hall Wheelock] said yesterday he thought it might be a two-volume set issued at $10. These are the Tom-Aline [Aline Bernstein, Wolfe's mistress] letters and I believe the Houghton Library has both sides of this correspondence, but those letters will have to be kept out of circulation for still awhile yet. . . .

Another thought I put into Wheelock's head was that after you have polished off the job of editing the letters, you might be induced to go on and do a biography of Tom. That job has been crying to be done these last ten years. Terry [John S. Terry], of course, is supposed to have been doing it but so far as Wheelock and I can discover, he inches forward like a glacier if he moves at all.[1] I do not believe, and never have believed, that he would really do the job; and even if he did do it, it wouldn't be a good job because he can bring no insight nor understanding to it. You could and would. So, just tuck that large thought in the back of your head until the time comes to take it and look at it.

My best to you as always and I do want ever so much to see you.

Ed

[1] John S. Terry had edited *Thomas Wolfe's Letters to His Mother* [New York: Scribner, 1943] and had been asked by Maxwell E. Perkins, Wolfe Estate administrator before Aswell, to write Wolfe's biography.

*

March 2, 1949

Dear Liddy,

In preparation for my meeting with Jack Wheelock and Mr. Randall [David A. Randall of Scribner's Rare Book Department] at lunch today, I have carefully re-read your several letters of February 12th, 13th, 18th, and 27th. I'll write you again after the meeting and let you know what decisions were arrived at about who will write whom about what. Meanwhile, just a private word about your question to me in your February 18th letter which I have not had time to answer until now.

The question of just what section of manuscript Tom actually worked on last is a hard one to answer. As you know, he didn't work on one thing consecutively. What I said in my Note on Tom about the section of manuscript on the Joyners as published in THE HILLS BEYOND is, I think, true although not the whole truth. In that Note, I was not trying to give a rounded and final judgment of Tom but was commenting chiefly on the pieces which appeared in THE HILLS BEYOND. Nevertheless, I did give what I wrote there a certain larger perspective and the whole first half of it pretty well indicates, it seems to me, that what Tom was growing toward is best to be found in YOU CAN'T GO HOME AGAIN. . . .

"On the whole, YOU CAN'T GO HOME AGAIN was a more satisfying book than its predecessor. It was much more complete, more nearly finished. It contained more of his latest writing, and even though those parts of it that had been written earlier had in many instances been revised and recast in his more objective style."[1]

Muller [Herbert J. Muller] pinned too much on my statement about the Joyner stuff. I do know for a fact that Tom reworded some of this Joyner material just before he left New York for Purdue. He talked to me about it then. Also, I have no doubt that he was working on what appears as the last part of YOU CAN'T GO HOME AGAIN at about that time, too.[2] One day, it would be one and the next day it would be the other. You know how it was, Liddy.

We can talk about this in greater detail when we meet.

What I am saying here, I suppose, is that I believe your theory is right and I think what I said about the Joyner stuff is also right.[3]

All my best,

Ed

[1] Herbert J. Muller, author of *Thomas Wolfe* in the Masters of Modern Literature series (Norfolk, Conn.: New Directions, 1947), questioned Aswell's statement that the manuscript Wolfe left at his death formed a "unity" that was an "extraordinary literary achievement," once the extraneous material was removed. Muller wrote, "There is indeed a unity. But aside from the fact that Aswell had to remove the extraneous matter himself, this is scarcely extraordinary, nor is it strictly a *literary* achievement. The unity is primarily that of a life, a personality. It might almost be reduced to the statement that all of Wolfe's work was written by Wolfe. . . ." (p. 27). Ironically, as we now know, some of Wolfe's work was actually revised or even written by Aswell, for example the Joyner family material, which Aswell revised and placed in *The Hills Beyond* rather than where Wolfe had originally intended it in *The Web and the Rock*. In this letter to Nowell, Aswell confirmed, because of Nowell's questions, that his "Note" had not told the whole truth.

[2] Aswell described the scene when Wolfe turned over the manuscript which was to become the posthumous material: "I went to his room in the old Chelsea Hotel on 23rd Street to get the manuscript. The writing was done and when I arrived Tom was sorting and arranging the pages. He sat at a table in his shirt-sleeves with a pile of manuscript a foot high in front of him. . . . Now and then he would decide that a chapter or a section didn't belong in the book and he would discard it, throwing it on the floor. All around him the floor was littered with these discards." Half an hour before Tom was due to take the train to the Pacific Northwest, he turned over to Aswell "probably one of the longest manuscripts ever delivered to a publisher" ("Thomas Wolfe's Unpublished Work," *Carolina Magazine,* October 1938, p. 19).

[3] Nowell recognized the Joyner material in *The Hills Beyond* as Wolfe's "Doaksology," written in the fall of 1935. In an undated letter to Aswell she said, "this is the Zach, Bear, etc Joyner stuff, isn't it, which was used later as The Hills Beyond. (But rewritten before used, so as to be Joyners instead of Doaks). Or am I all dead wrong about this Doaksology? If you are too busy, or not sure about your recollection of this yourself, I can go to the Houghton and look at the manuscript. But the only thing I'm really not sure of is the Doaksology. And if it isn't The Hills Beyond I'm damned if I know what it could be." It is no wonder that Nowell was uncertain, because Aswell, in his "Note," described this 1935 material as indicative of Wolfe's new maturity as a writer, calling it "the very last work he did."

*

March 4, 1949

Dear Liddy,

About the letter Tom wrote you from Portland venting his feelings about Max [Perkins], I think the thing to do for the present is to include it.[1] It belongs with the other letters having to do with Tom's relations with Max and his break with Scribner's. I think we'll have to see how all those letters shape up together, the kind of over-all picture they reveal. In the end, much will depend also on the editorial treatment you give these letters. Here, as in many other instances, it seems to me that you, as editor, will have to make some comment in order to set things in true perspective. In this letter, for example, there is evidence, it seems to me, of Tom's characteristic suspiciousness which caused him to over-color any situation involving personal factors. And I can't believe for a moment that Max instructed the Scribner salesmen to pass out stories about him in the way Tom has it here.

There will be a good many other instances before you are through of letters that will raise questions. My hunch would be to include anything that is interesting and important for purposes of your first draft, leaving the questions to be ironed out after you and Scribner's and I can see the whole picture.

Sincerely,

Ed Aswell

[1] On Sunday, June 19, 1938, Wolfe had written Nowell from Portland, Oregon. The letter reads, in part: "I'm sorry about M.P. Everything you tell me about him touches and grieves and hurts me like hell. Please — *please* don't tell him about me, or anything about me, if you can avoid it. For six years he was my friend — I thought the best one I ever had — and then, a little over two years ago he turned against me. Everything I have done since was bad, he had no good word for it or for me, it's almost as if he were praying for my failure. I can't understand or fathom it, but it is a sad strange thing" (*Letters,* p. 771).

*

Mar 25, 1949.

Dear Ed:

Well, it's 11:30 and I stopped work, put stamps on all my letters, put out the dog, turned out the lights, put down the thermostat, then turned on lights and started typing. I think it would be nice if you would write Edgar Lee Masters and ask if Tom ever wrote to him. I thought of him way back when I made my first list, then decided no, Tom only talked with him [at] the hotel.[1] But lately found a fragment, VERY formally and fancily embalmed at Houghton with the notation "The last thing Wolfe ever wrote" which is a hasty pencil paragraph written at the Hotel in Seattle about Old Masters and Tom telling him about the Am [American] Society of Artists and Writers or whatever the hell the name of it was. It ends up with the words Mr Masters (only a pseudonym) said "They're a bunch of shits."

It might just be that having penned these immortal words, Tom was overcome with love for Old Masters and sat down and wrote him, or that he wrote him at some other time. Probably not, but it would be a swell letter if he ever wrote one. This is the kind of thing I mean by saying I will rake through tons of junk, but might come up with a few jewels.

And so, Goodnight.

Love
Liddy

¹ The Hotel Chelsea. In a letter of March 7, 1938, to Mrs. J.M. Roberts (Wolfe's English teacher at the North State School in Asheville), Wolfe said: "I live here in a very old Victorian style hotel with enormous rooms and lots of other strange critters like myself. Mr. Edgar Lee Masters also lives here and has for years. I see him from time to time; in fact, he set me up to a glass of beer yesterday afternoon — but for the most part I just work" (*Letters,* p. 730).

*

April 6, 1949

Dear Liddy,

I have your last three letters, one of March 29th and two of April 2nd.

Terry does seem to present a real problem and I suppose I am the one who will have to smoke him out if he can be smoked out. He seems to be laboring under a misconception that he holds some sort of exclusive rights to the Wolfe material that has come into his possession in one way or another. So far as I have been able to learn, both from the correspondence in the files of the Estate and from a number of talks I have had with Mr. Scribner, Mr. Wheelock, and Mr. Cane [Attorney Melville Cane], no exclusive rights were ever granted him by Mr. Perkins. And it is even difficult for me to determine that any rights at all were granted him by Mr. Perkins. Mr. Perkins did certainly encourage him to write a biography and assisted him in many ways toward that end, but more than ten years have passed and so far as either Scribner's or I can learn, Terry hasn't yet written anything. Mr. Perkins really had misgivings about this project for he never gave Terry a contract for the book.

What to do? — That is the question. I have discussed this several times with Mr. Wheelock and we both know from past experience how tedious and difficult it is to get anywhere with Terry or to find out anything. Meanwhile, it would appear that he has come into possession of letters which ought to be considered for inclusion in the project you are working on. I wrote Terry about your project many weeks ago soliciting his cooperation, but I have not even had an acknowledgment of that letter.

11

For the moment, I think you had better not get involved in this problem. I shall make one more direct attempt with Terry, have invited him to meet me for a drink any afternoon next week, and if that fails, I shall try to enlist the aid of Mabel and Fred [Mabel Wolfe Wheaton, Wolfe's sister, and Frederick W. Wolfe, Wolfe's brother]. I suspect that Terry has Mabel's letters from Tom as well as other family letters. These were probably turned over to him by Mrs. Wolfe [Julia E. Wolfe, Wolfe's mother].

Today I received a letter from Clayton Hoagland [writer for the *New York Sun* and friend of Wolfe] in response to my inquiry about his letters and he says:

"I sent complete typed copies to John Terry some time ago for use in his biography, where I should certainly like to see them quoted if they are of any interest for that purpose. My immediate intention is to have some good photostats made shortly and as this will require my using the originals, I shall let you know then what arrangements I can make to get photos or originals to you. . . . Before this month is out, you should have some word from me."

So, be as patient as you can about Terry. It will accomplish nothing to get his back further up than it apparently already is. . . .

All my best,
Ed

P.S. Have just heard from Vardis [Vardis Fisher, novelist and former colleague of Wolfe at New York University (NYU)]. He will let me see the MS. of book 7 of his series, but meanwhile it is with Random House, he says. Vardis and Bennett Cerf [Random House editor] would be strange bed-fellows!

*

April 7, 1949

Dear Liddy,

This is in answer to your last letter which you said didn't require one, and it doesn't really.

I just wanted to say that I think you are doing a grand job — exactly the kind of job I knew you would do. By this, I mean to say that you have taken hold of this thing by the throat, going after it in a way that I think no one else could match. There are bound to be a lot of mysteries and loose ends to be cleared up. Between us, we'll do our best to clear them up as they come up and then in the end will probably have to give the recalcitrant people a second or third going over. . . .

Since my last letter to you, I have decided to confide in Mabel about the problem of John Terry and have written her a long letter explaining it all. At the same time, I asked her not to make any direct move until we see whether my last approach to Terry, inviting him to meet me for a talk, will produce anything. If it doesn't, then I shall ask Mabel and Fred to see what they can do. . . .

If we have to do it some other way, that will be different.

My best as always,
Ed

*

2 Prospect St.
So. Dartmouth, Mass.
April 8, 1949.

Dear Ed and Jack [Wheelock]:

Re: Terry: with Ed's permission I would like to sic Fred and Mabel on him. After all, the letters belong to them, not Terry, and they have a right to ask for them. They probably have a right to actually insist on same. If they think Terry is holding out on Tom and his estate, they may, of course, tear him limb from limb. But I think a row is justifiable, all things considered. Mama [Julia Wolfe] gave him whatever she gave him as trusted friend of Tom's and of the family's, and the family can best deal with him. Roughshod or not, as needed.

Wheelocks suggestion that I go camp on his doorstep and be "very persuasive" is no good. Terry will hate me more than anyone, as his deadly rival and supplanter. But his "dear friend Tom's own family" and Mama's own heirs and children should cut much more ice. If anybody can. If not, Mabel with a bottle of corn licker in her hand can make more of a row than anybody, except Tom. But I think Terry will surrender when he knows she's hot on his trail. He will if he has any sense. I'm not saying this to be catty about good old Mabel: she wrote me a wonderful-emotional letter, the kind only she or Tom could write. I just have a feeling that neither hell nor high water will keep her from getting her own letters, which, I think, is as it ought to be.

Only other alternative would be for Ed to phone him and ask him how about it pointblank. Terry is an awful putteroffer. He may be meaning to answer Ed, but just not have done it out of negligence.

If it's OK to tell Fred and Mabel (and I'll have to tell her anyway in answer to her worried queries about where her letters are), please give me Terry's address. This request addressed to either Jack or Ed.

I gather, that as long as Terry knows about this anyway, CSS [the publishing house, Charles Scribner's Sons] can go ahead with the announcement about me whenever they see fit.

Guess this is all for tonight. Let me know about Mabel-Terry business when you can, because I'll have to write her soon answering her letter or she'll be sitting on <u>my</u> doorstep.

Love and condolences
Liddy

If Ed cant bear to phone Terry, why not make Cane do it? That might scare him, even though we'd have no legal grounds to force him to surrender letters (unless the fact that they belong to Mabel is any sort of grounds). Hell, Cane might as well do something to earn his cut. L & K [Love and Kisses] EP. Poor Ed, between Scylla and Charibdis: me and Mabel on one hand and Terry on the other. Wheee!

*

April 13, 1949

Dear Liddy,

This will answer yours of April 8th.

When I finally decided to write Mabel about the Terry problem, I had a hunch she would get all emotional and worked up, and so she did. She called me at home last Saturday and talked for half an hour. Much of what she said was incoherent. Though it was early in the morning, she sounded as though she had already had a good nip or two. As the years pass, she seems to need to resort to the bottle more and more.

Anyhow, she made it clear that her letters from Tom are all in Terry's possession. She said she allowed her mother to talk her into giving them to him much against her will. Mabel indicated every desire to be helpful in this situation but, at the same time, she was full of apologies for Terry. She knows he is lazy and not doing much work on the biography, if any at all, but she also likes him. She kept repeating that he always treated her well. She wanted to know whether she should write to Terry immediately, but I repeated what I had said in my letter to her: namely, not to do anything until we see whether my last direct approach to Terry produces anything. If it doesn't, I will let her know and she says she will write him. I have a hunch, though, that she will not be very forceful in anything she may say to Terry. All he needs to do is to resort to the kind of heavy-handed flattery, of which he is master, and Mabel will melt like butter. It is a ridiculous sort of mess, isn't it?

Terry's statement about what happened to Tom's letters to his mother, as you quote it from his introduction, is as inaccurate as many of the other statements he made there. Mrs. Wolfe did not take those letters

14

back to Asheville at all. She left them at Scribner's. And after Mrs. Wolfe and Perkins both died, the Wolfe family worked themselves into a tremendous lather about gaining re-possession of the letters. They seemed to think, quite without foundation, that Scribner's wouldn't give them up. As a matter of fact, Fred came to New York, went to see Charlie Scribner and asked for the letters, and they were turned over to him. It was as simple as that. He then brought the whole batch of them to me and asked me to keep them in the Wolfe file in my office and there they still are. These are only the letters to his mother which went into that book. They belonged originally, of course, to Mrs. Wolfe and on her death, ownership passed to the four children. . . .

Guess this is all for now.

My best as always,
Ed

*

April 18, 1949

Dear Liddy,

You ask who the originals of Randy and Margaret Shepperton were. [1] Thereby hangs a tale.

When Tom decided to abandon the Gants and gave George Webber a very different family set-up than that of the Gants, he ran into a problem. Randy and Margaret Shepperton represent one of the ways he solved it. Margaret was essentially Mabel for whom read Helen Gant. But Tom wanted to make use of the disastrous experience Ralph Wheaton had had with, I believe, the National Cash Register Company, so he invented Randy for this purpose. In some of the factual material, Randy, then, was Ralph Wheaton, but in character Randy wasn't Ralph — he was simply the kind of friend Tom wished he had had at that time but didn't have.

At least, that's my theory.

All my best,
Ed

---

[1] Nowell, in her search for letters, had been trying to locate the "originals" of Wolfe's fictionalized characters, including Randy and Margaret Shepperton. Randy Shepperton appears briefly in *The Web and the Rock* but is given much fuller characterization in *You Can't Go Home Again*. According to David Donald, Randy is Aswell's composite of Ralph Wheaton and Fred Wolfe, or Lee and Jim in "The Company." Nowell recognized Shepperton as atypical of Wolfe's characters, but she did not realize Aswell's role in his creation. Even after Aswell's April 18th letter, Nowell continued her questions about Shepperton. For example, in an August 21, 1949, letter to George McCoy, editor of the *Asheville Citizen*,

she asked, "Do *you* think Randy Shepperton is a purely imaginative character, as Aswell does?" She wrote McCoy again in November that "Aswell asked Fred and Mabel and Mrs. Wolfe if Tom had any close childhood friend like Randy, and they said they couldn't think of anyone, so maybe he just invented the young Randy, as Aswell thinks he did." Nowell was also suspicious about Nebraska Crane (from *The Web and the Rock* and *You Can't Go Home Again*).

*

May 3, 1949

Dear Liddy,

I am having to hump to keep up with you. I thought I had cleared up everything with you in my last long letter. Then this morning three more from you, so now I'll try to hit the high spots of them. . . .

What you say about the notebooks sounds wonderful.[1] As you indicate, perhaps there will be another Wolfe volume to be made from these notebooks. Let's take one thing at a time, though. The editing of the letters is proving more exacting and time-consuming than I had thought and if it seems that way to me, I can well imagine how much more so it must seem to you who are really doing the work. Let's just tuck in the back of our minds the thought of doing something with the notebooks eventually. Meanwhile, I wish you would not say anything of this project to the people at Scribner's. Let's see how they do with the letters. . . .

About Terry: I didn't write you a report on my session with him because I wanted to think about it a bit first. I had Melville Cane sit in on the meeting because I thought something might come up in connection with legal matters, and something did. Terry's nose was out of joint because he claimed that Max Perkins had promised to let him edit the letters. Both Cane and I were able to call him on that one. I am sure Max never made any such commitment. Max had been planning to edit them himself. This is established both through Cane's knowledge and mine. There is no complication to be feared from Terry on that score. I think we can simply dismiss it. He indicated that the price of his cooperation would be that he (Terry) be named as co-editor with you on the project. I indicated there were difficulties in that and suggested that he talk to Wheelock which he said he would do immediately. To date, he hasn't gotten in touch with Wheelock. I have, though, and Wheelock and I both think the idea is completely impractical even if you would be willing to accept him as co-editor which I am sure you wouldn't. So, that is how matters stand at the moment. In other words, I haven't made any headway. Maybe in the end we will have to get Mabel to retrieve the family letters from Terry. What else he may have, I don't know. Aside from the family letters,

I rather doubt whether he has anything which would be a tremendous loss insofar as your project is concerned. . . .

I am worried about your being so tired. Can't you take it a little easier? No sense in killing yourself, you know.

My best as always,
Ed Aswell

[1] While working on the letters, Nowell realized that another project could be gleaned from a publication of Wolfe's notebooks.

*

May 25, 1949.

Dear Ed:

Separate letter. Now maybe I'm a prurient old ex-old-maid, but I do keep finding the most godawful things in Tom's notebooks. I know you said it didnt matter as long as the Wisdom Collection wasnt open to the public, but the trouble is that NObody is going to go through these notebooks word-for-illegible-word after me. I mean nobody in the Houghton Staff. And some day, sooner or later, the public will be stumbling over these things.

I found one and reported it to Bond [William Bond, curator of manuscripts, Houghton Library] because it was libellous. Tom said that Mrs. _____ called him up, he asked her to his hotel. He then says "(2 times) I noticed certain penal [penile] discomfort but thought it was only because I was all out" (last word illegible, but he meant he was exhausted: and no wonder what with all the other girls he had right then.) I wont go into names and details. Well, then it went on a page or so later to say that he examined himself, applied a prophylaxis, etc. Then two more pages later he had a cable to Perkins saying "I am sick, must stay here till I'm cured. Address Amexco, Copenhagen". I pointed out to Bond that Mrs. _____ . . . would not care to have it announced that she had probably caught something somewhat worse than a bad cold from Tom. I also pointed out that someday some smart student would start writing a life of Tom and saying he died of the Asiatic Zing instead of what he did. So I think Bond will fix that one.

But that afternoon I found two more, and Bond by then (and specially his secretary, who is the daughter of the Professor of Divinity at Harvard and was dying to know what it was all about) looked as if they couldn't take much more. So I told Bond simply that I found two passages which were not libellous, simply pornographic, the one was easily identifiable. . . .

That one is: I quote "with proud crowing love fondly he asked 'can you feel that?' 'God, can I feel it! That pole, that tree,' she panted." I spose it isn't bad. . . . [B]ut I dont think she'd like to have it preserved for posterity very much.

The other one involved only Tom. "Do you like to fuck Japs. Why not say the truth? Jew women will fuck anything if its in the mode. This was written at Marios when I saw the beautiful Jewess — she was with the Jap sculptor. You fuck Japs and Niggers. I will not fuck you. The worst thing I could think of in those days of a beautiful young girl was You like to suck off nigger pricks."

That's all for today. If you think they ought to be suppressed they are in a notebook that begins "Another party. We never got down to the point where they're thoroughly sold on a campaign". And has dates Feb 17 and Feb 18 a few pages later. Finally gives a date Friday, February 21, 1930. So I will put a note on it saying 1930 Feb-May on it: I guess I did already just before I left Tues night. [1]

Love,
Liddy

[1] On April 25, 1949, Nowell wrote Martha Dodd Stern, who had known Wolfe in Berlin, to ask if one of Wolfe's potentially libelous letters at the Houghton was to her (it was not). "Tom wrote things like this and, usually, never mailed them, so it may be all news to you. In some ways he was still a regular small-southern-town bourgeois jerk and anyone with any sense would realize that he was, from what he said in here. But going down in literary history, right or wrong, as Tom made people seem is tough on them" (Nowell files, Houghton Library).

*

2 Prospect St
So Dartmouth.
June 1, 1949.

Dear Ed:

You know, I wrote to Munn [James B. Munn, professor and dean at New York University] way back in the very early stages of this collecting, not knowing he was dead: he was on my list when we 3 divided up the most obvious and important people. I have just now had an answer to it, enclosing a copy of the letter Dean Pollock [Thomas Clark Pollock, NYU] wrote to you. I thought you might want to know how important these letters were, so I am writing you, though this, of course, is none of my business. . . . [1]

Well, now, maybe I am wrong: I'm only guessing. But I think I am slightly influenced by the feeling that Watt [Homer A. Watt, NYU English professor] had a hell of a nerve to think his correspondence with Wolfe proved enough to be published as a separate book, and make enough money for a scholarship.[2] I mean, certainly <u>his</u> letters to Tom wouldnt make more than about a hundred bucks. It seems to me that he is exploiting Tom's name with this bequest.

ALSO, and this is the important thing, if NYU does this, it'll be another case of "hold back the crowd". All the 50 to 100 other people who got better and more valuable letters from Tom will get the idea that <u>they</u> should publish a small separate volume: they'll go offering them all over to God-knows what publishers, (if you consent) and if you once consent it'll be harder to say NO to other people. Univ of NC [North Carolina] will want to publish their letters separately, Harvard (tho I dont think Harvard would be bothered): Basso, Julian Meade [Hamilton Basso and Julian Meade, both authors], Mrs Roberts [Wolfe's teacher in Asheville], well, you get what I am driving at. . . .

Love EP[3]

[1] Nowell went on to say that Wolfe's letters to "NYU bigshots" were "a little servile" and were not very valuable because they represented an adolescent phase of his life "before he ever really found himself."

[2] Homer A. Watt, chairman of the English department of New York University when Wolfe was an instructor, wanted to establish a scholarship in Wolfe's memory from the proceeds of their published correspondence.

[3] During her divorce in 1949, Nowell signed her letters with the initials LP or EHN. Thereafter, she signed herself EHN, EHP, ENP, EP, Mme. P, or most frequently, Liddy.

*

Wednesday June 8

Dear Ed:

Edna [Nowell's younger daughter] has, I spose, chickenpox: 104 last night but no rash yet. My contract is back from Fleisher [Attorney Sidney Fleisher] with a long list of legal details, most of which I wont make any fuss about. What this is about is something else: will try to write letter about contract later today or tomorrow or whenever Edna will let me.

I just got a letter from John Terry saying "I'm leaving for London on Wed to interview Tom's publishers and editors. I sincerely hope to get at some of the truths about how Tom fared with them. I hear that you are doing some editing of Tom's letters - What are your plans? I wonder if you'll write me a letter in London, Care of American Express Co, Haymarket, telling me how you inherited Tom from an agent you were working for - the one who tried so hard to influence Tom. Tom told me these things, but I'd certainly appreciate your giving me your facts. How long were you two his agents? etc and how did Tom seem to respond to your treatment of him? Its been a long time since we were together — glad you're a mother and wife. Sincerely yours, John Terry.

Well, in the first place, is Terry doing the official biography or not? It seems to me you ought to warn Frere Reeves [of Heinemann, Wolfe's British publisher] if he is not. [1] If he isnt, you dont want Frere turning over all their correspondence to him. Things are bad enough with all the family's letters and some of the NYU ones in his hands. Also, I wrote Frere Reeves last week, giving him a long list of all the friends Tom had in London, Mrs Barswell [Mrs. Donald Carswell] and about 20 more names which I dug out from his notebooks. I asked Frere if he could give me their present addresses so I could write to them for letters. Well, if Terry sails in and Frere receives him with open arms, it would be quite natural for Frere to hand my research list to Terry and send him to interview them all, and then he'd get their letters too.

Maybe you think I am getting a Terry-complex, but the whole thing is such a mess. And he gets everything so wrong. I did not "inherit Tom" from Lieber [Maxim Lieber]: Perkins gave me Tom but I was working free at Liebers for 1 year with the understanding I was to be either a partner or leave after that. We sold one story under Lieber's agency, but there was never any question but that Tom was my client, not his. Nor do I think Maxim tried "so hard to influence Tom"; that would mean that Terry thought Max was trying to make a communist of Tom, and Terry is a rabid reactionary. I hate to think how he would go to town and get this all mixed up. I suppose I'll have to answer him, but will wait until I hear from you. Main thing is I hope you can cable or airmail Frere a note telling him just what the status of Terry is at present. Probably Frere knows Perkins gave him permission to do the biography way back, and would fall all over himself to help him.

Love, Liddy

Also Terry wont get the facts about Tom's relations with Frere from Frere: the real dirt is in his notebooks and in a couple of letters to other people. I [Tom?] didnt like him: said he was crazy from the war, Frere got drunk and came and read the bible to Tom accusing him of seducing Pat, his wife. Which Tom says he never did, & I think rightly. Tom says "Why, he's even crazier than I." But I dont think Frere knew that: it is one of the things we will probably have to edit out of the letters.

[1] Frere Reeves, of Heinemann Ltd., had the British rights to Wolfe's novels, which the estate controlled. Nowell urged Aswell to make a decision about what was fast becoming another project, the biography: would Aswell choose Terry or Nowell for this important work?

*

June 16, 1949

Dear Liddy,

In recent weeks I have been in a jam and way behind in my correspondence. Several of yours remain unanswered and I can't get at them yet. Meanwhile, though, just a note in reply to the one you wrote on June 8th about Terry's trip abroad.

I shall write Frere and urge him not to turn over any letters. I shall make it clear to him that Terry is not the official biographer of Tom, whatever that phrase may mean. There is no official biographer that I know of. Terry, of course, can write a book about Tom if he wants to. He has had plenty of opportunity. So can anybody else. But getting a publishing contract is something else again and Terry does not have that.

My advice to you would be not to answer the letter Terry wrote. The mere fact that he did write you puts you under no obligation to answer. Or, if you feel you must write, the best thing would be just to send him a brief note saying something to the effect that you are hard at work on your job and haven't time at present to write out the full answers to the questions he asked you, but that you would be glad to talk to him sometime. That will put it up to him to arrange to come to see you which he will be too lazy ever to do. His laziness apparently is dictating the method he is employing. He wants other people to write out for him the full account of their relations with Tom. Then he can put his book together by simply quoting what other people have written him.

For your information, I have written to Fred about the whole Terry mess but now that Terry is abroad, I doubt whether anything can be done until he returns.

Very sorry to hear about Edna's chickenpox. Those children certainly seem to be running through the medical dictionary, don't they?

My best as always,
Ed

*

September 6, 1949.

Dear Ed:

This will be just a short one. I've already written and sealed up for you a long letter which is really addressed to Mrs. B [Aline Bernstein], but which I'm sending to you because I know you're going to see her anyway about some letters which you've picked out in hopes that she will let us use them.

But I got thinking about her, and I think we ought to tell her just

21

exactly what I'm up against. I mean, in the period after Tom left her, he wrote some pretty awful letters to other people about her: he seems to have had a sort of persecution mania that she was trying to get him back. And if we are going to do this book on the original platform: I mean with the solemn conviction that we have no right to suppress Tom's words except for reasons of libel or somesuch: well, if we are going to stick to that and publish all the awful things he wrote about Perkins and other people, we ought, I guess, to do the same with Mrs B. Some of it can be edited out on perfectly justifiable grounds but I cant get it all out without butchering & suppressing him outrageously. There is one long letter specially to Perkins in which he pours it all out, says he cant write because he's so upset, etc. (It was just after he'd seen her sister in London: I think the date is 1930). Then he sent a cable saying Perkins didnt have to help him in it after all: that he could and must help himself. Etc, etc, etc, etc. I cant list all the things like this offhand: I'd have to go back through everything and see just what was what. But this letter to Perkins from London is the worst: I am quite sure of that.

Well, I think Mrs. B will understand: she knows what Tom was like, and some of these millions of other people who have read her letters tell me that some of his letters to her were perfectly awful, in this same sort of way.

But it would be a pretty scurvy trick for us to go ahead and publish references of this sort without warning her ahead of time. I've been trying to prepare people he was brutal to, so they wont get a sudden shock. Have, for instance, talked over or written to Mrs. Baker [wife of Harvard drama professor George Pierce Baker] all the bitter things Tom wrote to him (and evidently never sent) and she now understands. I am very anxious to do the same with Mrs. B: but you know there's this silly business of I'm not supposed to write to her direct because Randall thinks she likes to deal with Men better than Women. I never knew her much but I always had a wonderful warm feeling for her: she is such a swell person: and she always was very swell with me and very frank. But this crazy Randall idea has sort of put up a wall between me and her. I wish the hell you'd give her this to read, if you think it is OK, and if she wants I'll send her a carbon of that letter to Perkins and any other thing like that that I'm confronted with. My God, she knew Tom better than anyone: she's sure to understand.

> Love to you both
> from
> ENP

22

*

September 9, 1949

Dear Liddy,

. . . . About Tom's letters to Aline: she turned them all over to me, as you know, just about a week before her son dropped dead of a heart attack.[1] She was so completely broken up by that that I felt I could not approach her about the letters until she had had time to adjust herself to the family tragedy. And, of course, this summer she has been out of town anyway. I still have the letters and will arrange to talk to her soon. There is no killing hurry about it. I am sure we will find something for you in these letters — something not too intimate and personal. And I am also sure that Aline will not object to the publication of that kind of thing.

You ask about my own letters from Tom. The truth is that there weren't any, or at least not many. During the period of my association with him, you will remember that he was in New York up to the time he left on that ill-fated western trip. Whenever he had anything to say to me, he would call me up and say it over the telephone or I would go down to the Chelsea [Wolfe's hotel] and spend an evening with him. Thus, there was no occasion for the writing of letters until he went out West. From various points in the course of his trip, he sent me postcards — perhaps a dozen in all. Like an idiot, I gave most of these away to people who came to me from time to time saying how much they admired Tom and couldn't they have a photograph of him or a scrap of his handwriting. I gave away dozens of prints of that studio picture he had made for Harper's and one by one I also gave away most of the postcards. I may still have two or three of them. They didn't say anything really. Just something like: "Drove through the Yosemite yesterday and am drunk on scenery. Having wonderful time. Wish you were here."

The only real letter Tom wrote me was something you know about — that forty or fifty typewritten page thing which started out to be a letter talking about the book he was writing and then gradually turned into parts of the book itself. He never sent it to me but Mr. Perkins found it among Tom's papers after he died and gave it to me then. I recognized large parts of it when I read it because he had incorporated the major part of it in the manuscript of YOU CAN'T GO HOME AGAIN.[2]

I do have quite a mass of interesting correspondence with the various doctors who treated Tom in his final illness and also with members of the Wolfe family, but these will be of interest primarily to Tom's biographer rather than to you for your present purposes. In any event, I promised Jackson I would give all these things to Harvard and I will do it as soon as I can get around to it. It is primarily a matter of finding time to get them out of my attic and sort them out.

I am glad Miss Wyckoff [Irma Wyckoff, Perkins's secretary] was able to confirm the fact that that business about Tom's joining the Communist Party was a joke. I am also glad you were foresighted enough to get a statement from Miss Wyckoff to give to Mr. Bond. After Tom died, Mike Gold and other Communists claimed Tom as one of their own. I know from many things Tom told me that this wasn't so but if some future scholar found that document in the Harvard archives and took it straight, you can imagine how the Communist brethren would welcome it and distort that whole phase of Tom's life.

Cordially,
Ed

[1] Theo and Aline Bernstein's only son died in March 1949.

[2] Wolfe's statement, in a letter to Aswell dated February 14, 1938, says, "This novel . . . marks not only a turning away from the books I have written in the past, but a genuine spiritual and artistic change. It is the most objective novel that I have written. I have invented characters who are compacted from the whole amalgam and consonance of seeing, feeling, thinking, living, and knowing many people." At Perkins's suggestion Aswell called the letter an "Author's Note" to serve as an introduction to *The Web and the Rock*. But then Aswell affixed the date of May 1938, creating an impression, as Richard Kennedy put it, that "Wolfe's book was more complete . . . than it . . . was," ("The 'Wolfegate' Affair," *Harvard Magazine,* September/October 1981, p. 53). In *The Window of Memory* (Chapel Hill: University of North Carolina Press, 1962), Kennedy also pointed out that Aswell used sections of the Statement as text for *You Can't Go Home Again*.

*

September 14, 1949

Dear Liddy,

Back from Washington to find your letter of September 10th. I spent an evening with Mabel and had an opportunity for the first time to see some of the things in her collection. But you know Mabel. She talked so steadily that there was no chance really to concentrate on the various letters and documents which she had gotten out of the attic for me and dumped pell-mell on the bed. Much of the stuff is in rather bad condition because of the consequent pawing over it gets and the careless way she keeps it. Not knowing how perishable most modern paper is, she thinks it is enough if she keeps all the documents locked up in metal trunks, but the stuff is just dumped in the trunks any old way. . . .[1]

P.S. A letter has just come from Fred. As you know, I have had to pacify him and Mabel because of the trouble John Terry stirred up which led them to think that our purpose was to dig up all kinds of dirt. I told them that Scribner's and you and I were all fully aware of the laws of libel and that the selections to be published would be carefully gone over by a lawyer to protect the interests of all concerned. I seem to have succeeded in soothing their anxiety. In this connection, Fred now writes "with the curb that you and Mr. Cane and I presume Mr. Scribner or Mr. Wheelock will certainly use in checking and editing, I don't see how anything could go wrong or be allowed to be hurtful to others and also to us. I think, so far as I am concerned, that we the members of Tom's family have a place for consideration, as well as what might concern outsiders or others. When I mention this, I am certainly not thin skinned! I think, and I believe you think too, that each of us, measure up to at least, the American average family group. Tom wouldn't want us or this misunderstood, and I feel you will watch this and see we get a square deal. That's all I ask for us, the family."

---

[1] The rest of the letter summarizes this meeting with Mabel Wolfe Wheaton in Washington, D.C., and suggests several other sources and means of obtaining letters for the collection. He wanted to clear things up with the estate (a job he found "exacting" and time-consuming) before he sailed for a five-week trip to England. Then he ends with this postscript.

*

> 2 Prospect Street
> So Dartmouth, Mass.
> November 11, 1949.
> (Armistice? Day?)

Dear Ed:

Separate letter about this "supplementary memorandum of agreement" to my contract, so that when I get what you charitably call "upset" and I call just plain hopping mad, I can rewrite it without retyping my other long letter of odds and ends.[1]

Well, I've sent the "supplementary memorandum" down to Eddie Colton [Nowell's attorney] of the Fleisher office to "negotiate". No sense in paying them to draw me a decent contract and then throwing the whole thing out of the window by signing some highly irregular ragtail agreement two months later. My God: I thought a contract was a contract. (And as a matter of fact, I still know damn well it is.) . . .

I agree that the basic rights to what Tom wrote belong to his estate, but a lot of these letters would never have come to light (or not without a helluva lot of work on someone's part) unless I had collected them. I dont mean the ones in the Scribner files: nor the carbon copies of typed letters at Harvard: any dummy could stick those together. But I do mean all these other ones from friends of Tom's that I've spent 11 months of intensive FBI work tracking down and am still tracking down. Likewise all the horrible hodgepodge of longhand fragments at Harvard: written on scraps of paper, in notebooks, on the backs of manuscript etc at Harvard. Likewise, the research into the correct dates on the letters, the background of them, which fragment hitches onto which, and often, who the letters were addressed to. Tom seldom bothered with a salutation: <u>he</u> knew who he was writing to, and that was all that mattered. . . .

You see, anybody else who might edit a later book of Tom's letters would have all my work to coast along on. Likewise for all the explanatory footnotes. Somebody else could rephrase them, but he certainly would be helped tremendously by what I had found out. Even if he checked back with my sources he'd be coasting on my work. Because in many cases I didn't <u>have</u> <u>any</u> <u>sources</u> to check back with: could only find them by my knowledge of Tom's life, by 10 months of deciphering those horribly illegible longhand notebooks, by writing to people who might be the sources and asking if they were — if and when I could find them by writing other friends of their's and Tom's.

So, all in all, nobody could possibly start again from scratch to collect and edit Tom's letters: not unless you could somehow guarantee that he would never see my edition.

Now maybe I have done this job too hard and too well. I realize that Scribners just meant for me to slap their letters together with the ones at Harvard that were clear, and call it good enough. But you wrote me that you were delighted with the way I'd started doing it and . . . anyway, I've done it that way and I still am doing it. <u>And</u> I have my contract for it. <u>And</u> I dont want to throw the whole thing out of the window without consulting Eddie Colton. When I get really steamed up, I want to refuse to sign this goddamned afterthought "supplementary memorandum" altogether. But maybe you and Eddie can work something out.

That's all, I guess. Eddie's address is 551 5th Ave, but he will get in touch with you in all due time. Meanwhile I will just try to keep my shirt on and keep working. But this kind of thing "upsets" me and drives me crazy, and I spend all my time composing letters of this sort to you, instead of pushing along with the big job.

Aw nuts!

Love,
Liddy

¹ This was just one of many letters Nowell would write during the next ten years about the details of her contract. A freelance writer and agent and a single parent consumed with money worries, she knew she had to fight for her professional rights in a male-dominated profession. She worried that when her edition of the letters went out of print "any executor" of the Wolfe Estate could take her half of the royalties. Her worry was partly in response to Aswell's complaints about his job with the estate (she feared he would get fed up and quit) and partly because of inexact wording in the "supplementary memorandum."

*

December 28, 1949

Dear Liddy,

Attached is a copy of a letter I have written to Professor Munn which may or may not accomplish something.

Yes, thank God, Christmas is over! Yours sounds as though it wasn't much fun. Mine, too, had a fantastic and unreal quality about it, the nearest thing to it being the Christmas Tom spent with me. I shan't bore you with the details of the one just passed, for it would take too long. Suffice it to say that it had to do with another attempt to mix business and family pleasure. I ought to know by now that that often doesn't work. . . .

Frankly, I doubt whether I have the right, legal or ethical, to look in the package containing Tom's letters to his mother. When Fred got them back from Scribner's, he brought them to me and asked me to keep them for his mother's heirs until the four children could make up their minds what final disposition to make of them. They are, therefore, in my physical possession, but are not my property, nor are they the property of Tom's Estate. When I took them from Fred, I put them in the steel cabinet, where the papers of the Wolfe Estate are kept under lock and key, and there they still are, wrapped up and untouched since that time. I hesitate to raise this question with Fred because he couldn't answer it without consulting all the others, and as you know they are rather touchy about their rights. I sometimes have to walk pretty much of a tight rope to keep out of trouble.

When you come down to New York, if you ever do, let's talk about the notebooks. I have always felt that something might be done with them. You might also let me know sometime what your present thoughts are about a possible biography. I sent you a letter the other day in response to one I had received from your young friend Kennedy [Richard S. Kennedy]. As you saw there, he is thinking about a biography. I cannot stop anyone from writing a biography if he wishes to do so, but I shall do what I can to avoid a duplication of effort.

The best wish I can think of for the moment for the new year is that I may see you in it.

Cordially,
Ed

*

December 29

Dear Ed:

Dean Munn letter (I mean Professor Munn nowadays) is a masterpiece, & I should think would melt a heart of stone, which I dont think Munn's heart is made of. So I will keep my fingers crossed and wait and see what he writes to you before I stir him up at all myself.

So sorry if your Christmas was too wild. I tried to imagine who you combined with family this time, but the only person I could think of was Boswell and I doubt if he was present at the festivities. . . .[1] Anyway we can all settle down now to a good long skiddy car-wont-start-y winter. Such is life.

Well, now you will rue the day you ever met me, but Gosh! how do we know that all of Mabel's missing letters arent in that wrapped up and untouched package that Fred brought to you from Scribners. I mean the letters that Mabel found the letter from Perkins about. I'll repeat all that information to you so you'll know what I am talking about. When Mabel started sorting out her letters just before she went to Asheville and Florida this time, she came across a letter from Perkins to her, dated June 1, 1945. I quote herewith from Mabel's letter to me about this. "In answering me he wrote 'I have typed copies of all your letters - not the originals. They were prepared by John Terry and your mother at Brooklyn and given me.' "

SO, when Mabel found this from Perkins she immediately stopped sorting out her letters and wrote Miss Wyckoff to send her those (or copies of them) so "I could ascertain here which had to be typed." Ever since Irma has been hunting throughout the length and breath [sic] of 8 floors of 597 Fifth for same and says she cannot find them. And of course, meanwhile Mabel has given up and gone to Florida.

BUT wouldnt the logical thing have been for those letters to have been wrapped up in that mysterious package which you have? I should think it would. I may be wrong. But I cant help feeling that there are all kinds of wonderful missing unknown treasures in that package: and suppose I'll dream of it until some time if and when you can look?? . . .

Love,
Liddy

28

[1] Nowell was referring to James Boswell (1740–95). Aswell, having just been appointed a member of the Yale Committee, negotiated publishing rights to the Boswell papers for McGraw-Hill. Five volumes of Boswell's journals were published during the years of the Aswell-Nowell correspondence (Frederick A. Pottle, editor).

Chapter Two

"I dont think devotion to *any*body is worth killing yourself over."

NOWELL, FEBRUARY 1950

*

THE JOB of collecting Wolfe's letters became more time-consuming and emotionally draining than either Aswell or Nowell had imagined. Aswell expressed weariness beyond weariness, as the demands of the estate seemed to take his energies away from everything else. Nowell made further demands on his energy, raising questions, seeking advice, asking him to write or phone people, proposing more Wolfe projects out of other un-sorted Houghton material. He complained that he got paid nothing for his position as administrator and hinted darkly that he had been a fool to take on the duties of Wolfe's estate.

For her part, Nowell found the letters project taking longer and proceed-ing more slowly than she had expected. She needed Aswell's prompt responses to her questions so that all references could be accurately anno-tated. Then, too, new letters kept turning up from Wolfe's friends, from his family, from Aswell himself. The British publisher Frere, for instance, having told Nowell that all his correspondence with Wolfe had been burned in the blitz by the Luftwafte, suddenly found twenty-five letters. And in September, Mabel Wolfe sent Nowell photostats of approximately 300 pages of Wolfe's letters. "Needless to say," Nowell wrote Jack Wheelock and Irma Wyckoff of Scribner's, "I am a little bit appalled."[1] After twenty months, the letters still remained unfinished.

The frustrations of the project caused Aswell and Nowell to develop distinct work styles. Oriented toward the future, Nowell wanted the letters project over and done with. Oriented toward the past, Aswell delayed.

---

[1] Letter of September 21, 1950, Nowell files, Houghton Library. Nowell later revised her estimate of pages downward.

31

His reluctance to confront issues caused Nowell real problems. He mentioned that he had a box of Wolfe material in his attic which he had never opened. Unable to find certain information she needed, Nowell suspected it might be in his box. When her chiding words failed to prod him into action, a chimney fire at the Aswell house finally did.

Between Aswell's style and Nowell's style lay Thomas Wolfe's style, simmering on the pages of letters and notebooks. If not scurrilous, many Wolfe passages were scandalous. In Nowell's view, such was the measure of the man. The possibility of lawsuits by Wolfe's "wimmin" — many of them still alive — meant that Wolfe's material required careful editing: on this they were agreed. But Nowell felt that to suppress the cruel things Wolfe wrote, notably about Aline Bernstein, would be to misrepresent literary history. Aswell did not see it that way. Saying he did not want to hurt Aline, he postponed decisions about segments of letters that might sully Wolfe's image.

The year ended amicably when Nowell and Aswell united, albeit for different reasons, against a common enemy. Once again, a former New York University associate of Wolfe's, Vardis Fisher, was the target. Nowell was angered by articles by Fisher fraught with Freudian interpretations of Wolfe. Nowell had been Fisher's agent in New York and had maintained her friendship with him, even trying to guide him as he wrote his article about Wolfe. However, reading what Fisher had written and knowing Wolfe's hatred of Freudian psychology, Nowell wanted Aswell to intervene on Wolfe's behalf. Aswell was quick to come to her defense, not so much because of a principle of scholarship as because of the articles' potential damage to a man whom he adored.

January 27, 1950

Dear Liddy,

Mr. Cane tells me that his second letter to John Terry produced a telephone call from him. Terry stated that he did not have Tom's letters to Mabel nor copies of them. He said he had seen them some years ago but that Mrs. Wolfe took them away "to put in a safe place." Mr. Cane thinks Terry was telling the truth and, if so, this gets us a little further in our search by the process of elimination. It is still my hunch that the letters are in Asheville among the mass of stuff Mabel said she cleared out of the house on Spruce Street and stored away without examination. If this is true, the chance of your getting them for inclusion in your book seems to me rather slight. Mabel seems incapable of carrying through the search and of putting things in order.

Cordially,
Ed

*

Jan 30, 1950

Dear Ed:

. . . Would you write to The Great Man ([William] Saroyan...) a kind of form letter and ask if he saved any letters from Tom. I know they corresponded in 1936 or 37 (when Tom was living on 1st Ave: Tom told me they did and showed me one letter from Saroyan which I think was in answer to an answer Tom had written to Saroyan's first. But I kind of think Saroyan would be greatly impressed by being approached by the estate, whereas he'd pay no attention to me. . . .

EP

Maybe I shouldnt say it: it may sound like sour grapes, but you know I was kind of disappointed in the Mrs B Letters (Tho dont tell her so). I'd thought they'd be the real Abelard and Heloise stuff, but Tom writes a surprisingly little amount about their love affair and an awful lot about himself which I'd already read, at least in fragmentary form, in notebooks. AND they dont carry the whole story of the affair very well: too spotty and far-between: almost all written from Europe in 26 or 28 and then a great gap and the trying-to-get-rid-of-her ones. I mean, I'm delighted to have read em, and to be allowed to ask for excerpts from them and they are damn good. BUT I dont think they stand up very well as a book by themselves: unless her own letters prove an awful lot.[1] Compared to them, the Perkins letters are MUCH more major: there you get the whole damn story of Tom's career and his changing relationship with M.E.P.

33

[Maxwell E. Perkins] from intense hero-worship to truculence and despair. [2] Oh well. Goodnight. EP

[1] These letters subsequently were published: Suzanne Stutman, ed., *My Other Loneliness: Letters of Thomas Wolfe and Aline Bernstein* (Chapel Hill: University of North Carolina Press, 1983).

[2] As most Wolfe scholars point out, it was difficult to maintain a friendship with Wolfe. Nowell wrote about this on March 13, 1949, to Richard S. Kennedy, whom she had met at the Houghton Library while he was a graduate student at Harvard: "I never got in a real row with Tom for 3 reasons. (1) Because I was never the person on the pedestal, only a secondary figure. (2) Because he died before he got around to me. He was beginning to show signs of making me his father-mother, the person he told everything to, after he broke off with Perkins and needed somebody to talk things out with. . . . (3) because in the few rows we had, I shouted him down, instead of being noble and patient like Perkins. But the real reason was that I was never the A 1 figure to advise him. I never was agent for his books, for instance, he didn't want me to be (he had Perkins and then didn't need anybody, tho he got free advice from me) and I didn't want to be. I knew that a job like that would kill me: it was too much on top of my regular job, and I didn't want to be responsible for his whole life & career, as he would have made me if anything went wrong" [Nowell files, Houghton Library].

*

February 7, 1950

Dear Liddy,

. . . Mabel and Fred have both just written that I may open the package containing Tom's letters to his mother, so I'll do it as soon as I can find the time. That's my trouble — time. I get up at 6:30 every morning, seldom go to bed before midnight, work at my desk at home almost straight through every weekend, and still I can't keep up with everything I am supposed to do. What a life! I frequently ask myself whether it's worth it, and the answer is no, and yet I go on doing it. And that, dear Liddy, is a definition of a damned fool. . . .

I hate to write Saroyan. Do you really think I should? If you say so, of course I will. . . .

I read the Mrs. B. letters a couple of years ago and missed the same things you miss in them. But then you remember Tom got a lot of his letters back from Aline and burned them — so she once told me. That may explain it.

Dean Munn sounds wonderful. I have never met him, but would like to. And so to bed.

Ed

*

[February 1950]

Dear Ed:

To get right to the heart of the matter, I <u>do</u> think you are a damned fool. I mean, of course, to keep on driving yourself so hard. I cant remember if I exclaimed about it when I saw you at Harvard or not, but you look at least 20 years older than you did in 1941. No kidding. AND if you ask me, being executor of Tom's Estate is an added and unnecessary chore. Sure, you're doing it because you were/are devoted to Tom, but I dont think devotion to ANYbody is worth killing yourself over. And I dont believe you get paid a cent for same: which means you cant hire anyone to help you or any such.

Well, it's none of my business, specially about the getting-paid part, but ever since I saw you I've felt kind of remorseful that I went and put my foot in it by suggesting you to Fred and Mabel when Mr Perkins died. And IF and WHEN you ever get to the place where you are ready to beg off on it, for Christs sakes dont think you have to stick to it just because I'm working on the Letters or somesuch. Sure, I would feel sunk without you, but that wouldnt matter: somehow it would iron out. The Letters are pretty well set now, anyway, and thats the only thing that counts. . . .

Love
Liddy

And I mean it about dumping the estate. But for Christs sakes dont dump it onto me. <u>I</u> wouldnt do it unless I got paid enough to hire a steog. [stenog.] to cope with same. Amen. EP

*

April 10, 1950

Dear Liddy,

. . . I remember very well that thing of Tom's which was called "A Statement."[1] It was something he prepared as a possible publicity release to announce his signing a contract with Harpers. It was, however, too long for the purpose and was not sent out.

I cannot remember the letter to me which is referred to in the statement. If it is not among the Harper papers at Houghton, it could possibly be in my attic. I have been meaning for weeks to get at the chore of going through those papers to send them on to Houghton. But somehow I never seem to have any time. I suppose I might just bundle them all up and ship them off, but it seems to me I ought to go through them first because I no longer remember what is there.

When your present job is done, you and I ought to have a talk about further possibilities. There is, of course, the possibility of a biography, which we have mentioned before. Then, too, I have a hunch that there must be things among the Houghton papers which could and should be salvaged for publication. Some, perhaps, in magazines; and then the notebooks for a possible book.[2] Ever since I became Administrator of the Estate I have hoped against hope that I might do this myself, but in three years I have managed only two visits to Houghton, both of them quite brief. What I have in mind, of course, is that perhaps you, with your vast knowledge of Wolfe and your present familiarity with the material in Houghton, might be interested in taking on such an assignment on some basis which we could work out. My ideas about it are very vague. You might turn the thought over in your mind and eventually let me know whether it holds any attraction for you. . . .

All my best,
Ed

[1] Nowell, in her second year of editing Wolfe's letters, wanted to tie up loose ends, finish this project, and get on with new Wolfe work. She wondered about a letter Wolfe wrote to Aswell, expressing his reasons for going to Harper. The letter is referred to in Wolfe's "A Statement," which Aswell used extensively in preparing the posthumous publications and which reads in part: "For two years now, since I began to work on my new book, I have felt as if I was standing on the shore of a new land. About the book that I am doing, I can only tell you that it is a kind of fable, constructed out of the materials of experience and reality, and permitting me, I hope, a more whole and thorough use of them than I have had before" (Richard Kennedy and Paschal Reeves, eds., *The Notebooks of Thomas Wolfe*, vol. 2 [Chapel Hill: University of North Carolina Press, 1970], p. 890; hereafter cited as *Notebooks*).

[2] All three projects they discussed in 1950 were subsequently published: *Letters* (1956); Nowell, *Thomas Wolfe: A Biography* (1960); and *Notebooks* (1970).

*

April 11, maybe, 1950.

Dear Ed:

. . . [1] About your own bundle of papers in your attic: shame on you: you are almost as bad as Mabel. And I do wish you would either go through them, or send them up to Jackson and let him/or me go through them. And do it pretty soon, if you can humanly manage same. Or if you cant, send em up and trust to his and my discretion. Or just mine, if there is apt to be any personal stuff you wouldnt want him to see. But maybe you can get a chance yourself. Anyway I wont dream of putting these letters to bed until you do look and see what you may have. Maybe there never really was a letter such as is referred to in that statement:

maybe you just said there was. But if there was, I need it: it is the only way that will express in Tom's own words his going to Harpers, especially now the one to me about it and about the Authors League is out at their request.

Future possibilities: well, I spose we'll have to talk about that face to face. But I can see ahead a way right now. I mean, I have the shape of a book of Travel Notebooks all in my head, and have at least a rough draft of the stuff it would be made from. I would like to do that very much: I've already done so much work towards it, and if you didnt use my work and laboriously deciphered copies of those notebooks you'd be nuts.

Also, did you ever consider publishing Welcome to Our City, which most people consider a much better play than Mannerhouse.[2] I have never read it: I know enough about it so I dont need to for the Letters. But I could some time. And there are several legible copies that were used for the Baker production which could be photostated easily. I'd say off hand, to get the Letters out. Then publish Welcome if you want to publish it. Then bring out the notebooks' book. Then, and not until then, would be time to dig around carefully and see what else was there that could be published. I don't think very much. Tho the Notebooks could go to two volumes if you thought the public would buy that much of same.

I know you have an idea that I could do a biography sometime, and I could do A biography right now. But it wouldnt be THE biography. For that, you could work for years. The essential facts of Tom's life will all be apparent, I think, from the Letters. After they come out, any dumb jerk can, and probably will, write a biography. And after the notebooks come out, the job will be all the easier. But I dont think that really matters: I think we ought to bring out the things Tom wrote himself first, and get that done. The other way would be to keep all this hidden till The Biographer had used them, so nobody else could do it first. . . .

So, well, sufficient unto the day the evil thereof, I guess. I will try like hell to get the letters done this summer. Would then like to rush right ahead and get the travel notebooks into shape. And then we could review the situation. Maybe by that time you'll know more about J Terry. He certainly wont do a very good biography of Tom: I keep finding the most horrible mistakes in Letters to Mama, due to just sheer laziness and lack of research.[3] And he doesnt know anything about Tom in the last days of his life and you and I wont tell him, and did I tell you about the NYU student who told Mrs B that Terry said she was "entirely unimportant" in Tom's life. My Gawd. But we dont even know, do we, whether Perkins wrote him a letter giving him official claim to be Tom's biographer: before

I undertook such a job I'd like to know exactly how things stood. I've run into several people just on this letters-job who I think have been influenced by Terry not to cooperate. (a) Albert Coates [Wolfe's roommate in Cambridge], (b) Chancellor Chase of NYU (c) maybe Archie Henderson [faculty member at UNC during Wolfe's undergraduate years], etc. etc. etc. It is OK on the Letters, we have got around em or are working on em: I'm still trying to get an answer out of Archie. But there might be a lot more like them in N.C. [North Carolina]. AND there is also Mabel!! If she got upset enough, she probably could get you fired, and then where would I be?

Aw nuts, lets get the letters and the notebooks out and maybe Welcome, and some other things, and see what has developed in the meanwhile: in the way of wars and pestilences and Mabel and J Terry. . . .

That's all for tonight. DONT answer any of it. Save your time and breath for the expedition to the attic.

EHP

[1] Nowell began her letter by saying she would not make the May 1st deadline for the letters but hoped to meet the next one, October 1st. She continued to write people who "might possibly have Wolfe letters" and to worry about "some tiny little almost unnoticed remark about someone with a tendency to nuisance suits."

[2] Thirty-two years later, *Welcome to Our City — A Play in Ten Scenes* (Baton Rouge: Louisiana State University Press, 1983) was finally published thanks to the effort of Richard S. Kennedy, who edited the manuscript and wrote an introduction to it.

[3] Nowell was referring to Terry, *Thomas Wolfe's Letters to His Mother (1943)*. This collection has been re-edited by Hugh Holman and Sue Fields Ross (*The Letters of Thomas Wolfe to His Mother* [Chapel Hill: University of North Carolina Press, 1968]).

*

April 19, 1950

Dear Liddy,

For my own selfish sake I'm glad the Ms. won't be ready till fall. That will probably be a much better time for me than summer. And of course Mr. Cane can now take his vacation when he pleases.

I agree with what you say about further publishing possibilities. We must talk about these things some time. About the biography. I do not see Terry as an obstacle. He'll never do it. He has not bothered to ask me anything about Tom's last year. He has never bothered to go to Houghton, and how can one write a biography without doing that? He seems to think he has all the essential stuff in what Mrs. Wolfe told him — which is foolish. Besides, he is lazy, and, Mabel says, ill. He will probably die without ever putting a line on paper. . . .

38

Ohio University Press
Swallow Press

The editors take pleasure in sending you a copy of

IN THE SHADOW OF THE GIANT: THOMAS WOLFE
Correspondence of Edward C. Aswell
and Elizabeth Nowell, 1949-1958

Edited by Mary Aswell Doll
and Clara Stites

xx + 256 pp., notes, photos, index.

Ohio ISBN 0-8214-0904-2 $27.95

Publication date: October 1, 1988

We would appreciate receiving two copies of any published review or mention of this book.

Scott Quadrangle / Athens, Ohio 45701-2979

Yes, you were in order to reprove me for not getting the Wolfe things safely out of my attic. There is not much there written by Tom, but there is the correspondence with doctors, Fred, and Mabel, during his final illness, which is all quite interesting. More meat for a biography than for your present job. I will definitely plan to clear it out and send it to Houghton this coming week-end. My resolve to do this was made before your letter came. We had a frightening chimney fire last Saturday which might well have burnt the house down. That was warning enough not to delay longer. Think I'll just pack the whole lot and let the people at Houghton make what they can of it. If I wait till I can find time to sort through it, God knows when it will get done.

My best,
Ed

*

Wednesday night.
April 24 or thereabouts.

Dear Ed:

. . . Am now in the middle of the notebooks: got about one-eighth of them done: should take 2 or 3 or 4 more days. I think there is easily another book to be got out some day from these: not the addresses or outlines for work, I mean the Western Journal kind of short snatches. Found one about Tom, who was then called not Eugene but Oliver, going to Beethoven's birthplace or some sort of Beethoven house and bursting into tears when he saw his huge brass eartrumpets and realized he had never heard his music. A funny sketch about Olin Dows [a printer and painter, a Harvard friend of Wolfe's, whom Wolfe often visited in Rhinebeck, New York] ancestors, a funny sketch about Oliver in Marseilles drinking wines, telling a hardboiled captain that everything looked crooked, had for about a month. Of course some of these may have been put into the novels and I have forgotten them (am rereading novels, but dont have much time for that, so do it only snatchwise). More about the head-busting-open incident, a wonderful Samuel Pepys kind of thing about going to Hollywood and meeting almost every celebrity with Joel Sayres [sic] and everybody drunk and never went to bed. A short piece about Vienna Wald. Well, those are just examples. [1]

As you can gather from the above, the notebooks are NOT in chronological order but they will be when I'm through: am clipping notes dating as well as I can to each and have made Bond promise to check on me and affix bona-fide Houghton dates as soon as I've made mine.

Any biographer of Tom is going to have a hell of a time as to what to say about all these babes: there are more than I had ever heard of, and they all are still very much alive. Once in a while en route to ladies room I stick my head in Mr Bond's door and say "My God, did you read the letters from So-and-So. And he says Yes, but did you read the one from So-and-So. His sec is the daughter of Divinity Professor at Harvard: once in a while she lets out a snort, half mirth, half shock and says "Were <u>all</u> those people crazy?"

Love
EP

[1] Wolfe wrote in his notebooks about Joel Sayre, a writer at the RKO motion picture studio: "Sayre had made some remarks so I offered to fight him" (*Notebooks*, 2:765). Olin Dows was the model for Joel Pierce in *The River People*. Dows was Wolfe's ideal of the young hero, "always grand, noble, and romantic" (*Notebooks* 1:137). Dows was also among Wolfe's list of those whom he knew best in the years 1920–30. The list begins: "Aline, Perkins, Wheelock, Baker, Olin" (*Notebooks* 2:476).

*

May 10, 1950

Dear Ed:

. . . What I'm writing about now is to say that I DO SO TERRIBLY WANT that letter Tom wrote Ben [Wolfe's brother], and the others you found in package with letters to Mama. And the whole thing seems to have gone into the state of limbo which is part of Wolfe life and family and affairs. DID YOU SEND FRED COPIES OF THESE LETTERS so he could see what they said and give approval or refuse consent? If you did, I can write to him again and jog him on it. If you didnt, will you, and will you let me know when you do, so I can write to him and jog him on it. . . .

Love
Liddy

*

June 4, 1950.

Dear Ed:

I dont believe you've ever got together with Mrs B about those fragments to her and what we ought to do about them. . . .

One thing I'm pretty sure of: that we couldnt possibly suppress everything he said and did about poor Mrs B of this sort. [1] It would be practically dishonest, because he did it so very much. And any number of literary people would point out that we'd misrepresented the whole thing. In all these letters I have got from people who knew him, they often mention that he told them all about it: often under the transparent disguise of saying he had "a friend" who had had a love affair with a certain woman and was trying to break it off. . . . If you would rather not bring it up with Mrs B but think it is all right to do so, I'd be perfectly willing to myself. I hate to upset her, but I think she certainly would rather know about it than not know about it: you know what I mean.

Love

Liddy

[1] At issue were sections of letters Wolfe had written to Perkins about ending the relationship with Mrs. Bernstein. Aswell was reluctant to publish these, since they would put Wolfe in a bad light and would cause pain to Mrs. Bernstein. Nowell saw Wolfe's cruelty as part of the man and the letter portions as old news to Mrs. Bernstein in particular and Wolfe readers in general. These differences in the way each saw Wolfe became more pronounced as the years passed.

*

June 27, 1950

Dear Liddy,

. . . In recent weeks, Aline has called me several times. She is in a very unhappy frame of mind and worried about many things. I thought I'd better tell you this because I know she finds it rather agonizing to have painful incidents from the past brought into her full consciousness again just at this time.

I know your great devotion to Tom and the heroic labors you are putting into this present job. I know that there are thousands of questions that must be answered one way or another. But they cannot all be answered now, dear Liddy. For example, I cannot possibly advise you, at this stage, whether to include some of things you mention in this present book or to save them for some future book. Nor, I think, can Aline answer that now. The only procedure that will be advisable is for you to use restraint in quoting from Tom's letters to Aline. You will remember it was a great concession we won in getting Aline's consent to quote any of them at all. Let's rest on that for the moment and not push her too hard. My advice to you in preparing the draft of the manuscript is to include the things you would like to use in the light of all the knowledge you have about each individual situation. It is no good my trying to advise you whether to put in or leave out some specific item which I have not even read. It can only be after the draft of your manuscript is complete, so that Scribners, Mr. Cane, and I can read it, that we can then give you our allied advice;

and because of the many problems involved, it seems fairly certain that some of things you would like to include will have to be omitted for one good reason or another. This seems to me the only possible procedure. It puts the initial burden of decision on you, but the final burden will have to be on us when we have all the evidence before us.

I am hoping desperately to get off for a vacation at the end of this week, to be gone until about the middle of July. I am swamped with work and weary almost beyond weariness. Whether I shall succeed in catching up with everything before I go, I don't know. At this moment it looks impossible.

Cordially,
Ed

*

July 29, 1950.

Dear Ed:

Well, this is what I didn't have the time or strength to write you night before last when I sent you that little hasty note clipped onto the Harper stuff. What it boils down to is this: that I am very broke and kind of tired and nervous and discouraged and — well — I suppose Tom would call it "desperate" but that's a pretty strong way to put it. I guess just tired and fed up is more my way of saying same. This damn job has dragged on for 20 months now — count 'em — Jan 1949 to August 1950, and there is still no end in sight. I've been indexing by dates and working on all the million things that need research and foot-noting, I've filled up 4 of those big mottled cardboard files with letters to and from people. And every day when I think "Now I can go ahead and index and do footnotes so I can put the thing together in comes a pile of letters or of questions I must cope with: and so goes another day, and weeks and weeks and months. . . .

<u>And</u>, of course, there is the inexplicable and imponderable factor that I should have known would be connected with anything to do with Tom, sheer mass and utter unbelievable confusion. Fragments, total lack of any dates, letters which he wrote and did or did not send, or rewrote in different forms and sent, letters with both no date and no salutation, so you can only guess at who and when they were written, and why. Also constant mysterious references to "a friend" or "a young lady" or "a piece of writing" etc. etc. It was part of his suspiciousness and defence, I guess, that kept him from ever saying anything right out by name. . . .

SO, ANYWAY, I'd better get to the main point. Which is that I am BROKE and have been ever since Edna had virus pneumonia and all the rest of us had virus not-pneumonia. I was beginning to get "desperate" about it when you wrote me that terribly exhausted letter saying you were trying to get off on a vacation and get some rest. So I sold Dr. Perkins' [Nowell's father-in-law] desk and my Celadon china to an antique dealer and got along somehow, but then got up against it all over again. Wrote Charlie Scribner saying so: I thought maybe if he couldnt advance me any more against the Wolfe (I got my $3000 long ago in 1949) I might be going to get something on Nancy Hale [writer for whom Nowell was the agent], but no such luck for months if ever. Charlie said that he would be willing to give me $500 more and that you would not have to be consulted. Wait, what he said was "With regard to the Wolfe, I do not see any possible reason why I should have to consult Aswell, if I gave you an extra $500 advance. It is true that, as a representative of the Wolfes, he put up one thousand dollars against your advance, whereas Charles Scribners Sons put up two. Presumably he would not care to put up any more, but, if we did, it would be on our heads and for us to worry as to whether the royalties we paid you would return the same — no wonder you are such a meticulous girl in making contracts, since you seem to understand the simple wording of them so little."

To which I say Oh yeah. I mean of course I know that legally I have a perfect right to take any money which Scribners may think safe to advance to me against my own account. But still I'd be damned if I'd do it unknown to you, behind your back: you know what I mean.

So there the matter stands: and I wish the hell you'd write me about all this as soon as you can get a minute, because I havent answered Charlie definitely yet, was waiting till you were back and I could write to you. And, oh you know, he might be jealous if he thought I insisted on consulting you even when he assured me it was unnecessary, and all that sort of thing.

Well, to hell with it. Let me know if you ever need an editor for the General Letters of Calvin Coolidge, and meanwhile

Love,

from

Liddy

*

August 1, 1950

Dear Liddy,

. . . Believe me, I sympathize with your feelings to the fullest degree. I know exactly what it is like to be exhausted and discouraged. But a spot of rest, if you can manage to get it, will do wonders for you. At least it did for me. It distresses me greatly to learn that you are in financial difficulties. Since Mr. Scribner is willing to advance you another five hundred dollars, I urge you to take it. He was, of course, quite right technically when he said there was no need of consulting me, but just the same I am glad to know of the situation.

Please be assured, dear Liddy, that I understand the many difficulties that have faced you since you began work on this book project. None of us, I think, quite realized the magnitude of the job. Certainly, I didn't. If anybody knows the full extent of your own labors, I think I do. It is not often one meets with such devotion and conscientious work as you have put into this.

I suppose anyone who devotes as much of himself to a task as you have devoted to editing these Wolfe letters must derive his chief satisfaction not from the monetary reward, but from the particularly personal satisfaction that there always is in a job well done. I think back to the three years I spent editing Tom's posthumous manuscripts. It was necessary to carry on my full-time job at Harpers while I put Tom's manuscripts in shape, working every night and every week-end, literally during the whole three-year period. I never received a penny for it. And yet, while I was doing it, and now as I look back on it, I am still glad I did it. Even Max Perkins did not realize what was involved, just as I am sure that people at Scribners do not fully realize what is involved in your labors now. This is not meant as a criticism of them. Unless one has done that kind of thing oneself, it can't be comprehended.

Comfort yourself with the thought that you are nearing the end. There will have to come a time when you will say to yourself that the business of writing to people and collecting letters will have to be considered done whether it really is or not. It will never be possible to round up all the strays. . . .

I am returning herewith the two fragments you sent me, and I shall answer your questions about them to the best of my ability. . . .

In the fragment called "A Statement," where Tom referred to "a letter written to his publishers," I think this should not be taken literally. I don't believe there was such a letter. Tom simply cast his statement in this form to make it appear that the publisher had prepared the release. . . .

The second fragment I am pretty sure is part of that "Statement of Purpose" which Tom began as a letter to me, but when he got going he found he was actually writing part of the book. So he never sent the letter to me, and I received it only after his death when Max Perkins found it among his papers. It existed, I believe, in several different drafts, and I believe, also, that this fragment was part of one of the drafts. When

I edited YOU CAN'T GO HOME AGAIN, a couple of the chapters in that book were taken from this "Statement of Purpose." I simply took a pair of scissors and cut the pages out and pasted them up. That is probably why this fragment is so brief.

There is no point in writing Harpers to look through their files again. Before I left there I went through the files personally and took out all of the Wolfe stuff and sent it to Harvard. This was done with the approval of the president of the company. [1]

Cordially yours,

Ed

[1] Although Aswell had gone beyond the bounds of editing in preparing Wolfe's posthumous works and although he did not always tell Nowell the whole truth about what he had done, he made certain that all of Wolfe's manuscripts, complete with his own notations, changes, and additions, went to Harvard's Houghton Library. Nowell, who was originally working only with Wolfe's correspondence and notebooks, apparently never had time to examine the original manuscripts closely.

*

2 Prospect Street
So Dartmouth, Mass.
August 3, 1950.

Dear Ed:

As a matter of fact, I began to feel better as soon as I got all that long long mess of complaining off my chest to you. And now I feel sort of like a heel to have made you take so much of your own time and strength to sympathize, exhort, and comfort me and all. So I wont take any spot of rest: taking care of C&E [her daughters] aint exactly what you'd call a rest at any rate, and I do want to get the damn thing done and off to you and Jack. Meanwhile, as long as you think OK, I'll tell CS he can send me the extra $500 bucks when its convenient. I honestly feel sure the letters ought to make a whole lot more than the advance: they are so swell and anything of Tom's is bound to sell at any rate. But I do want to get it done and out especially before any kind of war conditions or paper shortages gum things up: paper shortages are poison to T.W. of course, the way he let words rip.

Well, OK, to hell with it, and I will plug along, and try to fortify myself by thinking of how you almost killed yourself working on the novels. And will try to get the thing together but still open enough for the insertion of Mabel's photostats when they are done. And thank the Lord you have them and have sent them to Bond and they are being done.

That second fragment doesnt fit into a Statement of Purpose, which flows right along, sounds to me as if Tom dictated the whole thing in one big hunk without even pausing to draw breath. But I can stick it next to it with some kind of footnote saying maybe it was another version of it, as long as you feel sure that some bright guy at Harpers wont suddenly turn up an unknown letter containing it.

Well, never mind, it'll be all right and I will try to leave you in peace for quite a spell now. And thanks a lot and

Love
from Liddy

Oh, PS I wasnt fair about one thing. I forgot that Irma did type some of the longhand photostats of Wisdom material for me way back: it was so way way back that I didn't remember it till I came across one she had typed after I had written you. In other words, she typed longhand letters to Scribner people and in Wisdom Collection (some of them) and I typed typewritten letters or am just going to use the photostat, and did all the things collected from everybody else. It doesnt really matter except I wasnt fair to CSS on that.

DONT answer any of this. Wait till I have something you really need to answer.

*

August 21, 1950

Dear Ed:

Here is a babe you had better deal with in your most official but velvet-gloved manner. I wont answer her at all: you can write and explain to her that she couldnt publish Tom's letters without your consent, etc. You know the general answer to people of this sort.

There are quite a lot of letters from her to Tom, so supposedly she should have quite a lot from him: maybe 5 or 10 or thereabouts. She was a girl of his all right: is mentioned occasionally in his notebooks and is also included in some of those famous lists of babes he made. I never had any proof that he was deeply in love with her, dont think he was: but he evidently saw a lot of her at any rate. If you can get em from her, OK, fine. If you cant, to hell with her.

That's all and there's no hurry about this. I'm just writing it to dump it on your desk instead of having it clutter up my own and maybe get lost in the shuffle or filed by mistake.

Love,
Liddy

*

August 30, 1950

Dear Liddy,

. . . I met Tom for the first time at a cocktail party in the spring of 1937.[1] We didn't talk about his work at all but did discover that we had a number of friends and interests in common. I can't remember the exact date of this meeting. It was probably in March, because I left on an automobile trip through the South toward the end of March 1937 and was going to Chapel Hill, among other places, and I remember asking Tom about some of the people I was planning to see there. Of course, he knew them all. I was gone on the trip about six weeks, returning to New York around the end of the first week in May. Tom's phone call to Lee Hartman [Harper's editor] occurred after I got back because I was out to lunch when the call came through, and that's how the mix-up occurred; and Lee Hartman was put on the line because I was not in the office. I would say, then, that the call could have been sometime in May, though I think it was more probably in June, and may even have been as late as July.

I hope this will help you solve the mystery.

Cordially,

Ed

[1] Nowell and Aswell's wife, Mary Lou, were also at the party, as Nowell had reminded Wolfe in the fall of 1937 when she wrote to him of Aswell's interest in becoming his publisher.

*

August 31, 1950

Dear Liddy,

Your thought about the title seems to me to head in the right direction. As you say, the book (or books) will be something more than the usual collection of letters because of the simple fact that Tom was usually so preoccupied with himself and with the events of his life. Let's both continue to think about this title problem. In the end, of course, Scribners may have their own ideas and may not agree with us, but I think they will be more likely to agree if you and I can come up with exactly the right suggestion.

I don't think "The Story of a Novelist" is quite right. As you say, it may cause confusion with THE STORY OF A NOVEL. Also, isn't it perhaps too limiting? May it not be true that the book will present a fairly complete story of a life? That is, of the man as well as of the novelist? Tentatively I suggest "The Life of Thomas Wolfe, as Told through His Letters."

This is perhaps too sweeping, but if the words can be refined down to

47

greater exactness I think perhaps the general idea conveyed here may be valid. And certainly some such title would, as you say, give the book the greater importance which it deserves.

In thinking about this problem, let's not worry about Terry one way or the other.

My best, as ever,
Ed

*

Sunday Sept. 4, 1950.

Dear Ed:

Thanks again for many letters on my behalf. About a possible title for the letters, we all seem to be more or less in accord. I now have an answer from Jack to my letters to him similar to one I wrote to you. Of course it is subject to the usual qualifications of "I will talk it over with the others here" but he more or less agrees, as definitely as he ever agrees unless I send him a "Yes" or "No" question, and he gets C.S.'s definite consent or refusal.

I almost think your rough idea is going too far: though of course I know it was just to suggest the general lines. I mean "The Life of Thomas Wolfe, as Told Through His Letters." I have a feeling that if I could get a good title from Tom's own words, that would pass the buck a little bit: I mean, instead of you and me and CSS claiming that these letters presented Tom's life, we would be just sort of hinting at it. But maybe I'm too shy. I looked up his list of discarded titles for <u>The Story of a Novel</u> which is in a notebook. Other ideas he had for that were:

The Apprentice Years	
An Apprenticeship	
My Apprenticeship	
An Artist in America.	(Which is a <u>good</u> title, I think, but didnt someone use it for a life of Audubon or Currier & Ives or someone?) Maybe not. maybe I just think they should
A Man and His Book.	(it would have to be "books" here)
Of Making Many Books,	which Scribners swiped for their own book later. . . .

New subject: Vardis has written a pretty stinking article for Tomorrow about Tom and Perkins.[1] It was sposed to be about Tom in his N.Y.U. days and friendship with Vardis, and V said he'd send it to me in case I needed any of the facts for background about NYU period. If he had limited himself to that, it would be one thing, but he's gone ahead and tried to deduce all sorts of conclusions about "what would have happened to Tom if he had lived" about the merits and weaknesses of his books, etc. etc. In the first draft, he said that he thought Tom would have gone insane, and like a damn fool, maybe, I sat down and started writing 3000 word letters in argument. You know how hipped on Freudian psychology and psycho-analysis etc. Vardis is. Well, he contends that Tom had certain neuroses and phobias etc and that "he never faced himself" and that people who dont are apt to go insane. (Which I think is just psychiatrists sales talk swill.) I talked him out of that some: he now mentions it but doesnt make it the main point and climax of the piece. Well, I couldnt even begin to list all the false premises and things that probably would make you mad. You know Vardis was bitter about Tom in later years, I think because he had a greater success. Also V was always very bitter about Perkins: because Perkins turned him down for Scribners twice. (3 times in all now, I wrote CS about him after you declined Solomon [novel by Vardis Fisher] and CS turned him down again.) Vardis says all this stuff about Tom, also says that Perkins was "not the best editor for Tom" because Tom needed an editor to "make him face himself" and Perkins didnt, and that "Perkins never faced Perkins." Goes on to say Perkins and Tom both had strong "feminine identifications" in early life: that Perkins expressed scorn of women came from that and that if he "had faced himself" he would have realized it and got over it. Says Perkins wearing a hat is another indication of childhood phobia etc. Does the same thing, but more with Tom. Tells about Tom was worried about leaving cigarettes burning in NYU days and "had a phobia of fire." To which I answered that he may have had a phobia of having his only longhand ledgers of the <u>Angel</u> get burned up, but that I never saw the least evidence of it later, and that his apartment, furniture, manuscripts, etc. etc. are lousy with cigarette burns: that sometimes that is how I can tell which page follows which, by degree the cigarette burned through. Oh, to hell with it: its another instance of a person who knew Tom in his early days and assumed that Tom went on from bad to worse, instead of, as I know was true, that Tom "found himself" in some ways as he matured. There is nothing you have to do or could do about this. I have seen 2 drafts, finally wrote Vardis I wish I had never seen it in the first place, or anyway never tried to argue with him, because he is focused grimly on his basic first false premises and so there's no sense arguing with him. Told him I washed my hands of it and that he was not to quote any of my counterarguments. He may revise once more and show it to me, but I hope he doesnt. It only takes up about two days of my precious time, and makes me furious, and does no good.

Goombye. Dont answer.

Love

from

Liddy

---

[1] Vardis Fisher's articles, "My Experiences with Thomas Wolfe" and "Thomas Wolfe and Maxwell Perkins" appeared subsequently in the April and July 1951 issues of *Tomorrow*. Fisher's psychoanalytic approach to Wolfe in these articles infuriated both Nowell and Aswell. Nevertheless, Nowell corresponded regularly with Fisher, who had known Wolfe at NYU, and in 1954 she became his literary agent. Many of the Fisher-Nowell letters are now at the University of North Carolina, Chapel Hill.

*

September 7, 1950

Dear Liddy,

Your letter of September 4th has just come.

Yes, I realize that the title I suggested was too broad and, in fact, said so. I was merely groping toward something. It is good to know that Jack Wheelock is favorably disposed toward the general idea. The perfect solution, as you say, would be to find some phrase of Tom's that would fit. Over and over again he said in various ways that a writer had to write about what he knew, about the experiences of his own life, since that was all he had to write about. There must be some phrase in that connection that would serve. When you have time you might reread his note to the reader in LOOK HOMEWARD, ANGEL. I don't have it handy. Maybe there is something there. As I remember it, though, it seems to have been written as a protection against libel suits and thus was not quite straight since it accepted the charge of autobiography and disclaimed it in the same breath. There are probably better and stronger statements about this same thing elsewhere in Tom's writings. I'd be surprised if there weren't a number of such statements in his letters.

Too bad about the Vardis Fisher piece. This is the first I had heard of it. But we must try to be philosophical about such things. People are free to write whatever they like, which means among other things that they are free to be as foolish as they like. Without reading Vardis' piece, I would be quite convinced that he would have very little illumination to offer about Tom. Vardis has narrowed his life down to a set of tight little theories. Tom's growth was in the opposite direction, one of constant expansion. His desire was to embrace life; and for this reason he had to

50

reject pretty much all the theories, because there was too much of life they did not take into account. So, as I say, it's too bad about Vardis, but let's not worry unduly on that score. What he has written will do no good, but in the long run it will also do no harm.

By now I suppose I must be a close runnerup to Scribners in Vardis's disesteem, for I too have rejected him three times. He has said nothing to me about the Wolfe article. Yet, within the week, I have had two friendly letters from Opal [Vardis's wife], who is sending me, at Vardis's suggestion, a historical novel she has written. Please say nothing about this. Whether the book is any good remains to be seen.

My best to you, as always,
Ed

*

September 21, 1950

Dear Liddy,

Enclosed is the Estate's check for the vast sum of $1.93 representing your commission as agent on the Wolfe transactions I recently reported to you. I am glad to know that Mr. Perkins paid you for the transactions which occurred before I became administrator. The present check, therefore, clears the record to date. I send it now because if I don't I'll forget it.

Ah me, so I'll have to tackle Aline about that letter of Tom's to Max Perkins? I hate the thought because I don't like to hurt people, and this letter will hurt her deeply. One final plaintive plea to you before I do it. Is it really necessary? If you think that the letter or portions of it should be used in the book to fill a gap in the record that is not otherwise filled, I would much prefer to have you put it in and then leave it to Mr. Cane and me to try to clear it with Aline later when we have the complete text of the book before us and can show her just how you have handled this delicate matter. Her reaction will be less pained and more cooperative if she can consider the whole problem in its context. Don't you think this is really the better way to do it? When the time comes, Cane and I will undoubtedly have to consult Aline about more points than just this one, and we may as well cover everything in one session.

Too bad that Scribners have closed their minds about the title. As far as I am concerned, the question is still open. Let's not worry about it now. Keep thinking about the kind of title you have been groping for. If you come up with the right one, I'll go to bat for it. Of course, such things are often considered the final prerogative of the publisher, so it wouldn't be wise to try to force a title on Scribners to which they had strong objections. After all, theirs will be the job of selling the book, and we don't want to dampen their enthusiasm. . . .

All my best,
Ed

*

October 6, 1950.

Dear Ed:

Sometime in the near future, no terrible emergency, I wish you'd cast your eye over the enclosed correspondence and tell me your reaction to it. What it boils down to is this: In two letters to Perkins, as proof of his loyalty to CSS, Tom refers to the fact that another publisher offered him a large sum of money and he didn't pay any attention to him. Well, I know that that was a Cap Pearce [Charles A. Pearce] of Harcourt, and that the sum was $10,000 and I am quite sure that Tom told you as much, also Linscott [Robert B. Linscott of Houghton Mifflin], also me, also 100 other people at one time or another. Didnt he tell you that?

I saw no reason why I shouldnt put a footnote to it saying that in 1933 or 1934 Tom was approached by Charles A Pearce, who was then editor for Harcourt Brace and offered ten thousand dollars advance for his next novel, sight unseen. [1] I almost wish I'd gone ahead and written said footnote, but I thought I ought to consult with Cap and at least warn him. Result, enclosed letter from him, which I know is a deliberate playing-down of the whole thing because Charlie Scribner called Harcourt on it and Harcourt spanked Cap pretty hard so Cap backed down. What the hell, I was Tom's agent then (with Lieber) and was right in the midst of the whole mess.

Well, again I wish I hadnt but I did — sent Cap's letter down to Jack and Charlie. And got the enclosed ukase from the throne of Sanctity of Publishers from Charlie. [2] Was so mad I didnt dare to write him back, or not yet anyway, so wrote to Jack and blew off steam. As third person enclosure. To which Jack, bless him, answered soothingly that "I suppose Charlie feels that, while you are responsible for what is said in the book, it might be construed as an unfriendly act on the part of Scribners to publish a book with such charges, and might give rise to all sorts of unpleasantness. Publishers have to play ball together, in many ways, and discord has to be avoided."

Which is OK fine if publishers want to "play ball together" but I dont want to play in-field or out-field or anything with same. AND if I minimize this, I am almost making Tom out to be a liar: I mean, if I imply that he really wasnt offered any "vast sum of money" (which is a lie — he was.) I spose I can just leave this reference unfootnoted, as CS wants me to but it is going to be very obvious that I have not footnoted it, because I've been working till my eyeballs pop right out to footnote all such other references, as I think a good job on letters ought to do. OR I could write a footnote saying "Wolfe was approached tentatively by two other publishers after publication of Look Homeward, Angel, both of whom had declined it previously. He was offered ten thousand dollars advance by one of these for his next book, but chose to stay with Scribners. The names of these publishers are omitted here by request of Mr Charles Scribner." WHOOPS! THAT would fix him. Or should I just subside. Well, think it over for a while: I guess you had better be my arbiter and balance-wheel on this.

Love,
from
Madam P.

[1] *Letters* contains no such footnote.

[2] It was typical of Nowell to be aboveboard in her three-way dealings with Scribner's and Aswell, always letting Aswell know what transpired between Scribner's and her. It is also typical of her disdain of the old boys' syndrome that she would refer to the letter from Scribner's as a "ukase," or edict from the czar.

*

October 10, 1950

Dear Liddy,

. . . No, I do not recall that Tom ever told me a definite figure in connection with Pearce's approach to him. Nor did he mention a figure in connection with Houghton Mifflin. Your letter was the first indication I had had of this. I had thought I was the only one to name $10,000.

Pearce is soft-pedaling the whole thing now, of course, but don't let that disturb you. For your footnote why not leave the name of the publisher out since it could well have been Knopf.[1] And word the footnote in such a way so that it will not appear to have been Harpers that approached Tom at that early date. As you well know, I did not get into the picture until quite late after Tom's break with Scribners was definite and his manuscripts had been at one point turned over to Houghton-Mifflin. All I'm saying is that in protecting Pearce from the specific charge, don't word the thing in such a way that the reader will jump to the conclusion that you are referring to Harpers. This would be a natural inference since Tom did go to Harpers. . . .

My best,
Ed

53

[1] Blanche Knopf had tried to lure Wolfe to Knopf, without success. At a publisher's luncheon that year, Alfred Knopf reflected angry disappointment with their failure when he said, "The publisher who took Thomas Wolfe away from Max Perkins should hang his head in shame" (Edward C. Aswell, speech to Harvard Club, October 13, 1953).

*

October 11, 1950

Dear Liddy,

Thanks for your letter of October 9th and for the check for $11.53 representing the Estate's share of royalties on Thomas Wolfe's short stories in The New Yorker anthology.

I am a little puzzled by your saying, "Herewith I repay the compliment of the dollar something you are going to pay me later." The check for $1.93 representing what the Estate owed you was mailed you on September 21st and has already come back from the bank with your endorsement and the bank's cancellation. I assume you must have received it and forgotten it — and no wonder, since it was so small.

Cordially,
Ed

*

December 20, 1950

Dear Liddy,

I have forwarded today to the Harvard Trust Company the Estate's check for seventy-five cents covering the cost of photostating one letter.

A very merry Christmas to you, too, and a happy new year!

Sincerely,
Ed

Chapter Three

"You are not free to reveal
my confidences."

ASWELL, APRIL 14, 1951

*

THREE YEARS into the project, Nowell expected the letters collection to run to two volumes containing seven to eight hundred letters, depending on how many must be cut because of libel or space restrictions. In her effort to be accurate she sometimes spent as much as five hours researching and rewriting a single footnote. As she told Jack Wheelock, "The legend of Tom has become enormous — and enormously full of errors and misinterpretations. Well, here he is himself, and every bit as fascinating as the legendary Wolfe, but portrayed with the verity of his own words, so nobody can 'get him wrong.' "[1]

On February 16, she sent volume I to Aswell, followed by volume II on March 20th. But Aswell did not read the manuscript and did not respond to her questions about it. Instead, he explained patiently that both he and Wheelock were overworked and in poor health. Nowell felt that, before she could finish the book, she must know from Aswell and Scribner's whether they wanted the letters to be the life of Wolfe as told through his letters, with ample editorial commentary, or simply a collection of letters with brief commentary from her. As the deadline for fall publication — Nowell believed it was May 1st — came closer, she became more and more frantic in her efforts to get Aswell to read and react.

She also wanted to know about other Wolfe projects she could work on. In February she suggested a book of reminiscences by Tom's friends, and she continued to urge Aswell to consider publishing sections of Wolfe's notebooks. Aswell and the Scribner's people had business lunches together in New York but did not always inform Nowell of their decisions — or

---

[1] Letter to John H. Wheelock at Scribner's, February 28, 1951.

even whether or not they had discussed the questions she had asked. Nor did they tell her until too late that the book had missed the deadline for fall publication — a deadline they finally told her was April 1st, not May 1st.

For his part, Aswell was intrigued by the projects Nowell proposed. From a purely practical standpoint, he saw no reason why he (and McGraw-Hill) should not be the publisher of these new Wolfe works. It would make his efforts for the Wolfe Estate worthwhile — an argument Perkins had used, Aswell told Nowell. But rather than tell Scribner's outright what was in his mind, he thought it best to "feel his way along" during the lunches and phone conversations in New York. One project at a time, one volume at a time, one reading at a time was the best, most practical course to follow, he stated. Confiding these matters to Nowell, Aswell asked her to say nothing and to leave all questions concerning the estate entirely in his hands.

What was a practical matter for Aswell was a painful one for Nowell. She felt bound by years of friendship to Scribner's. To follow Aswell's suggestion and leave them would be like a divorce. She felt "married to two guys at once," unable to choose between her loyalty to Scribner's and her loyalty to Aswell. Adding to her pain and frustration was Aswell's passivity about the notebooks project. Nowell described the project as a baby growing within her, difficult and painful to carry. Now, because of Aswell's reluctance to act, she feared that the work she had done on the notebooks would become worthless.

Nowell's anxiety and persistence forced a rift. When Aswell went on a business trip to Dallas, having delayed answering Nowell's questions for four months, their two styles clashed. Nowell demanded that he express her paste-up of the letters to Scribner's and that he allow Scribner's to publish the notebooks. He responded by telling her she was not free to make decisions about matters she did not understand. Then Aswell suddenly disavowed interest in the notebooks, clearing the way for Nowell to proceed with Scribner's once the letters were published.

Dear Ed:

Ever since I finished writing you this morning, I've been trying to write my threatened letter to Jack and Charlie about the title of the letters. But I think it would be better to consult with you a little first. Do you think there is anything in this (taken from the introduction of LHA: you suggested that there might be something there, and with your tentative title as a subtitle):

THE FABRIC OF HIS LIFE
The Life of Thomas Wolfe
As Told Through His Letters

Of course, if Jack is going to stick to his second opinion that the book should be called just "The Letters of Thomas Wolfe" I guess he would object to this. But I am not at all sure that he would stick to it — he began by more or less agreeing with me: then wrote later saying "The feeling here is very strong that your main title should be 'The Letters of Thomas Wolfe.' " But it depends on whether the people who had that "strong feeling" were the hams in the advertising dept or whether they were Charlie himself, and if Charlie, whether I could argue him and Jack out of it.

If I cant argue them out of it, I think we ought to try your title of The Life of Thomas Wolfe As Told Through His Letters. Or maybe even try for "The Life and Letters of Thomas Wolfe" IF that didnt mean that I would have to take three more years to expand my expository material into a real biography (which would make the book too long — just the letters themselves make it long enough, God knows.)

But in your letters of condolence, written after I told you what Jack said about "the feeling here is very strong" you quite sensibly suggested my keeping casting round to try to find the perfect title. And I think "The Fabric of His Life" is as good as I can find. I had a great long list of phrases culled from here and there, such as

"An Artist in America" with your subtitle (taken from Tom's list of ideas for titles from which he chose The Story of a Novel). But this makes me think of Audubon. NO, wait, it was the title of a book on American Etchers pub by Knopf in 42.

Penance More. From the letter to Volkening [Henry T. Volkening, New York University English professor]. V put in the "No" himself.

"The Worm Gets In" or
"One Lamp Forever Lit" both from letter to Mrs Roberts, but I think a little hammy.

To Wreak Out My Vision (letter to MEP) not bad, but a little far removed

Well, I had several more but none of them were very good. I may be wrong but like "The Fabric of His Life" because it is a straight quote from Tom, but also is a phrase describing what his letters are.

Guess I'll stop. Write me your thoughts on all this when you get a chance and I wont write Scribners till I hear.   E.N.

*

Sunday.
Jan 7, 1951

Dear Ed:

I've decided to send you down the manuscript of the notebooks anyway, without waiting to hear from you, so am expressing it to you marked Personal tomorrow, Monday. I need some money for myself and for the kids, and if you and Scribners want to do the notebooks book, OK. But if you dont, likewise OK. However in that case I will want to start looking round now for some job or other work that I can start on when the letters book is finished.

About the title: I think it should be either

The Fabric of His Life
As Revealed in the Letters of Thomas Wolfe

or

To Wreak Out My Vision
The Life of Thomas Wolfe As Told Through His Letters

or simply

The Life of Thomas Wolfe
As Told Through His Letters

Revealed is kind of a hammy word, but I dont think you can tell a fabric. Wreak is a wonderful word, really. If the Wreak title wasnt too long, I think I would prefer it. But the third simple one might be more palatable to CSS.

The quote which would go on the title page with the Fabric title would be this: "The author has written of experience which is now far and lost, but which was once part of the fabric of his life. . . . We are the sum of all the moments of our lives — all that is ours in them: we cannot escape or conceal it. From the introductory note to Look Homeward, Angel.

The quote which would explain the Wreak title is a beauty, and does not have the disadvantage of the Fabric quote, which is that anyone really familiar with Wolfe would know that the Fabric quote really went with the Angel.

Here is the Wreak quote: "My whole effort for years might be described as an effort to fathom my own design, to explore my own channels, to discover my own ways.... I have at last discovered my own America, I believe I have found my language, I think I know my way. And I shall wreak out my vision of this life, this way, this world and this America, to the top of my bent, to the height of my ability, but with an unswerving devotion, integrity and purity of purpose that shall not be menaced, altered or weakened by anyone. (From Wolfe's letter of December 15, 1937, to Maxwell Perkins.)[1]

The word Tom actually used before Wreak was "shall" not "to" but I dont think that would matter, do you? OK, I'll stop now. Let me know what you think of the rough notebook manuscript.

Liddy

---

[1] The Letters opens with what Nowell calls "the Wreak quote" beneath a photograph supplied by Wolfe's friend Belinda Jelliffe, with whom Nowell carried on a lively correspondence during the 1950s. The quotation is from a letter of December 15, 1936, from Wolfe to Perkins. In her letter, Nowell incorrectly dated the Wolfe-Perkins letter 1937.

*

January 10, 1951

Dear Liddy,

Since writing you yesterday about my proposed trip to Boston later this month, your letter dated January 7th has come, and I also have your later letter which accompanied the typescript of Tom's notebooks. This project makes it all the more important, I think, for us to have a talk, so I do hope you can arrange to meet me in Boston for that purpose.

And please don't write Jack Wheelock or anybody else at Scribner's about the notebook project. I shall have to decide for the Estate about any publishing arrangements that are to be made, including the publisher who should do it. And at the moment, I am strongly tempted to do it myself. I shall, of course, read the material before I go to Boston so I shall be primed to discuss it more or less intelligently.

My very best, as always,
Ed

PS - I think the proposed titles for the volumes of letters should be put up to Scribners. Somehow I don't like any one of the three. They promise too much, or seem to. They might be more appropriate, or at least equally appropriate, for a biography.   ECA

*

Thursday
Jan 10, 1951, I guess.

Dear Ed:

Well, all right, if we have to do nothing about the notebooks book, we have to do nothing about the notebooks book until I see you in Boston. But I'm pretty sunk about it now. For one thing, I hoped we could go ahead and find out if I could have an advance on it or not right now, and for how much. And for another, I guess maybe I'll have to drop it altogether, which will mean all the work of typing out that script is prac- tically wasted. (Except for the reference value to me for work on the letters.)

I mean, I realize that you have to choose the best publisher you can for Tom's estate, and if you think the best publisher is yourself, well, maybe you are right. But that brings me to the precipice of choosing between Scribners and yourself which, to quote TW, will cause me "untold grief and anguish". If I hadnt got a job there in the first place: if Charlie Scribner hadnt let me work up gradually from job to job: if Perkins hadnt done all kinds of things to get me out of an intolerable position with Lieber and start my own agency:[1] hadnt helped me with it as I went along (also Charlie) — well, I wouldnt ever have been whatever I was and am now. For one thing, I wouldnt have been Tom's agent so wouldnt be fitted to edit his letters, notebooks, or anything. Also there is the incalculable amount of good will and childhood sentiment involved — which applies not just to Perkins but to Charlie, Miss DeVoy, Gilman, Jack, way down to old Charlie Wilcox in the retail store and Stanley in the shipping room and — well — say somewhere between 20 and forty of my old and best friends.[2] I would have to think very long and hard about it, but, I kind of think I'd rather kiss any more work on notebooks or whatever goodbye, get some kind of regular job in a store or library or something here, and stay friends with both you and CSS. And of course there's the business of being Nancy's [Nancy Hale] agent too. I'd have to give that up besides. You dont realize what bitterness there would be if (to quote Perkins this time) I "turned my back on Scribners".

Well, maybe I could sell you my rough typescript of the notebooks outright and you could hire somebody to go on with them from there.

That way, I'd get a little bit back on it and you wouldnt have to start all over. Besides, the idea is mine, tho I spose somebody else might have thought it up too.

I guess I'd better stop: I keep getting tears in my eyes, dammit. I was kind of counting on a nice advance and a chance to do the work I'm fitted for and know so much about now, but I guess it is no soap and I'd rather write this to you now than go bursting into tears in some Italian restaurant in Cambridge. Aw nuts, and I was hoping to start pasting up today. Well, maybe I still can get back to it after I calm down.

Love and see you anyway,
EP

[1] Nowell had gone to Lieber's agency on the understanding that she would work there for a year without salary and then become Lieber's associate. Perhaps Lieber did not see the agreement in the same way; in an interview with Clara Stites in 1985, he described Nowell as "just a secretary." At any rate, Nowell realized the arrangement would not work as she had hoped. In addition, she was concerned about Lieber's alleged communist activities. In fact, the FBI has a file (FOIPA No. 256,955) on Nowell because of her relationship with Lieber. Apparently FBI investigators interviewed Nowell at least twice in 1949. According to the FBI records, she told them about her business relationship with Lieber and explained that her breaking off with him was the result of her prolonged illness during the summer and fall of 1934 and the fact that Lieber was apparently involving himself with the communist party and expected her to do likewise.

[2] Although she left Scribner's editorial department in 1933, Nowell remained lifelong friends with many of the people she had known there.

*

January 16, 1951

Dear Liddy,

Over the weekend I read all the extracts you sent me from Tom's notebooks. As you said, there is much good material here. There is also some of it that for one reason or another should not be published now because of possible libel, invasion of privacy, and that sort of thing. Just the usual Wolfe problem. One general thing in the notebooks puzzles me, and you'll have to explain it when we meet. Over and over again, there are mere jottings, a kind of shorthand, as it were, and I don't know whether they appeared that way in the notebooks, being thus Tom's mere reminders to himself of what happened, or whether the foreshortened effect is because that is the way you jotted things down merely to remind you of what is there.

About the general plan for a volume based on the notebooks, I think you are right in wanting to include certain things not actually in the notebooks themselves. I gather that during the last year or so of Tom's life he seems to have made less use of the notebooks than he did earlier. The entries for this period are certainly more sketchy. This may be because he was learning to make better use of a secretary, and things that would formerly have gone in the notebooks were written up separately, first in longhand and then typed. It is interesting to observe how many purposes the notebooks were made to serve. Here are the records of where he was and what he did. Here are names and addresses of people he met. Here are dozens of examples of his passion for making lists of countries visited, books read, people met, the women in his life, etc. Finally, and very importantly, the notebooks also served to record trial drafts of things he meant later to use in his books. In connection with this last purpose, as I said before, he began toward the end to do less of that because he was using a secretary more for his trial drafts. This would justify, it seems to me, including in such a volume as we are talking about various manuscript bits which are still unpublished and which are good enough to publish. You have mentioned one or two. I also thought of that piece on Bridges which he called "Old Man Rivers." It has been published in the <u>Atlantic</u> but never in a book. [1] Then there is that last little skit he did about Edgar Lee Masters on the front and back of the receipted hotel bill in Victoria, British Columbia. All I am saying is that there is quite a bit that might be considered for inclusion in the volume in addition to what the notebooks actually contain, and that the inclusion of such things can, I think, be justified.

Since you were worried that your typescript might be lost, I am having it returned to you today by first-class mail in a separate package. You may want to bring it to Boston with you to discuss specific points.

On getting back to the office today, I found your rather disturbed letter of January 10th indicating your belief that you would have to bow out of the picture if the notebooks were published by anyone other than Scribners. I confess I cannot follow your reasoning. It would take too long here to attempt to answer your argument, but I shall set myself that task when we meet in Boston. For the moment, at any rate, please don't close your mind to any of the possibilities. I shall want to discuss the whole problem with you very frankly. Not only will I try to give you advice, but I shall also want you to give me advice too. Being Administrator of the Wolfe Estate is not the easiest job in the world.

At the end of last week I got an undated letter from you about our meeting in Boston. Since Tuesday the 30th will not be a good day for you, suppose we have lunch on Wednesday the 31st. I shall be staying at the Statler, so why don't you come directly there as soon as you get in.

Let me know ahead about when to expect you so that I will not make any other date that will cut your time short. Let's plan to spend as much time together as we will need to spend to cover all the ground that will have to be covered.

I am looking forward very much to seeing you. Meanwhile, cheer up.

Ed

[1] Robert Bridges, a former editor of *Scribner's Magazine,* was the first Scribner's person to be fictionalized by Wolfe in "Old Man Rivers." Perkins's reluctance to let Wolfe publish stories about Scribner's was one of the reasons Wolfe left Perkins. Aswell wanted to include the piece in *The Hills Beyond,* but Perkins refused permission on the grounds that Bridges was still alive, although (according to Aswell) senile at the time. Aswell then offered the piece to the *Atlantic,* which published it — much to the dismay of Perkins. "Old Man Rivers," about Robert Bridges, should not be confused with "No More Rivers," about Scribner's editor Wallace Meyer.

*

January 17, 1951.

Dear Ed:

About Boston. . . .

The earlier in the day on Jan 31 you could start arguing with me, the better it would be for me. I have to get up at 5:30 and get so damn sleepy after eating lunch that I never make much sense. But even so, you dont have to Receive me at 8:35 if its your one good chance to catch up on sleep.

Guess that covers that subject, except maybe I should add something you doubtless know: that if and when I think my conscience is involved I can be as stubborn or even stubborner than Perkins. For the same reason: that I have a false but unshakeable conviction that God is right at my left elbow.

As to the mere jottings. I guess those are Toms. All the words in the notebook typescript are his except words like "illeg" or "After Chickenpox," and a few odds and ends like that. Tom wrote those notebooks at great speed on trains, in bars, etc. a good deal, and often just jotted down the highlights for his own memory to fill in. Also, some of the outlines in the NYU years are notes on a course Munn gave, lists from a college composition book of theme subjects etc. I have a good idea of what is what from interviewing Munn and showing him samples. And the composition books at Wisdom. I have found most of the lists of themes there but some are missing, and I think maybe the missing ones were made up by TW himself. Anyway research would clear this up.

As to including Old Man Rivers, I think not. For various reasons. Because I think the unifying theme of the notebooks book, if there is one, should be "Of Wandering Forever" (and the earth again".) Even if we skip all the fancy titles and just call it the Notebooks of TW. In other words, only pieces about what Tom saw, smelt, ate and thought and dreamed. But not things he actually created like that story. A great many of those fragments he wrote into the notebooks appear in his novels. Kennedy made a damn good guess at when Tom was writing what from finding the passages in the notebooks and finding dates of actual appointments. But sometimes Kennedy guessed wrong: sometimes Tom would write a fragment in a notebook, leave it deep-frozen there for a long time, then thaw it out and use it. ANYway, this would take more research — to take each literary passage that I might want to use and make sure that it wasnt in a novel.

HOWever, there are some semi-autobiographical semi-literary passages that were more autobiographical. The two which stand out notably in my mind right this minute are the fragment about Tom being deeply moved by the sight of Beethoven's ear trumpet and about Tom with Dr Dubois after the Oktoberfest fight. In these two, Tom calls himself Eugene (He was thinking of using this material in The River People). But it is really Tom and his actual experiences in Europe, as I can prove by similar factual passages in letters to Mrs. B. So these few fragments I would want to put into a notebooks book, especially since the bulk of The River People came out of T & the River.

Well, to sum it up: I think a notebooks book should be travel and autobiography, and I think with careful winnowing it could be given the kind of lyrical descriptive magic that Tom's descriptive passages in his novels have. Sort of in the class with The Face of a Nation or that sort of thing.

BUT I think the other reason we shouldnt start putting stories like Old Man Rivers in are these. One, they would make the notebooks book too long.

Two, there are an awful lot of unused pieces of stories, hunks out of Time and the River etc. Just taking the hunk of stuff Old Man Rivers came from there is No More Rivers, of which you used only a few paragraphs. And The Lion at Morning (or did you use that in You Cant Go Home Again, I dont believe you did). Well, if I get going on the unused fragments from all the books, this letter will go on forever. ANYway, I think there would be another book sometime in unpublished fragments of his writing, as separate from his more personal jottings in the notebooks book. There would be things wrong with lots of things, and lots of them might have to be omitted on account of libel. But I think there would be something anyway. And my hunch is that its better to hold up Old Man R and finished pieces of writing of this sort. (Also the Masters gem) and put them into that book. Maybe that book could be called Portraits and Caricatures or something. Maybe not.

But I think it ought to be a separate project.

And I think it would make the notebooks too much of a hodgepodge, too unbalanced, if you know what I mean.

Thats all. See you in Boston Jan 31, and will phone from Back Bay [Back Bay Station in Boston] round 8:35 to 9. (Depending if the train is late). Of course if anything dire should prevent my coming I might try to persuade you to come sleep with Thomas Wolfe in the diningroom-downstairs bedroom where the crates of letters are. In which case Mother or I could meet you in Prov [Providence] and drive you over and back. But lets hope and pray that Edna will avoid pneumonia till after Feb 1st.

Love,
Liddy

About the title of Letters, sure I agree with you those titles sound like a biography, because I think the letters are an Autobiography. But will let it slide till you read the mss: if you think they arent an autobiography, OK. But only way to convince you how much they are is to show you. Have got 65 pages pasted up. Only about 200000000 to go.

*

January 22, 1951

Dear Liddy,

This will answer your two letters of January 17th.

On Wednesday morning the 31st, I suggest you take a taxi and come straight to the Statler as soon as the train gets in. I'll delay breakfast till you arrive and suggest you breakfast with me. One who gets up at five-thirty as you do can probably manage a second breakfast by nine. We shall have all morning to discuss our many problems, and then can lunch together to forget them.

As I see it, the problem of who is to publish the notebooks has nothing to do with conscience — yours, mine or anybody else's. It is just a question of what is best to do. You can tell me your side of it, and I'll tell you my side of it, and we'll see where we get.

I have no fixed ideas about what should or should not go in a volume based on the notebooks. Your conception certainly makes sense. We can discuss all that, too. . . .

Marjorie Fairbanks' [a Cambridge friend of Wolfe's] letter to you is

65

returned herewith. Only one thing in it surprises me, and that is her statement that she has spent several days going over the new acquisitions of Wolfe material at Houghton. She never had access to all the Wolfe material at Houghton with my permission. I gave permission for her to see only certain specific items, perhaps half a dozen, in all, which she said she wanted to look at to verify certain facts during the period when she knew Tom. I am writing to Jackson today to find out just how freely she has used the stuff at Houghton. When I gave her permission to see the few things she said she wanted to see, it was on the basis of her statement to me that she was not writing a life of Thomas Wolfe but was merely writing an account of her recollections of him. I would never have authorized her to do a life, and if that is what she is up to, I shall have to do what I can to stop it.

When Mrs. Fairbanks was in New York about two weeks ago on the point of sailing for France again, she telephoned me and said she had come to an arrangement with Houghton Mifflin about her book.[1] I reminded her then of her earlier promise to show the manuscript to me for approval before anything final was done with it, and once more she agreed to do this. To make certain this was clearly understood all around, I then wrote Paul Brooks at Houghton Mifflin and told him what my understanding with Mrs. Fairbanks was. Since then I have had a very nice letter from him saying that her script would certainly be shown to me before it was set in type. I shall see Paul Brooks when I am in Boston to find out definitely from him whether he has contracted for a life of Wolfe or merely for Mrs. Fairbanks' memoirs about him.

I think your note about Mrs. Fairbanks says too much and that it should be changed.

I'll have another go at Mr. Moe [Henry Allen Moe, secretary at the Guggenheim Foundation].

I'm looking forward very much to seeing you next week.

Ed

[1] The unpublished biography Marjorie Fairbanks was working on has been acquired by the Houghton Library.

*

Friday, Feb 2, 1951.

Dear Ed:

Round about 1 AM last night I was wishing fervently that you hadnt told or asked me about that Harvard University Press idea for a book, because when I finally stopped pasting up the letters, I got to thinking that I ought to give you my later-than-telephone ideas about the Harvard Press thing.

Well, it seems to me that their idea is one phase of a whole general idea which we all are fiddling with. They evidently are planning to collect and publish only pieces about Tom which have already appeared in magazines, newspapers etc. Miss Champion [Myra Champion, librarian at Asheville] is going them one better, and is collecting statements from other people who knew Tom, but who, to date, have never written their reminiscences of him down. Both of which things lead me to think that there could be a book called "Thomas Wolfe as I Knew Him" by Fifty of His Friends (or a hundred or any number). And I know damn well I have the first groundwork for a book like this right here in my five fat cardboard files of correspondence with his friends.

I wont tell you who or how many — I couldnt without digging back — but a good many people have written me reminiscences about Tom in the course of correspondence about his letters. And various and sundry of those people have said "I've always meant to write down what I know about Tom but have never got to it. Do you think, Miss Nowell, I could sell such a piece to some magazine if I should write it." To which I've answered yes, but only in a few cases have given advice about specific magazines. A good many others have written me the highlights of their reminiscences in actual letters. A great many others have said "If you ever come down my way, I do hope I can see you. I'd like to tell you about Tom and Such-and-such, but havent time to write it all down here."

Well, IF I ever had the time and financing, I could write to all these people, and ask them to write their reminiscences up for a royalty-per-page division of earnings from an anthology, with some sort of provision about serial rights etc. By financing, I mean if a publisher would want to undertake that kind of complicated shared-profits-deal and also to pay me some to get the people organized. Of course this material is also material for a biography — its what I said maybe Terry had been trying to collect, and what I thought I'd have to do some measure if I ever did try a biography, and which would necessitate endless travelling and listening to people's aimless talk.

Anyway, you get the general idea, and we should kind of mull it over from time to time, I think, to see how this goldmine of material should be approached and used.

Last night, when I first got to thinking about it, I had the idea of trying to persuade the Harvard University Press to do that kind of book, instead of simply a collection of the things which have already been printed. But this morning I think probably not — that it isnt the idea they had, and that if there is anything in it, you might want whoever-is-Tom's-regular-publisher then to do it. Therefore, if and when The Harvard Press man (is it Wilson?) writes to ask me that one question you said he probably would, I guess I wont say any of this to him. BUT if you want it said to him, you can either send this letter to him, or you can tell me to say it to him.

The trouble with his own book, to me, is this. That for the most part, the people who knew Tom least were the ones who rushed into print with their reminiscences about him. Whereas the people who knew him best and realized how complex he was, have kept their mouths shut, for the most part. Witness you (I mean as far as anything personal goes), me, Perkins (except for the very brief things in Chapel Hill memorial issue of Carolina Magazine, Harvard Lib Bulletin or whatever it was, Basso, etc. etc. But unless we should want to try to persuade Wilson to use only the GOOD things that have been published, and commission other GOOD things which have not as yet been written, well, see, that leads back to the other idea again.

Assuming that Harvard Univ Press wants to use simply the things which have been published, I have these remarks to make: First and foremost, they should have Somebody who Knows Something to edit the collection of these published reminiscences and gently point out absolute falsehoods in footnotes. I'll give you just one very glaring example. Desmond Powell wrote a piece about Tom in the Arizona Quarterly. When he was talking about things which Tom said to him or did with him, it was pretty good. But at the end he announced that Tom died of a brain tumor, and that as early as July 1935 (when Tom met Powell in Arizona) he showed signs of the insanity which goes with an incipient tumor. Which of course is absolutely false, and which I'd hate to see spread and given authority by publication in a book like this Harvard Press one for students etc. It should be gently but firmly footnoted with the statement which Dr Dandy [Wolfe's doctor at Johns Hopkins Hospital] wrote to you about Tom's condition, and which you sent out to the press. How many other cockeyed things have been said by people in magazine articles, I couldnt tell you without rereading them and making a long list. But there are a good many others, tho the Powell one is, I think, the worst.

ALSO, I trust that the Harvard Press isnt going on the assumption that the Wisdom Collection has everything of note which has been published about Tom. Because they havent — they only have what they happen to have picked up here and there. I've sent them some things that I heard about and got, but even so there are lots of important things missing.

Somebody ought to make a list of the important things, with reference to the Wisdom Collection, but going far beyond it. And no sense leaning on Preston [Wolfe bibliographer], either, because he lists some things, and omits others which are far better.

NOW therefore, if you and the Harvard Press people think there's anything in what I've said in the two paragraphs above, I suggest that they get Dick Kennedy[1] to edit their collection for them. He has already been published in the Harvard Library Bulletin, would be highly recommended by Professor Munn, and probably also by Howard Mumford Jones, for whom he is writing his Phd Thesis on Tom. It would be a nice thing for him (to be editor of a collection for the H Univ Press) but would be a much nicer thing for them, because he knows where these various reminiscences go off the beam, knows whats been published where, or could complete his knowledge in a very painstaking and thorough way. He also could find them the different versions showing the development of one theme in Tom's work, since he has been through the notebooks, all the various drafts of manuscripts etc. I should think he could do it in his summer vacation, coming back to Cambridge when the University of Rochester closes, but of course I'm only guessing — I dont know what he's planned to do this summer, except wind up his thesis in the final typed draft.

If, on the other hand, anyone should ever want to do the book I talked of first — the one for which somebody would write all Tom's friends who have something valuable to say — I think I would be better. Because of my five fat files of beautiful friendships with these people which I've conducted by correspondence (to my sorrow, sometimes) for the past two years. Kennedy could do that too, of course, but I have the five fat files headstart on him, and my own cockeyed way of writing people usually begets more intimacy than a more formal, cautious kind of letter such as he would write. I think when he interviews people about Tom they are all very fond of him and open up and tell him things and end up by writing me that they hope he gets good and drunk sometimes and has some fun in his life. He also writes me nice warm humorous letters (about TW, his baby, everything in general) but he might be too formal in letters to comparative strangers. Tho whether his way of doing it is better than my own cockeyed way, is, of course, a question for debate.

Thats all. When I hear from Wilson, I guess I'll just answer the question he is going to ask me (according to you). Unless you've had a chance to answer all of this, and tell me whether to suggest Dick to do the job or not. Or whether to mention the Good but as Yet unwritten book. Of course, to be perfectly honest with you, I cant see how showing the development of one theme of Tom's fits into a collection of printed reminiscences about him. It is something DIFFERENT, and to me, should be done in something else: something which would be a study of Tom's ways of work and work. You might as well print a facsimile of his left toenail in a book of reminiscences of the kind that have come out in magazines etc. But that is none of my business.

L & K

Be a good boy and do your income tax NOW. I am up to Sept, 1927, so hot on your heels. (I hope.)

Don't blame me for all these thoughts above. You asked me what I thought of the Hvd Press idea. Well, now you know — about 2700 words worth of what I think. EN

[1] Nowell's friendship with Richard S. Kennedy began in 1949, when she wrote to him about reading his seminar paper on Wolfe's years at Harvard (published later as "Thomas Wolfe at Harvard, 1920–1923," *Harvard Library Bulletin*, 4 [Spring and Autumn 1950]). Nowell and Kennedy remained friends until Nowell's death — a friendship which Kennedy described in his introduction to *Beyond Love and Loyalty*. Kennedy was a promising young Wolfe scholar Nowell liked and trusted, someone to whom she could pass on all she knew about Thomas Wolfe. As Kennedy explained in his introduction, "whenever she acquired a new Wolfe letter that reflected on his literary work in any way, she immediately made a typewritten copy and sent it to me; whenever I sent a query or two about an episode in Wolfe's life, I got back a two-or-three-page letter of single-spaced, accurate, and hilariously phrased information" (p. xi). Kennedy closed his introduction by describing Nowell as "tough, life-loving, always ready to do something for a friend. When my wife and I had our first child, we named her Elizabeth after my wife's favorite aunt. But we always called that little girl Liddy" (p. xxii).

*

February 6, 1951

Dear Liddy,

Your letter of February 2nd contains a very interesting idea. I am inclined to think, offhand, that quite a good book could be made of reminiscences of Tom written by those who knew him well enough to have something important to say. Let's think further about it because it is something that probably ought to be done before the people who could contribute to it die or forget. And I can't imagine anyone better qualified than you to go after these people and pull the book together. It is a real idea. The only reason I suggest waiting just a little while is that I want to see how it will fit in with the various other ideas you and I discussed in Boston.

Your suggestion would not overlap or conflict with the Harvard University Press volume. I guess I didn't make it clear to you that Mr. Wilson, director of the Harvard University Press, has the typescript in his office. It was put together by Richard Walser of the Department of English of North Carolina State College, Raleigh.[1] It is simply a compendium of what Walser thinks are the best things that have been written about Wolfe, practically all of them published in magazines. Some of the things are critical and some of them, such as Ma Wolfe's piece from the <u>Saturday Review</u> are reminiscent. But there is not enough reminiscence in the whole lot to interfere seriously with the idea you have proposed. So don't speak of your idea to Wilson when you write him. Somehow I doubt whether a university press would be the proper outfit to publish such a book. Those people just don't have the sales facilities to do a proper job. . . .

Your thought to have someone like Kennedy go through the Harvard University Press script to check up on possible errors is a good one, and I am passing it along to Wilson.

It was certainly good seeing you in Boston.

All my best,
Ed

[1] See Richard Walser, ed., *The Enigma of Thomas Wolfe* (Cambridge: Harvard University Press, 1953), which contains biographical and critical selections.

*

February 14, 1951.

Dear Ed:

. . . I never did hear from Wilson. Anyway, I will not mention the reminiscences-by-Tom's-friends book.[1] I had one wild and wicked thought re same: that it could be "something else" which I could do for Charlie Scribner if I ended up by having to kiss you and all work on Tom's own stuff regretfully good-bye. I mean, it is my own idea and doesn't call for anything of Tom's own writings, so I should think I could do it for almost any publisher, as long as I explained conscientiously to everyone that I wasn't doing it for the Estate. But, oh goddammit, it would be much nicer if it was for you and the Estate, and anyway the thing I want to do next and first and foremost is <u>the notebooks book</u>. I've been pregnant with that for two whole years and am beginning to feel the strain.

And when I say pregnant I dont just mean that it was I who waded through those notebooks, sorted them out, dated them and conceived the idea of doing a book from same. I mean that all those endless days when I got up at dawn and strained my eyes on that Execrable longhand were just like the early stages of real pregnancy: same feeling as if hit over the head by a piece of lead pipe: same queasy feeling in the stomach, same general discouraged feeling that I would never never live to see the glorious end. Well, I wont go into any more of the unpleasant details: you have never been pregnant, but you have a rough idea of what it's like. But honestly — to carry the metaphor even farther — if I dont get to do that book I'll have the same discouraged, embittered, frustrated feeling that you get with a miscarriage — all that blood, sweat, tears and agony for naught. Even if you (the estate) bought my rough typed manuscript from me, it would never make up for all said agony. It looks easy now that it is sorted out, dated, pieced together, typed, but you have no idea how horrible those notebooks are, and still would be, even with my first rough draft. Chiefly through sheer maddening illegibility.

Well, anyway, part of my wild and wicked thought was this. Do you suppose that if you do do all Tom's own books yourself, we could make some kind of a deal whereby I could do the notebooks book for you — then do the reminiscences-of-friends book for both you and Charlie? I could do a biography that way, too, maybe, IF I ever do one and you didnt mind. Of course, the reminiscences-of-friends book is one more step toward a biography — it would be getting the material for one, but publishing it separately first, in the people's own words.

Now maybe you are wondering why I am back on this tune. But when I first read your letter about going to see Charlie and "feel your way along and be governed by the mood and feeling that develops in my meeting with him", my heart leapt up with hope that maybe you and he could hash things out so that you'd be willing to go along with him, so I could work on all Tom's stuff for both of you. I sat right down and began a letter to you, saying the only real trouble was that you two didn't know each other, so were like two strange dogs, circling warily around each other with your hackles standing up. That I wished you two would get a little drunk together, and relaxed and friendly — that you and Perkins got to love each other over a few martinis, and that there was no reason why you and Charlie couldnt do the same. But then I tore the letter up because I realized you probably hadn't meant anything like working out a way to stay with CSS at all — had just meant that you would "feel your way along" about how to break the news to him that you wanted to do Tom's books yourself. I also realized that my own terrible anxiety to stay with CSS as well as with you was Purely Personal, and quite unfair to you. I can't help feeling as if I was sort of married to two guys at once, like a Mrs. Enoch Arden, but that's my hard luck. But I'd better stop, or I'll be writing the-letter-I-tore-up all over again.

However, there is one minor business detail that you might want to discuss with CS about the letters. To wit: who is going to pay for revised galleys. . . .

Just between you and me, Ed, I think Charlie would say oh what the hell: I'll pay for revised galleys for the sake of haste and efficiency, as I've known him to do before when the author was somebody he loved and wanted to keep happy. But if he loves me and wants to keep me happy, and then it turns out that I am going to "divorce" him (even with his consent, if he gives it) for the sake of doing the notebooks book.... Aw nuts, there I go again. But you see what I mean. It doesnt seem fair to me to accept favors-granted-for-the-sake-of-long-term-good-will whilst keeping a guilty secret from him that this is the last Wolfe book (and maybe Nowell book) that he will ever have. But I cant tell him what you've said to me. Oh Christ, I guess it'll just have to be part of your "feeling your way along."

Ed, please realize that I realize that it was you who suggested my doing this letters book and that I will always love you for the same. Also that with the exception of Nancy [Hale], it has been you and Nordstrom [the publisher] who have given me every job I've had since I got married.... But, dammit, I want both you and Charlie — I am grateful to you both. OK now, I'll stop, and I'm sorry that this letter is so long and agonized and involved. Will send you a postcard when I express the letters manuscript. And will address it to you as Administrator of the Estate, so it wont get mixed in with the McGraw Hill run-of-the-mill submitted manuscripts. . . .[2]

Love from

[1] Although Nowell did not have time to edit a book of reminiscences-by-friends, many books in addition to the one by Walser have been published. See Maurice Beebe and Leslie Field, "Criticism of Thomas Wolfe: A Selected Checklist," in *Thomas Wolfe: Three Decades of Criticism*, ed. Field (New York: New York University Press, 1968), pp. 273–93 for material through 1965. See also Elmer D. Johnson, *Thomas Wolfe: A Checklist* (Kent, Ohio: Kent State University Press, 1970); and John S. Phillipson, *Thomas Wolfe: A Reference Guide* (Boston: G. K. Hall and Co., 1977) and *Thomas Wolfe: A Reference Guide Updated, Resources for American Library Study* 11 [Sp. 1981], pp. 37–80. Then too, the *Thomas Wolfe Review* (begun in 1977 as the *Thomas Wolfe Newsletter*), edited by John S. Phillipson and Aldo P. Magi, features numerous reminiscences, as well as "Additions to Wolfe Bibliography," by Theodore V. Theobald, the *Thomas Wolfe Review* 5 (Spring 1981): 42–50.

[2] Aswell, editor with McGraw-Hill's trade book division, Whittlesey House, received the sort of manuscripts to which Nowell refers, but, in justifying his past record, he mentioned that Josephine Winslow Johnson, whose *Now in November* had won the Pulitzer Prize in 1934, had been one of his authors at Harper.

*

February 15, 1951.
5:10 PM.

Dear Ed:

I decided you would want to read Welcome right off as soon as possible, before you talked with Charlie, so I knocked off re-reading the letters for small mistakes, and hastily galloped through the photostat of Welcome. Mother has just taken off now for the New Bedford express office with it, addressed to you as Administrator of the TW Estate, not as a member of McG Hill. I also put in the photostat of Purdue Speech because could get it in same package. Will pass on to you by lettermail any information from College English if and when I finally get that about said speech.

I still think Welcome is stronger, hence better, and more individual stuff than Mannerhouse, which was diluted Chekhov. Welcome has wonderful Asheville stuff in it (including old Looky Thar in one brief scene). I have just finished it and have an awful itch to cut and edit Welcome — it is too heavy, too talky in lots of places — to bring out the more dramatic parts. But it is good strong satiric bitter Wolfe, and that is why I like it.

Anyway, you'll see. Will now go back to re-reading letters manuscript. Should think I'd have it done by tomorrow night: at any rate will be shipping it by Monday at the latest. But will drop you a line when it starts.

Love, bleary-eyed,
EP

*

February 19, 1951

Dear Liddy,

. . . About the problem of Scribners, the main consideration from my point of view is that there just isn't time enough for me to do my own work and give a lot of time to projects which some other publisher is to bring out. I suspect, but do not know for a fact, that this consideration had a great deal to do with Perkins' decision to do the Letters himself. That is, in working to get the Letters together, he could feel that he was working for Scribners as well as the Estate. This is something I think I can tell Charles Scribner without causing embarrassment either to him or to me. It is a purely practical problem. And some awareness of this must have been in the minds of the people at Scribners when they tried to block my appointment as Administrator. When Mr. Scribner gets back, I'll talk to him as best I can and will report to you immediately afterwards. . . .

All my best to you,
Ed

*

February 20, 1951.

Dear Ed:

Once M.E.P. paid me the greatest compliment I ever got in my whole life, by saying that I "argued like a man" (Though it was only in a comparative degree, as compared to an argument he'd had with poor Mrs P about the Immaculate Conception or Divine Grace or something of the sort.) But anyway, I guess I'm slipping. Because I sure am arguing with you about the leaving-Scribners-business like a Woman, and nothing else.

Having apologized for same, I shall now go right ahead that way, and say that you wouldnt have to do much, if any, work for the notebooks book. Because that doesnt depend on other people as collection of the letters did. It depends simply and purely on many many weary hours of staring at totally illegible words at Houghton: of sorting and resorting all those loose pages torn out from the notebooks (some of which I've done already, but every time you look at the damn things you wonder if they go here, here, or here): of reading and rereading all Tom's books to see what jottings were used where, or what were taken from Donne or whoever. But all of this is up to whoever works at Houghton — not to the Administrator of the Estate and his official hand and seal and letterhead. . . .

Well, hell, just see what happens when you see C.S. I have written him a letter which I enclose for your edification in carbon copy. Dont be alarmed: it doesnt say anything about any of this stuff, except that it ends with an exhortation to get drunk and cheerful with you when you meet. Naturally he wouldnt like it if he knew I'd sent you a copy, but I thought I would, so you wouldnt think I'd said anything indiscreet behind your back. . . .

Goombye. Back to page 411.

Love and apologies from
Liddy

*

February 21, 1951

Dear Liddy,

The three parcels have safely arrived — two of the boxes containing Tom's Letters from 1908 through December 1928, the third containing photostats of the Purdue Speech and of "Welcome to Our City." Since all these things come at once, my question is to determine what to tackle first, and, of course, the Letters must come first. The photostats will simply have to wait a while. They have waited all this time, so a little longer won't matter. Meanwhile, Harvard's bill of $52.00, to cover the photostating, is being paid. I'll simply pack all these things up and take them home with me and work on them as I can.

Since the material arrived, I have received your three letters containing matter to be inserted in the Letters. I'll put these with the typescripts of the Letters and take care of them as I come to them.

If you discover any more insertions or other changes that need to be made, I suggest that you hold them in a neat little pile and let me have them later, all at once. This will save time and may possibly avoid some confusion.

When I telephoned Scribners last week and asked for Jack Wheelock, he was still out of the office ill. There are a number of small questions of procedure that I ought to discuss with Scribners and I am quite handicapped by the absence of both Jack and Charles Scribner. Please be as patient as you can, knowing that I, for my part, will do my best to hurry things along.

By the way, did you see Alfred Kazin's long piece ["The Writer's Friend," The New Yorker 27, February 17, 1951, pp. 88–92] in the book review section of the current New Yorker It is ostensibly a review of EDITOR TO AUTHOR, but actually Kazin uses the book simply as a springboard to jump on both Perkins and Tom.[1] It made me quite angry, and I thought for a moment of writing a reply to it; then I realized that the New Yorker probably wouldn't publish what I wrote. To reply adequately, one would have to do so at some length.

All my best to you,

Ed

[1] While Kazin describes Perkins's letters as "unctuously clever," revealing a mind that seems "amazingly schoolmasterish," and Perkins himself as "intellectually threadbare," the gist of the article is not as Aswell describes it. Kazin's point, rather, is to explore the "utterly unexpected and quite touching" devotion that Perkins had for Wolfe. Kazin concludes that the Perkins-Wolfe letters bring home "the satisfactions of a friend who must always live in the shadow of another's writing."

*

March 14, 1951

Dear Liddy,

This letter will inevitably disappoint you because the purpose of it is to report no progress at all in my reading of Tom's letters. I took them home with me to read just before Washington's Birthday and then promptly came down with influenza. I have only just now returned to the office and am still feeling a bit weak. The Wolfe letters are of tremendous importance and interest to me, and I shall certainly read them now just as soon as I can. But I wanted you to know about the delay and the cause of it.

Your letter of February 28th to Jack Wheelock, in which you wrote him your synopsis, so to speak, of the letters is a wonderful document.

My best to you,
Ed

*

March 15, 1951

Dear Ed:

Just got your letter and am sorry as all hell that you've been so sick: I had a slight touch of same myself and know it leaves you feeling as life was too much of an effort, and it does seem to do something strange to one's eyes as well as nose. So take it easy: in a few more days you'll suddenly begin to feel lighter again. To tell you the truth, I myself, for my own sake, am only too relieved to hear that the reason I hadnt heard from you was because you had the flu: I've been imagining you writing long, long lists of things you thought were wrong about the letters and hesitating to broach same to me....

I dont know if this will be too much for you to bear or not, but I have just finished pasting up the rest of what-I-am-pretty-sure-now-will-be-Volume I. Through publication of Of Time and the River, ending with Tom's long letter to Perkins about it, written from London. The total on first pasting up was 258,367 words. I am going back over it now, cutting all I can. Doubt if I can get it down to an actual 200,000, but Charlie said it could possibly go to 500,000 for both volumes, or 250,000 for Vol. I. And I can surely get the necessary 8,367 words out, probably a little more.

It'll be several days before I finish — probably will ship it to you some time next week. Will drop you a postcard when I actually take it to the Express Office.

That's all for today, Vardis writes that his article on Tom is in the April issue of To-morrow, out, I think, this week. This is the one I tried to argue with him about and regretted bitterly doing so ever since, because he is still prejudiced and bitter, and is now undoubtedly going to misquote me besides saying all the stuff I tried to argue him out of saying. But what the hell — one more wrong article about Tom wont make much difference: Tom can weather these and a helluva lot more.

Take it easy if you can.

*

March 20, 1951

Dear Liddy,

Thanks so much for your sympathetic letter of March 15th. You have been much on my mind and conscience, and I can't tell you how my bout with the flu has complicated my life since. I have talked on the telephone to Jack Wheelock, who says he is feeling all right again, and it has been arranged that I will pass on sections of the Wolfe script to him after I have finished my own reading, without waiting until I have finished the whole thing. Thus he will be able to be reading some of it while I am still reading some of it. He will also pass the script along to Melville Cane in sections in the same way.

I have a date to lunch with Jack tomorrow to discuss some of the other questions of procedure which you and I talked about. Incidentally, he told me over the phone that there is no need to have volume one and volume two exactly the same size. One can be longer than the other provided the difference in length is not too great. . . .

All my best,
Ed

*

March 21, 1951

Dear Liddy,

Just to report quickly on my luncheon today with Jack Wheelock.

First of all, I was pleased to find him looking so well. He seems to have stayed out long enough to get back on his feet in good shape.

The procedure which I outlined to you earlier was confirmed. That is, the script will be read in the order: Aswell, Wheelock, Cane; and will be passed along in sections to save as much time as possible. Even so, it is going to take quite a bit of time. Jack confessed to me that he is overwhelmed with work, just as I am, and each of us will have to fit this in as best we can. Jack points out that, since the book isn't to be published until the fall of next year anyhow, we need not feel under too much pressure. I doubt if there will be very much point in our taking up any problems that may occur to us until after Mr. Cane has examined the whole script. It will be simpler for all concerned to deal with Volume One as a whole rather than with individual points.

Jack Wheelock feels very strongly, and so do I, that the book could not be set in type until all the legal problems have been ironed out, because otherwise the production charges might exceed the cost of composition.

By the way, I mentioned to Jack that there was another Wolfe play and asked him whether he would care to see it. He said he would, just as a matter of personal interest, but that he had grave doubts whether it would be something Scribners would want to publish. When I can work around to it, then, I will read "Welcome to Our City" myself and then will show it to Jack and see what he says.

All my best to you,
Ed

*

Dear Jack and Ed:

Maybe you will think this is a "Woman" changing her mind and messing things all up, but it is really (hah!) a woman seeing things more clearly as she works her way along.

ANYway, after you two and Cane have finished reading Vol. I, will you ship it back to me for a few days before you send same to press. Because by that time I am quite sure I will have finished pasting up and estimating Vol. II, and can therefore get to work and cut more out of Vol. I. Which will save a lot of money that would be caused by cutting in the galleys.

That's all. Up to May, 1936 to-day, but still 2 cartons full of letters to go before the end.

Love,
Liddy

Am sending copies of this to you both at the same time.

*

April 6, 1951

Dear Liddy,

Just a hurried note to let you know that the two new boxes of Wolfe letters have arrived safely, and I have them at home with the first two where I am reading them as I can.

Tom's cousin, Elaine (Westall) Gould, telephoned me one day recently and sounded very nice over the phone. Unfortunately, I was unable to see her, but I did put her in touch with the right person at McGraw-Hill who has charge of copy editing and proof reading. Whether anything definite will come of that, I don't know. [1]

Cordially yours,
Ed

---

[1] Not much is known of Aswell's impressions on Gould or others. But his literary portrait

at McGraw-Hill was painted unflatteringly by William Styron in *Sophie's Choice* (New York: Random House, 1976, pp. 15–20). Calling Aswell "the Weasel — a near-anagram of his actual surname," Styron wrote, "The Weasel had been brought in to give to the place some much-needed tone. At that time he was chiefly known in the publishing business for his association with Thomas Wolfe, having become Wolfe's editor after he left Scribner and Maxwell Perkins, and following the writer's death, having helped assemble into some sort of sequential and literary order the colossal body of work which remained unpublished. Although the Weasel and I were both from the South . . . we took an immediate dislike to each other. The Weasel was a balding, unprepossessing little man in his late forties. I don't know exactly what he thought of me . . . but I thought him cold, remote, humorless, with the swollen ego and unapproachable manner of a man who has fatuously overvalued his own accomplishments. In the staff editorial conferences he was fond of uttering such locutions as 'Wolfe used to say to me . . .' Or, 'As Tom wrote to me so eloquently just before his death . . .'

His identification with Wolfe was so complete that it was as if he were the writer's alter ego" (pp. 15–16).

*

Sunday

Well, now, listen, boys. In about a week's time I am going to need to know the answer to my question in my long fresh letter which is in with Box I, Volume I about the title. Because I cant write the introduction OR the explanatory text, unless and until I know what kind of book this is I'm writing same for — the routine uninteresting, under-promoted "General Letters of Thomas Wolfe," or the <u>life</u> <u>and</u> letters of Thomas Wolfe, either with that title or the Wreak Out My Vision title I'm so fond of. If its the latter kind, the kind I want, I have to write the introduction to explain that it <u>is</u> this kind. And I'll have to make the explanatory text much fuller — and you are supposed to tell me how much fuller. If its the won't-sell-anyway, dull, musty general letters of TW, well, then, I'll write an introduction to harmonize with same in dullness, mustiness etc. (Threat!) And write very brief explanations. For that kind of book there really is no explanation needed — the footnotes and the text make everything clear as day light. But either in explanatory text OR introduction I want to ring in Tom's own snatches of apologia for the way he was in various stages of his life. But again my hands are tied until I hear from you in answer to my fresh letter.

So please for Christs sakes step on it a little, or I'll be held up here twiddling my thumbs and we'll end up by missing the deadline anyway, after my half-killing myself to make it. For all I know, I may have to do all kinds of research for the introduction and explanatory text (if any) —

sure I've done the research for the footnotes, but when (if) I sit down and try to write a brief biography of Tom there are going to be all kinds of things that I wont know exactly — that were not called for in a footnote but that I'll need to know exactly for the sake of making my exposition SHARP, not vague and muzzy.

Well, as you can gather from all this, I am half dead and so wound up that I dont even know it. Worked till midnight last night, started in at 7 AM this morning, so as to get an hour, anyway, before the children woke up. I feel as if I was the Harvard Varsity Crew rowing the shell all by myself and you boys were backing water while I did. Excuse it please.

Oh dear, I know this is a stinking letter and I ought to write it over and be nice. I know you've both been sick and are overworked and everything, but Jack said way back that December 1st was the latest possible, then Charlie finally said May 1st. Well, it now is April 8, so only 3 weeks to go. I have been killing myself to make it for over 2 years now and will still keep on but if you hold me up my hands are tied.

But I DONT want you — either of you — to make a jump-conclusion about the title of the thing and kind of thing it is. You've got to read it, or anyway a big hunk of it, or you wont know what to say — whether to agree with me and Dick [Kennedy] that it does tell the whole story of his life or to disagree.

Thats all. . . .

> L & K and apologies from
> You-know-who

Of course I'd also like to know if it is any good or not. I dont see how it can help being because it isnt me, it's Tom. But its my baby too and I'd like to know if it is masculine, feminine, a Mongolian Idiot, a Clubfoot or the-most-beautiful-baby-that-was-ever-born.

Oh Lord. Well, dont get sore — just tell yourselves that Liddy is highstrung and all wore out. Of course if I hadn't suppressed this so sternly for the past 7 weeks I wouldnt be exploding with pentup impatience now.

*

April 11, 1951

Dear Liddy,

Your Sunday night letter came this morning, and I telephoned Jack Wheelock to talk over the problem with him. I fully realize how tired you must be and what a natural right you have to feel impatient. All I can say is that Jack and I are both doing our best, but you must remember this is not an ordinary manuscript. You are familiar with every line of it, but we are not. It takes time, time, time to encompass it, and it is one of the damnable things about publishing that one never seems to get very much consecutive time to give to anything.

Tomorrow I must leave on a business trip through the South that will take me as far as Dallas, Texas. I won't be back here until the 30th. As proof of my devotion to you, let me tell you that I am taking part of the Wolfe letters with me, since I will have some time on the train. Now don't jump to the immediate conclusion that I will lose them, for I don't think I will. This will be my best chance to get in some consecutive work on the letters. . . .

Jack Wheelock said on the phone today that in his opinion your book should carry a subtitle such as "The Life of Thomas Wolfe as Revealed in His Letters" and he thought the main title might well be some phrase of Wolfe's own, but he did not like "Wreak Out My Vision." I agree on both counts. Perhaps this answer will be enough for the moment to enable you to go ahead with your explanatory text.

My best, as always,
Ed

*

Written in pencil at 4 AM
Friday a la Thomas Wolfe

recopied on the typewriter
at 8AM after a nights
sleep if you can call it that.

Dear Ed:

I'm going to put it straight to you. Here goes:

In view of the fact that you have got me in this awful jam, through your failure to read boxes 1 and 2 in seven whole weeks and boxes 3 and 4 in three weeks — and through your failure to even tell me that your slowness has made me miss a deadline which I made 7 and 3 weeks ago — I think you ought to do the following, just out of fairness to me:

1 Send by <u>air</u> <u>express</u> to Jack immediately Boxes 1 and 2.

2. Wire Mrs. Aswell to express boxes 3 and 4 to Jack immediately.

3 Wire Jack where to airexpress you boxes 1 and 2 of the carbon, if you want it.

4 Consent to Scribners showing all four boxes of Vol I to Cane immediately and setting up galleys as soon as he has read it. With any changes you think absolutely necessary being made in the galleys at the Estate's expense.

5. Consent to my submitting my notebook idea and manuscript to Scribners.

. . . I've got to cut this Gordian knot of secrecy an do-nothingness and get some money and I've got to do it now.

That's all. Please wire me the answer to this . . . ultimatum.

Love from

General MacArthur

*

WESTERN

UNION

BAL24 DA220

D.AJA049 PF ET OL CHG PD = AJ DALLAS TEX 14 513P

= MISS ELIZABETH NOWELL =

= 2 PROSPECT ST   SOUTH DARTMOUTH MASS =

= AGREE YOU SUBMIT WOLFE NOTEBOOK MANUSCRIPT TO SCRIBNERS TO LEARN WHETHER THEY INTERESTED IN PUBLISHING, BUT INSIST YOU NOT COMPLICATE POSSIBLE ARRANGEMENTS BY DISCUSSING MATTERS YOU DO NOT UNDERSTAND. YOU ARE NOT FREE TO REVEAL MY CONFIDENCES. AIRMAIL LETTER FOLLOWS =

= ED ASWELL =

*

Hotel Adolphus

Dallas

Sunday, April 15, 1951

Dear Liddy,

This will answer your airmail letters and telegram. I'll have to be brief because there is no time to go into details.

Your questions 1, 2 and 3. No, I will not deliver the typescripts to Scribners until I have read them. There are many problems which require careful thought, and I will give them as much time as they require. This is not any ordinary kind of publishing project, as you ought to know, and I will not permit publication to be unduly hurried at the expense of proper care. If this causes you inconvenience, I am sorry but I can't help it.

Question 4. No, I will not consent to showing the typescript to Mr. Cane until I myself know what all the problems are to which I must direct his attention.

Question 5. I wired you last night approving submission of the Notebooks to Scribners, but cautioning you not to go beyond an explanation of their

83

interest. If you fail to heed this advice, you may well defeat your own purpose. You threatened in your telegram "to explain whole mess to them, but will be as discreet as I can." You are free to explain anything you like in so far as it concerns your own problems, but you are not free to talk about things I told you in confidence. Whether you do it discreetly or indiscreetly is not the point: you are just not free to do it at all. I insist on the right — the sole right — to handle my end of it. There is a lot more in this situation than you have any knowledge of. Your telegram and my reply have not changed my essential position in the slightest. As I told you in Boston, I am trying to make decisions in the best interest of the Wolfe Estate, and I shall continue to do so regardless of pressures from anyone. It may surprise you if I say that this includes McGraw-Hill. It also includes you.

What it all boils down to is that you found this project more time-consuming than you anticipated. So, now, do I. You have simply got to face the fact that everything wasn't finished the moment you put the boxes in the mail. I, too, have a job to do, and by God I'm going to do it. Whether it will take weeks, months, or years doesn't matter in the least. And I will not be pushed and rushed just because you want to build a house.[1] That is your affair. It has nothing to do with Tom Wolfe.

You say I got you in "this awful jam." Really, Liddy, you are in a state. You told me nothing of the house deal. And why should you? But now I am supposed to know all about it, and am somehow responsible. Nonsense. Even if I had known, what difference could it have made? I phoned Jack Wheelock the day the first section of the ms. arrived and he said not to hurry — that Scribners couldn't publish until next year anyhow. True, I did not report this to you. I assumed you knew, that it was part of the understanding between you and Scribners. It was their business to tell you. The publisher is the one that controls publication dates.

Sorry if this letter sounds brusque. It is not so meant. I am here on other business and have to squeeze this in. The whole situation is far more complicated than you realize. I have written to Mr. Scribner for an appointment on my return, May 1st. I hope things will work out right — but believe me, they will work out better if you will remember that there are many situations in life in which one cries out for an immediate answer, and cries in vain, because sometimes — as here — time must be a factor in the answer. I wish it were not so. But it is. Let's face it.

My Best,
Ed

---

[1] Nowell had purchased land where she hoped to have a home constructed for herself and her two daughters. As a result, she felt financial pressures more strongly than ever.

*

Monday noon. Ap 15.

Dear Ed,

. . . I realized all along what you said in your wire — that I had no right to tell them anything of what you had said to me in Boston. In fact, that is one of the reasons why I have had to keep writing and rewriting my letter to them since Friday — I kept verging on implying something of the sort, and having to rip the letter out of the machine and start it over.

Of course I am not sure if you really mean that you will now be willing for them to do the notebooks book (if they want to do it) or that you are only willing for them to read it as a prelude to going to the mat with them about the whole problem. Surely if you had no intention of letting them do it anyway, you wouldnt have wired consent to their reading same. Well, I can only wait and pray and hope that everything will all work out, and I can do it for somebody anyway. [1]

Ed darling, if I am acting like a combination of a horses arse and a virago, please forgive me. . . . I suppose I feel that way because the book is sort of like a baby. Oh to hell with it. Forgive me if I've said anything in the past few days that I should not have — and I am afraid I did in that letter which I wrote at 4 AM on whichever agonized day-and-night that was. If I can just get this stuff into the mail and get a little fresh air and exercise and sleep, I will calm down. And I am SORRY.

Love and K from
Liddy

[1] Nowell sent her typed manuscript of Wolfe's notebooks to Wheelock in mid-April, saying, "My idea would be to begin it with the 1925 'Log of a Voyage' . . . and to end it with 'A Western Journey.' . . .

"There is still some confusion as to proper dates of certain portions of the manuscript. Tom ripped several notebooks apart and changed the dates on them from 1928 to 1924, with the idea of including them in Of Time and the River (and a few were actually included there, but only a very few). I have tried to put these ripped out pages back where they belonged, but need to check the whole thing over carefully once more.

"Some of the things I've put in here were not written in the notebooks but on loose sheets of paper. For instance 'The Return' (written in Asheville in 1937) and the answer to a critic about his lack of Marxian propaganda, etc. I've put in here whatever I thought could be suitably included. Maybe Tom's Purdue speech (May 1938) could be included too, and could take the place of Western Journey if needs be. . . .

"But the main thing is that I am convinced that a swell book could be winnowed out of all this rough inchoate mass."

*

April 27, 1951.

Dear Ed:

I suppose if you get back and find no letter from me you will think I have dropped dead or something, so here is a very brief (Maybe) report on Charlie's answer to my letter of April 15 (the long frantic one I sent you a carbon of in Dallas). I have now run down to the point where I don't want to yap about it or even think about it any more, which no doubt is OK fine with you. I realize your instant reaction to this will be that you wish I'd reached that point before, but — well — I guess you understand.

Anyway:

(1) Charlie offered me an extra $500 against my share of the letters which I refused for reasons which you understand. If I should be completely and helplessly unable to get out of debt, I might ask him for some later, but will try to make out without.

(2) He said that he had thought all along of doing both volumes simultaneously, which certainly was news to me! but which now makes me palpitate with hope. But of course it's up to you and him.

(3) Jack thinks the notebooks are "extremely exciting" in "the glimpse they give into the workshop of a writer's mind". I gather they would like to publish them but they were very punctilious in pointing out that although the typescript of the notebooks belonged to me, all rights of publication of said notebooks rested in your hands. (As if I didnt know it!)

(4) Other questions in my letter of the 15th remain unanswered except for agreement that everything should be discussed with you (about dead-lines if you agree to both volumes in Feb, 1952, etc.) and vague but emotional protestations of undying love twixt them and me, especially me, because all this brought out the kind of paternalism which Charlie does have for the old hired help. Oh dear.

(5) One more thing — and this may make you say I am still crying out for an immediate answer which it is impossible to give — but I cant help hoping that things will get hashed out as much as possible in the next month. Because if Clara and Edna are going to keep on going to Friends Academy, I have to enter them and pay part of their next year's tuition by the final deadline of June 1st. Also because if the bottom drops out of all Wolfe work and I get fired, the best time to get a job round here is before "The Season" starts in June.

Well, what the hell. The only thing I cant help feeling is that you and I have always been allies on everything to do with Tom for thirteen years,

86

and now there seems to be a rift or something. But I suppose that's my own fault for lashing out at you at 4 A.M. in my first desperation. Well, what the hell. I said that before, but it seems to be about the only thing to say excepting

Love
from
Liddy

*

May 8, 1951

Dear Liddy,

Today I had a very good lunch with Mr. Scribner and Jack Wheelock, and there was a complete meeting of minds about the volumes of Wolfe letters. Mr. Scribner said he would write to you, so I think I had better leave it to him to do so, so that no lines will get crossed. Perhaps one thing that has made for misunderstanding in the past has been that Jack or I would write you at frequent intervals and each would sometimes assume that the other had told you something which the other somehow forget to tell you. If the sense of our meeting today is conveyed to you by Mr. Scribner, there can't be any possible opportunity for misunderstanding.

I hope things are easier with you now that you are getting a bit relaxed. If I blew my top a bit when I wrote you from Dallas, it was only because I was under such damnable pressure, and I hope you understand that. Nothing whatever has occurred to change my great admiration and genuine affection for you.

Cordially yours,
Ed

*

May 10 ? 1951.

Dear Ed:

All day Tuesday I kept thinking it was D Day and wondering what was happening between you and Jack and Charlie. Now I have very nice peaceful letters from all three of you, but I can't see that much of anything got settled. All Charlie says is:

(a) That you are all agreed the letters should be published both volumes simultaneously, which is OK fine with me.

(b) That you can't tell yet just when they can be published.

(c) That he thinks it would save me time to come to New York and confer with you and Jack about what you've cut for libel's sake before I write the commentary.

(d) That "I" (Charlie) "talked to him" (you) "about the work books and Jack thinks that something really interesting could be done with them. However, they both agree that this volume should not be published until at least two years after the letters."

(e) That he would gladly advance me some more money, which I have again declined. . . .

. . . Charlie seems very fond of you in his letter: a great deal of it is interlarded with remarks that you are "a good fellow," and how terribly over-worked you are, and how you no sooner got back from the South than you had to go to New Haven, etc.[1] If you had told him, or even hinted to him that you had no intention of letting Scribners do the notebooks, he surely wouldn't sound so happy and devoted.

So I am at a loss to guess whether you tacitly agreed that they could do the notebooks book, or whether you are still "feeling your way along," as you once put it, or are resolved that they shan't do it but dont want to break it to them till you have to, or maybe havent been able to winnow it all out in your own mind. . . .

Of course, the business of postponing it till two years after publication of the Letters doesn't bother me at all. It would take me about a year to get the manuscript in shape anyway — if I get the job and can take it without causing too much bitterness on their part. Well, hell, the music goes round and round.

. . . As for all and any correspondence twixt you and me when you were in Dallas, lets just forget it: certainly I blew my top more than you or anybody else.

Love,
Liddy

[1] Among those pressures on Aswell were numerous trips to Yale Library concerning the James Boswell papers.

*

May 15, 1951

Dear Liddy,

. . . The situation about the notebooks is quite straight. You needn't look around corners for there is nothing around the corner to see. I have thought a great deal about that project since you and I talked in Boston, and I found that as time passed I became less enthusiastic about attempting to publish the notebooks at the present time or in the immediate future.

88

This is based in large measure on my growing feeling that there is a great deal in them which for one reason or another is unpublishable or is of little general interest; and that what remains would be of rather special interest, and that to make a book of it might seem like scraping the barrel. I told Mr. Scribner that this was my view, but Jack Wheelock indicated that his own view was more nearly like my first reaction immediately after I had read your typescript. If, then, Scribners should decide that they eventually want to do something with the notebooks, I am more or less prepared to say all right and to withdraw my reservations. But even in that event, Mr. Scribner, Jack, and I do not want to rush into that project right away. The letters are still an immense problem, especially for me, because I have to fit them in with all my other work, and in the last several months the pressure on me has been greater than I have ever known it to be. If I were two people I could just about keep up. As things stand now, I can't even hope to do that.

For example, over the past week end I had a number of very urgent problems to deal with. One night I stayed up till two-thirty in the morning and another night till five when the sun was up. I mention these facts merely to indicate that my situation is at times almost intolerable. Sooner or later something will have to give, and if I am not wiser or less conscientious or something the thing that gives may well be I. All of which is simply to say that right now I am dog tired. For this reason, if for no other, I hesitate to commit myself to the problem of the notebooks when the problems of the letters still confront me unsolved. . . .

My best to you as always,
Ed

*

May 19, 1951

Dear Ed:

I'll try to keep this very short to save you time and spare you more fatigue, but I do just want to write and thank you loads for your last letter and say how wonderful it is that you think now it would probably be OK to let Scribners do the notebooks some day in the distant future. . . .

Nor am I really worried about your thinking the book might be scraping the barrel. You're just too utterly worn out now and have forgotten how you felt about it in the four months of dreadful pressure since you read it. And I do know Tom always wanted to publish the travel parts: you'll find places in the letters where he says so, in 1925, 1935, 1936, 1938 etc., and Perkins always said they had some wonderful stuff. I advertised for and finally got the famous Chekhov notebook, but — My God! that's

<u>thin</u> compared to Tom's. But I promised to make this short. And please dont think I'm trying to argue with you. Just forget it for a while and get some rest.

Ed, there's no sense in my saying it because you know it and feel it, but you cant go along that way. And you really shouldn't for Duncan's and Midgie's sake: you and I are in somewhat the same situation on that score: we have to stay alive until our children are no longer minors. And if you get so terribly run down, you could pick up some infection and have no stamina to fight it off. I did it at least twice in NYC, and the second time I said to hell with it and gave the whole thing up. I realize you have got to support them but you cant kill yourself in doing same. . . .

Goombye, <u>dont</u> <u>answer</u> <u>this.</u> I'll try not to write to you at all now for a good long while. And get some rest! and

Love and thanks from
Liddy

*

July 23, 1951

Dear Liddy,

To answer your post card, I plan to go back and reread your entire text, starting with the first box, as soon as you have finished your present chore. As I understand it, you are writing in connective tissue where it may be needed to give background to the letters, and in the process are eliminating a lot of your footnotes. This I think is the main point which Mr. Scribner, Jack Wheelock, and I agreed upon at the meeting we had after my return from Texas. It is difficult to evaluate the letters and to judge the dangers of libel which may exist unless the letters are read in the exact context in which you propose to present them. . . .

Yes, I saw that Struthers Burt piece, and it made me quite angry. At first I had a strong impulse to write a reply to it, but after thinking about it for twenty-four hours I decided not to. Burt's charge that Tom betrayed Max and that this killed Max is simply fantastic.[1] Then, too, Burt said somewhere in the piece that too much had been made of the break between Max and Tom, and then went on to make more of it than anybody else ever has.

I just don't understand the <u>Saturday</u> <u>Review</u> and the way they operate. If Harrison Smith says he was disappointed in that Burt's article failed to prove its most sensational statement, why didn't the thought occur to him there might not be any proof? Also, why didn't he telephone me to check on it? To publish such charges without proof and without checking seems to me irresponsible journalism.

Cordially,

90

¹ Struthers Burt argued in "Catalyst for Genius" and "Letters to the Editor," (*Saturday Review of Literature* [June 9, 1951]: pp. 33–42 and [August 11, 1951]: pp. 22–24) that Wolfe's break with Scribner's was not only a betrayal of Perkins but the cause of Perkins's death. Aswell worried that such irresponsible claims were libelous to himself and to Harper and required an immediate public response.

*

August 14, 1951

Dear Ed: This is going to be a long letter full of very minor details, but we want to have your answer to Burt absolutely air-tight, so nobody can discredit it by picking tiny errors in any part of same. Nor will I pause to say that it is swell. . . .

. . . The thing that occurred to me was from a different slant: from that of Perkins. That he was ecclesiasticus, and a Vermonter, and too full of philosophy and of Vt Granite to die of a broken heart even if anybody had betrayed him. I think the thing you referred to was some trouble about Mrs. Perkins and I have vague ideas about that which would more or less bear you out. But I dont think that even that, or anything, could turn Perkins into a Dame aux Camelias who would pine away. . . .¹

Ed, I dont think Burt really libelled you and Harpers, but I think he was close to it and needs answering anyway, on general grounds. . . .²

Now something more important. When I got to the part about Houghton Mifflin asking me if I would edit Tom for a fee, I was at first thunderstruck: I didnt remember a thing about it. But now that I think it over, I guess MAYbe they did ask me, but very informally, almost undoubtedly through Paul and probably not on the phone but in a by-the-way conversational manner when he saw me as he often did. (Paul Brooks, I mean.) But I couldnt swear to it and certainly Paul would vehemently deny it now, and I have never mentioned it in all my correspondence with Linscott and he could point that out if he wanted to. (And he is pretty touchy about it, tho I have just got him satisfied about my comment in the Letters). Ed, are you sure of this? I guess you may be right, but I ought to warn you that I had totally forgotten it and still couldnt swear to it. Nor is there any documentation of it at Houghton.

Now enter ECA into the picture. My letter to Tom conveying your first phone call is at Houghton. I'll tell you what it says, and I hope you will blush a pretty posey red about it all. It is dated

November 10, 1937

"Dear Mr. Vulfe: (Which was what his nice old German cleaning-
woman at 856 1st Ave always called him)

"It seems that Ed Aswell at Harpers had just heard the 'rumors' that
you are free of C.S.S. You know, he's the one that I said I knew was
honest that you met with his wife at a party once, and who is a personal
friend of mine. He is Saxton's [Eugene Saxton, editor in chief at Harper]
assistant and one of the few people that I really trust, because even if
Harper's is like any publisher, maybe sometimes even more pennypinching,
Ed has always done what was fair by the one Harper book-author I have."
(Ed: This was Judy [Judith Kelley]: Vardis didn't come to you till 1938).

"Well, I guess you remember my telling you about him and saying that
I knew he'd jump at the chance if you wanted to tell him, but you said
you'd talked on the phone with Hartman, so that was that. I swear by
all that's holy or something that I never let out so much as a peep to
him, but this afternoon around five oclock he called me up out of a clear
sky and said he'd heard the 'rumors' and asked me if it was true. I told
him that it was and that he could write you in my care and I'd forward
it to you special (I didnt say whether you were in NY or not, but used
the old line about you hadn't settled down anywhere) and he said OK,
he'd write you but would I write you in the meanwhile to-night so as
not to lose any time.

"He was sort of hurt and reproachful that I hadnt told him before,
especially that time I was out at their house in Pleasantville for dinner a
couple of weeks ago, so I explained that part to him — that I had told
you there was nothing I thought he'd like better than to hear about it,
but that you had said you'd talked with Hartman though I didn't know
what the outcome of that conversation was."

Well, unfortunately, that is as much as I copied out from the original
at Houghton. I guess the rest was unimportant. . . .

I think you are dead right in saying Tom felt nobody wanted him, but
I am not sure that he was absolutely dead-stony-broke — he said he was,
and says so in letters, but you know how he was about such things. . . .

Are you sure Tom said "You Can't Go Home Again" the night you first
met him round November 10–12? I would say he didnt get this title till
around dawn on Dec 2, on the way home from Sherwood Anderson's
party — Tom walked Ella Winter home to her hotel opposite Grand
Central station, and according to her she said it to him and he seized
upon it. And she didnt volunteer this — I had always heard from Tom
that she said it to him first and wrote to her for confirmation.

That's all. I hope all this hair-splitting wont drive you absolutely wild. But I do want to be sure nobody can catch you up on any tiny minor detail. Hell, you'll understand. Going to stop this now, reread it after supper, mail it to you quick. GOOD LUCK.

EP

[1] The reasoned tone of Aswell's reply to Burt ("Thomas Wolfe Did Not Kill Maxwell Perkins") was the result of suggestions made by Nowell. Aswell drew directly on what Nowell had said, writing, "In the end his (Perkins') literary judgment prevailed over any personal feelings he may have had; and to say, as Mr. Burt does, that his hurt was so vital that it sent him to the grave is to ignore the granite elements in his otherwise sensitive nature. Max was no Camille to cherish his wounds, real or fancied, and languish from a sense of injured pride" (*The Saturday Review of Literature,* October 6, 1951, p. 17). Aswell's refutation of Burt's claim was based on the fact that Wolfe had appointed Perkins administrator when he drew up his will on April 17, 1937 — an appointment which Perkins knew about, did not refuse, and was faithful to for ten years until his own death.

[2] Omitted sections of this letter — approximately three pages — go into extensive detail about "Tom's approaching or being approached by other publishers," including Knopf, Harper and Harcourt Brace, and about Wolfe's one packing case and nine packages of manuscript left at the Houghton Mifflin offices with Bob Linscott. Nowell, tracing the steps Wolfe took in his break from Scribner's, "doing it all wrong as he was bound to do such things," recounted Wolfe's reason not to go with Bob Linscott: If Houghton Mifflin couldn't take responsibility for his manuscripts he would take them away.

*

Sunday, Oct 1!

Dear Ed:

At that first meeting with Tom, you expressed your own great personal admiration of his work in some words which he never would repeat to me, but which I think influenced him more than the $10,000 advance, or anything. When he discussed the whole business with me afterwards, Tom would wind up by saying "If Aswell really believes what he said he thought about me — and he must believe it or he wouldn't have said it the way he did. . . ." Then he would break off and make that sort of wry pursed up mouth that he did when he was deeply moved, would shake his head, and repeat "Well, anyway, if he does believe all that of me . . ." etc. I always figgered you told him you thought he was the greatest writer in America or somesuch. God knows just exactly how you put it. God also knows if you remember, or if you do, if you could put it down in black and white so that it could be quoted, likewise in black and white. . . .

EP

*

October 3, 1951

Dear Ed:

All my questions to you are coming thick and fast, but that is just because I'm card-indexing my rough-draft material about 1938 right at the moment. So I'll leave you alone after — well — I guess I have 1 more days work at this material in the letters.

So, here is the question for to-day. You know the final paragraph of You Can't Go Home Again "Something has spoken to me in the night, burning the taper of the waning year," etc etc through "Whereon the pillars of this earth are founded, toward which the conscience of the world is tending — a wind is rising, and the rivers flow".

Well, that was originally the end of I Have a Thing to Tell You: dictated by Tom to me around 3 AM in October or November 1936. And what I want to know is, did Tom transpose those paragraphs to wind up Farewell to the Fox (wind up You Can't Go Home Again) or did you? I think you did. That Tom never really did finish Farewell to the Fox — intended to do more work on it after he got back from Purdue (says so in a letter dated May 3, 1938 to me). But that you had to find some good ending for the whole book, so hit upon the bright idea of moving this over from I Have a Thing to Tell You to the end of the whole book. Am I right, or am I right? ? ? ? ? Or maybe you can't remember, but I guess you can.

Love,
Liddy

*

October 4, 1951

Dear Liddy,

This answers your letter of October 1.

It would be impossible for me to remember exactly what I said to Tom at that first meeting with him. I remember fairly clearly many of the things he said, but what I may have said to him is gone from me. My words, whatever they were, were prompted by the circumstances and feelings of the moment, although they were certainly genuine. All I can tell you specifically is that I tried to reassure Tom by stating exactly how I felt about him, which was that he was, in my opinion, the greatest writer of his generation. I still think so, too.

I have just looked up the contract Tom signed with Harper's, and the title of the book as it is listed there is, "The Life and the Adventures of Bondsman Doaks." Of course, at that time we weren't thinking of a specific volume but of the whole work then in progress. I remember Tom's saying that it would be my problem, as editor, to decide what part of it should go in the first volume. It was a little later that I persuaded him to abandon the Doaks name.

All my best,
Ed

*

October 8, 1951

Dear Liddy,

If I don't answer at once your letters of October 2nd and 3rd, they may drift to the bottom of the pile and then God knows when I'll be able to answer. So here goes:

Sorry that I don't remember the date of the day Tom telephoned and announced his decision to go with Harper's. Nor do I remember what day of the week it was. Isn't it odd what tricks the human mind plays on one? For example, I remember all sorts of things from 'way back which are of no consequence at all, but this event of Tom's phoning, which was a matter of such tremendous importance to me, had gone from me entirely until your letter came reminding me of it.

Yes, I remember saying to Tom that if he held out for $15,000 advance I was sure I could get it for him from Harper's. Our discussion at this point was casual, and I believe it came up only once. He never pressed at all. The offer was ten thousand, so that, of course, was the amount named in the contract. . . .

Yes, you are right about the ending of YOU CAN'T GO HOME AGAIN. As you know, the manuscripts had no form at all when Tom turned them over to me because he wasn't anywhere near finished with them. After his death I had to do the best I could to give them form and order according to the internal evidence. Those final paragraphs were transposed from "I Have a Thing To Tell You" so that the book would have a proper closing. . . .

Cordially,
ED

PS- Since the above was dictated, your card has come. I guess I wanted to hear from you more than anybody, and I do greatly appreciate what you say. There has been another bunch of letters in the afternoon mail, all of which is rather heartwarming, for it shows that a lot of people still do care tremendously about Tom.[1]

My lunch with Linscott went very well. He was very cordial in his gruff, shaggy-dog way. Not one word of complaint about the way I handled him. Quite the contrary. He seemed appreciative, and everything he said showed that he had a true feeling for Tom.

[1] Among the letters Aswell received about his *Saturday Review* reply to Burt was one from an actress, Hilda Vaughn, who wrote, "I wanted to write a vituperative letter to Mr. Burt — about fleas and elephants, etc. — but to what purpose? I had no facts beyond my knowledge of Thomas Wolfe's greatness and that would not count — alas — in the whole unworthy debate." Aswell quoted her comments in omitted parts of this letter.

*

December 7, 1951

Dear Liddy,

Sorry to be slow in answering you again. I had to spend most of last week in Boston, and I am so tired of traveling that I hope I won't have to make another trip for months and months and months.

The passage you quote from the italics section on page 706 of YOU CAN'T GO HOME AGAIN was my own thought and was not quoted from anything Tom wrote nor even from anything he said. I put in that thought about the backward pull of the dark ancestral cave and of the womb simply to suggest that Tom's phrase, "You can't go home again," had a very wide and universal application. [1]

My very best, as always,
Ed

[1] Aswell's words, italicized in the beginning of Books II – VII of *You Can't Go Home Again,* give third-person summaries of the first-person narrative. The passage which Nowell questioned states that the evil effect of Hitler's Germany can be traced to "something primitive in man's ugly past" that must be eradicated. The passage continues, "When George realized all this he began to look for atavistic yearnings in himself. He found plenty of them. Any man can find them if he is honest enough to look for them. The whole year that followed his return from Germany, George occupied himself with this effort of self-appraisal. And at the end of it he knew, and with the knowledge came the definite sense of new direction toward which he had long been groping, that the dark ancestral cave, the womb from which mankind emerged into the light, forever pulls one back — but that you can't go home again" (p. 706).

Chapter Four

"Wheels within wheels. But maybe it will all get us and Tom somewhere some day."

NOWELL, SEPTEMBER 11, 1952

*

Two MAJOR EVENTS transpired which set the tone for the year. The first event was the sudden death of Charles Scribner III on February 11, 1952. He had run Scribner's since 1932 and had been Nowell's good friend and loyal supporter since 1928. His death marked the end of a generation and a style with which both Aswell and Nowell were comfortable. Scribner's death also moved Aswell to write long letters from his home, conveying a personal warmth and anecdotal skill not evident from his office letters. Charles Scribner, Jr., took over the firm from his father and treated Nowell very differently. She reacted with anger and indignation, referring to him incorrectly and demeaningly as CS IV. Nowell's ties to Scribner's were weakening and, except for her loyalty to Jack Wheelock, she had fewer qualms about leaving Scribner's for McGraw-Hill.

The second event concerned Nowell's work on the letters. In writing the expository material, she realized that she had a great deal more to say about Wolfe — enough for a full-length biography. Aswell was Nowell's chief supporter in this endeavor; he had long wanted her to write Wolfe's biography, and now he encouraged her again. She replied full of gratitude to him for believing in her abilities. But she saw "wheels within wheels": the spectre of Terry, also working on a biography, stirring Fred and Mabel against her; the need to withhold material from curiosity seekers, so as not to drain interest from the biography.

Both Nowell and Aswell had vested interests in their Wolfe projects and sought to "hold back the crowd," which now included Professor Oscar Cargill of New York University, George McCoy of *The Asheville Citizen*, and Nowell's "young friend" Richard Kennedy. As before, their different manner of handling a growing number of Wolfe enthusiasts arose from their different personalities, as well as from the different Wolfe each had known. Nowell had known Wolfe as far back as his turbulent NYU days. Aswell had known Wolfe only one year, when he was maturing as a writer and a man. As administrator, Aswell acted almost as Wolfe's guardian, protecting Wolfe from the errors of his youth. When Aswell said, for instance, that a critic's motives were malevolent, he was protecting Wolfe's reputation. Meanwhile Nowell, saying she wanted to "get Wolfe right," was concerned with historical accuracy. Each was hounded by "truth," although they saw this truth differently.

Dear Liddy:

. . . I ran into Charles one evening last week, and he mentioned that you were still worried about possible libel and that he had given you assurance that you needn't worry. I agree with him. It is my understanding that the clause in your contract, exempting you from any libel risk, refers to the book as a whole and everything in it, which of course would include your notes and biographical material as well as the letters themselves. . . .

I do not remember that Tom had a cold when he left New York for his trip out West. I do know that he had a heavy cold at sometime during that previous winter, for I recall a large assortment of bottles of all sorts of patent medicine junk which he had in his bedroom and out of which he dosed himself. It is my best recollection that he got over this cold before he went West, but I could be wrong about this. The only thing I can say with complete assurance is that I was with Tom as you know on his last night in New York and left him only a short time before he went to catch his train. I have a clear recollection of that evening, and if Tom had really been suffering from a cold then I think the fact would have stuck in my mind along with my other impressions of that occasion.

All my best,
Ed

*

Feb 15, 1952.
Dear Ed:

I spent most of Tuesday writing you a long letter which, when I finished, turned out to be only an anxious repetition of all we'd said on the telephone. So I tore the damn thing up. But I still just cant get over it. [1]

I know I said I'd let you know if I heard anything about young Charlie, and I just got a letter to-day, in answer to my own really broken-up letter to Jack about Charlie's death, which I had already written before you phoned. Jack's answer is, alas, poetic rather than definite. He says "Fortunately we have the leadership of young Charlie and we shall all rally around him. He has rare ability and character, and will carry on the great tradition of the House.". . .

Ed, you dont <u>have</u> to read it, but if you should ever want to read any of this biographical stuff I've done to date, so you'd have something to confer about as an opener. Well, if you ever should, just let me know and I'll send down as much as I've got done. Am in within 2-3 pages of finishing the 2nd chapter, TW at Harvard, and have the first all done, as you know. Was hoping to finish the 2nd one this week, but this Charlie business sort of knocked me for a loop and I spent a lot of time writing highly emotional letters to people who were already highly-emotional enough and then some. . . .

You dont have to answer this at all unless you want something.

Love,
Liddy

---

[1] Nowell is reacting to the news of the sudden death of Charles Scribner III, whom Nowell calls "my Charlie." There are five Charles Scribners: Charles Scribner (1821–1871); Charles Scribner II (1854–1930); Charles Scribner III (1890–February 11, 1952); Charles Scribner, Jr. (1921–), to whom Nowell refers as Charles Scribner IV; and Charles Scribner III (1951–). When referring to the publishing firm Charles Scribner's Sons, Nowell calls it either CSS or, as Aswell does, Scribner's.

*

February 19, 1952

Dear Liddy,

Your letter of the 15th reached me at home yesterday. I wish you had sent me the longer letter you said you wrote and tore up, even though it did repeat, as you indicate, only what you had said to me over the telephone last week.

I too was greatly upset and disturbed by Charlie Scribner's death. I had come to be very fond of him and had seen him several times in recent months, the last time less than a week before he died. I still find it hard to believe that he no longer exists.

I myself have heard nothing directly about Scribner's plans. Whitney Darrow [vice president of Scribner's from 1931–1953] told me over the telephone that they were going to try to get young Charlie released from the Navy so that he could come in and head things up, and Whitney said he thought they had a very good chance of doing it. Maybe, as you suggest, they have already succeeded in this, although if that is so it is the quickest action I have ever heard of involving anything to do with the Navy.

When I talked to Jack Wheelock the day after Charlie's death, he was very gentle and sweet, but said that everybody at Scribner's was completely stunned and dazed, which of course I could well believe.

To answer your question about the biographical material, I think I had better not tackle it piecemeal. It will make a lot more sense to me to read it in context. I probably told you a long time ago that Charlie Scribner had agreed to let Melville Cane act for Scribner's as well as for the Wolfe Estate in giving advice about libel in the book you are working on. Charlie also agreed to divide Cane's fee fifty-fifty with the Estate. While it is true, then, that both Scribner's and the Estate would have to depend chiefly on Cane's advice about libel, I feel that I cannot go solely on the advice of anyone. I have had a good deal to do with libel problems myself and may possibly have at least a few questions to raise with Cane which he may miss. Libel sometimes has as much to do with the context in which a statement is made as with the statement itself. In other words, it is possible that there could be some libelous implication in your biographical stuff in the light of what may appear in the letters. Both Charlie and I have separately reassured you that you are not to be held responsible for libel in the book or in any part of it including the biographical stuff. That, of course, makes my own responsibility all the greater and is the reason why I would prefer to read your biographical material in context.

Cordially yours,
Ed

*

1177 Hardscrabble Rd.,
Chappaqua, N. Y.,
February 27, 1952.

My dear Liddy,

Bless you, I did not mean that you should write over again the letter you tore up. But now that you have, I am grateful. Reading it was almost as good as talking to you. But I see now that I was an ass. The night of Charlie's death, when we talked on the telephone, I should either have been more explicit or I should have said nothing. Since I did tell you part of it, I'll now tell you the rest. My apology is that Charlie's death upset me greatly — more, in fact, than Max's death did — and that is strange, for I knew Max much better and his going was more of a personal loss to me. I can't explain this paradox. Perhaps it is simply that I am older now myself, and therefore nearer death, and the loss of one I had come to know and love strikes closer home.

The business about Scribner's had a very nebulous beginning. I am not sure I can put my finger on the exact point where it started. There was a time, not long ago, when I felt that my relations with Scribner's were rather strained. I think I may have written you letters which conveyed that sense. Then, rather quickly, everything cleared up. So far as I can remember, it came about in connection with your book. You will recall that I was rather slow in dealing with it, and was unable to get around to reading it until I went away, almost a year ago, and took the manuscript with me to Texas. At that time, Charlie wrote you something to the effect

101

that he could control Jack's time, but not mine. Well, as you know, when I came back from that trip I had a session with Charlie and Jack and certain things were agreed upon. And at that meeting I said something to Charlie which I think struck him as news, in the sense that he had not thought of it before. I pointed out that my position as Tom's administrator was quite different from Max's, in that Max could work for Tom and for Scribner's at the same time, while I could not. For me, the rather onerous and thankless work I do for the Wolfe Estate has to be done largely on my own time; and if I am hard pressed, as I usually am, it always has to take second place. Charlie saw this at once, and I think he realized for the first time that what I do for Tom's estate is a labor of love and nothing else. Somehow that brought us closer together.

From that point I can't trace the exact sequence of events. Charlie was a rather solitary person and often lunched alone. I can remember seeing him at a table all by himself in various restaurants, and it always rather surprised me, for, to me, a solitary lunch is an abomination – yet he seemed to prefer it that way. However this may be, he and I came to know each other better, and I got the impression that he rather liked me, and certainly I came to like him very much. So, from time to time, always at his suggestion, he and I would lunch together. I was his guest a couple of times at the Racquet Club, and a couple of times he was also my guest – at my insistence – at the Century.

I have been told that Charlie was a fairly heavy drinker. I don't know whether this was true. With me, he always had two cocktails before lunch, and after two drinks his personality seemed to change. His rather excessive shyness would vanish and it was as if, suddenly, he was able to become the person he really was. I could be quite wrong about this, but I got the impression from things he told me that he was a victim of a father who seemed to him so everlastingly right, so dynamic and sure of himself, that he, as a boy, acquired the notion which he never outgrew that, no matter how much he tried, he could never measure up to the family pattern of what was expected of him. It was a strange thing. I had encountered it twice before, once in young Teddy Roosevelt (whom I knew rather well), who lived his whole life in his father's shadow and died a "hero" in France in the last war because that was what his father would have expected of him; and, again, in Elihu Root, Jr. [son of Elihu Root, secretary of state, 1905–1909] who was and is a different kettle of fish altogether, and has allowed himself to be completely flattened out by the oppressive weight of his father's greatness. The truth is, I think, that Charlie was much more of a person than he ever allowed himself to believe.

Anyhow, Charlie would become expansive and communicative when he had two drinks under his belt, and it was at such times that he spoke to me in a confidential vein. He was worried about Jack. Jack had a heart condition. Last winter he had a serious bout with pneumonia. He was not strong. Charlie was concerned about him as a friend and long-time associate. He was also worried about the business. If something happened to Jack, what then? No one had been brought in when Max died, but if Jack popped off something would have to be done. Charlie told me that he was concerned and had thought about the problem for some time, and he said he had tried to figure out what he ought to do. He flattered me greatly when he said he had surveyed the field and – I quote him as exactly as I can remember – "If anything happens, you are the man I would naturally turn to." It was said tentatively, conditionally, as if he were sounding me out and wanting to learn whether I would be available. There was no commitment in it, no definite proposal. I am as sure as I could be of anything that Charlie was thinking of the future, and laying his lines, and wanting to know whether, if something happened to Jack, he could count on me, or whether he should look elsewhere.

I told Charlie as straight as I could that I was honored that he should consider me, and that "I would give my right arm to work for him." I reminded him of something he had forgotten – and I don't know whether I ever told you of this: that I had once applied to Scribner's for a job. That was in the days just before I left the <u>Atlantic</u>. I knew I was going to get out, but I didn't know where I would go; so I looked around, and, knowing nothing then except magazine publishing, I concluded from such evidence as anyone could see from the outside that <u>Scribner's Magazine</u> was going on the rocks; and I came down to New York and went in cold to see Max Perkins and told him, cockily, that I thought I could save <u>Scribner's</u>. I thought then, and I still think, that it could have been done. And Max at least took me seriously enough to call in Charlie Scribner, and the three of us talked about it. That was the first time I met both Max and Charlie. To me, it was a memorable occasion. But it made little or no impression on either Max or Charlie. Once when I reminded Max about it, I learned that he had forgotten it; and so, as it proved, had Charlie. I still think I had some sound ideas about the magazine, but that phoney Logan [Harlan Logan, last editor of *Scribner's Magazine*] was the one they turned it over to. I have frequently puzzled about this, and I now have the notion, rightly or wrongly, that Max didn't really want to save the magazine; he thought it had outlived its time and ought to die; so, subconsciously, he was more interested in Logan who quickly killed it, than in me who wanted to put new life in it. . . .[1]

The way things were left was that Charlie, who always spoke of himself deprecatingly, mentioned his son and asked whether I had ever met him. I told him I had not. He said, characteristically, that the genius in the family missed a generation and skipped him, but that his son had it; and he asked whether I would be willing to meet the son the next time he came home on leave from the Navy. I said I would like to meet him. But Charlie died before the boy came home again. And this is the whole story as far as I know it.

You said in your letter that I knew Charlie had not discussed this with Jack. This is not quite accurate. I don't <u>know</u> anything more than I have told you. But I strongly suspect that he did not discuss it with Jack. It would have been an indelicate thing to do. It would have been like saying: "Look here, Jack old boy, I'm worried about you and I'm afraid you may pop off any time, so naturally I've been thinking about it, and what would you think of Ed Aswell as someone to come in here when you die?" Charlie just couldn't have done that, or anything like it.

As for Whitney Darrow – well, somehow I doubt that Charlie said anything to him, either. So far as I can remember, Whitney's name was never mentioned in any discussion I ever had with Charlie; and I got the impression, rightly or wrongly, that Whitney stayed on on sufferance, and didn't really cut much ice.

If Charlie spoke to anyone about his conversations with me, I rather imagine it may have been either to his sister, whom he mentioned to me as a co-owner of the company with himself, or to his son, to whom he may possibly have written something. Yet I doubt this last, too. You see, it was all very vague and indefinite. I don't think Charlie ever had the notion of bringing me in while Jack was still there. He gave me the impression that he was simply thinking ahead, about what he should do when Jack died. And that being the nature of the situation, I rather guess that he did not even write his son about it, but simply planned to bring the two of us together for a meeting when the boy came home again. But Charlie died before that happened.

So where are we? Nowhere, I think. It is just one of those things that might have been. I have written you, of course, in confidence.

My best, as always,
Ed Aswell

---

[1] This letter foreshadows Aswell's letter about Max Perkins (10/29/53), to whom Aswell ascribed dark subconscious motives.

*

March 6, maybe,

Dear Ed:

I've been meaning to answer your long letter about CS but there is really very little I can say because you've said it all so very beautifully. In fact, you've said a lot of things that I'd been thinking myself, and it is amazing to find that you were thinking them too at the same time. I mean, for instance, you said that his death upset you more than Perkins' did and then you said "and that is strange". I'd been thinking that myself and wondering why: thinking perhaps that I'd forgotten a little of how I felt when M.E.P. died — that it had sort of got dimmed by time. Because I did know Perkins better, and I also had persuaded him to be one of two executors of my own will which I had drawn the first year after Charles [Nowell's husband] got back from the war when I had all those operations, and was terrified that I might die. . . . Well, I did feel Perkins death, but I think the difference is that I wasnt as sorry for him, Perkins, as I was for Charlie. Because Perkins, in his own eccentric way, had a pretty good and happy life. Whereas poor Charlie . . well, you've said most of it in your letter. I mean, I think you are dead right about his father, "flattening him out". And I dont think (just between you and me) that Mrs S did anything to help rebuild his flattened ego. I dont know her very well, but the one time I went out with them and some extra man they needed a girl for at the last moment, she was pretty impatient with poor Charlie. And, oh, its hard to say: she is very very attractive and good-looking, but she carries herself as if she had a steel reinforcing bar threaded through her vertebrae, and then curved around over the top of her head to dangle a piece of very aged fish an inch or two before her nose.

Well, maybe that's unfair. For all I know, they were devoted, or anyway, I know he was to her. But he was sort of like a collie dog: if you patted him on the head he was so inordinately pleased and grateful and affection- ate. I think those solitary lunches you noticed Charlie having were not from choice but just because nobody had asked him to have lunch. I know, when I would suddenly hit New York in the war, I'd call up and Charlie could almost always meet me if I phoned him. But Perkins was apt to be busy, and would have to work and wangle things if he was going to meet me. Of course there were lots of people at CSS who would have loved to lunch with him — I know damn well that everybody there was devoted to him — but they might not want to impose on him by suggesting it, and he wouldn't suggest it to them, probably, unless for some special reason. And the brief, shy, but very charming appearances he'd make in Perkins' office when some famous author was in there. Perkins always made a point of asking him to meet them, but Charlie would come in, stay only a second, then go out so Perkins could discuss whatever had to be discussed. Poor Charlie was no sort of a creative critic, and I think that was one reason for his sense of inferiority: he left all that to Perkins I cant help wondering if young Charlie is any kind of critic himself: I am inclined to doubt it, knowing his father and his mother. But of course I hope he is.

About his being a heavy drinker. I dont think he was. At least I never saw him when he seemed the least bit tight in business hours, and I couldnt say the same for MEP, bless his heart. I think Darrow spread that rumor round about Charlie when he, Darrow, had been halfway pushed into retirement. It is one of the reasons I dont like the guy and do not trust him. But of course I never did. It may be that Charlie did drink quite a lot when he thought he had cancer of the throat, which was around that time. (I think it was just a little while before Perkins died, because I remember his, Charlie, telling me that it was not anything malignant after all when I saw him right after Perkins' death.) I think it scared and worried him half sick, and he might have tried to ease the acute horror of it by drinking more than usual.

Well, does any of this build up your own picture? It is only random thoughts. About the magazine: I think Logan put a lot of money in it, whereas I dont think you could have offered to at that time. But maybe I am wrong. Though I dont think Perkins was (even subconsciously) interested in Logan as an exterminator. I think Perkins was very sad to see it go, and – well maybe I am wrong, but I think Charlie and the more purely business – people were the ones who picked Logan. I dont see how Perkins could have chosen him himself: he was too good a critic and too canny in such things. But I dont really know. All I know is that Charlie couldn't bear to fire Dashiell [Alfred Dashiell, editor of *Scribner's Magazine*], and went abroad and suddenly told Perkins to do it. We were all a little sore at Charlie for ducking out on it that way, because it was terribly tough on Perkins, as you can imagine.

About you and Charlie yourself, Ed, I can see the whole thing perfectly, and I just cant possibly say how sorry I am. There was a hint of it in a letter he wrote me once, though nothing definite. In the beginning he had been sort of jealous of you, somehow: I think partly because Tom went to you, and partly because I myself was fond of you. Charlie was quite jealously possessive about people like me, and he used to call you, in letters to me "your friend, Aswell," or even things like "your boy-friend, Ed". But after that long conference with you, when you had just got back from Texas, he called you simply "Ed" and then said parenthetically "you see, he's my Ed now too" or words to that effect. I'm pretty sure those are the exact words he used. Or maybe he said it on the phone to me. I cant seem to find it, but I'm sure that that was it.

Oh dear. Well, it is none of my business, but if I were you I'd keep in touch and have lunch or something sometime, occasionally, with Jack. I dont mean to see if he shows any signs of dying, but — oh just to keep in touch. I agree with you that Charlie couldnt have said what you gave the gist of to Jack, but he did pour out all kinds of things about people and his plans; he might possibly have said something about you as a person junior to Jack to him. Oddly constructed sentence, but you see what I mean.

And to think that before that conference (when you got back from Texas) I was worried sick lest you'd be cold and shy and formal, and Charlie'd be the same, and you two wouldnt get along. Well, I most certainly am glad that you two did get to be such good friends.

The end. Again this is all poured out in one big mess. But you will understand.

Love,
Liddy

*

March 6, maybe, 1952.

Dear Ed:

Couple of things I need to know.

First, Mr Bernstein didn't die, did he? I had a letter from Mrs. B about a week ago, saying he had had a second shock and was "fighting for his life". And I ought to answer it but dont dare to, for fear he died and I just dont know it. If he should, would you let me know? Do you read the paper on the train and can you glance at death notices? Nice cheerful duty I'm suggesting, but if he should die, you would want to know yourself.

Other thing, which is more in the direct line of duty. I have now finished the Harvard chapter, and am beginning to collect my wits about the next one (1924–1926) which is the one that worries me about libel possibilities, I am quite sure I shouldnt identify Helen Harding [Boston friend of Marjorie Fairbanks] nor Marjorie Fairbanks by name in the part about Paris in 1925. Aren't you? (You know, they were the two babes with Raisbeck [Kenneth Raisbeck, Professor Baker's assistant in the 47 Workshop and a friend of Wolfe's] who are Anne and Elinor in Of T & the R.)

But what about Mrs B? Do you think it would be safe to use some of Tom's own words from Of Time and the River and The Web and the

Rock about her, IF they are complimentary ones and do not imply that she was actually his mistress? For instance, would it be safe to quote the passage from the end of T & the R, where Tom looks down from the ship and says "He turned and saw her then, and so finding her, was lost, and so losing self, was found, and so seeing her, saw for a fading moment only the pleasant image of the woman that perhaps she was, and that life saw. He never knew: he only knew that from that moment his spirit was impaled upon the knife of love." etc not all of it, but the gist of it up to the last 3½ lines of the entire book.

The thing is, if I dont say enough about Mrs B, I'll sort of be insulting her by slighting her and her great influence on Tom. And her influence was not so much artistic, nor financial, nor anything except the fact that they were in love with each other and (as she said somewhere) added to each other's stature. But if I quote any of the really beautiful and touching things Tom wrote about her, I'll be implying that Esther is Aline in the novels. And is that safe or not?

God! What a mess! What do you think? Would it be all right for me (or you, if you'd rather) to ask Mr Cane?

Love,
Liddy

PS I realize it'll be very hard for you to give any definite answer offhand, and I dont expect any <u>definite</u> answer. But I just cannot possibly write the goddamned thing unless I know which way to go about it: i.e. by avoiding any quotes at all from Tom's books about Esther as Aline, or by quoting judiciously from his books about her.

*

1177 Hardscrabble Rd.,
Chappaqua, New York,
Saturday afternoon,
March 8, 1952

My dear Liddy:

This afternoon I ought to be working on the papers of Sir Joshua Reynolds that turned up in Boswell's archives. Ted Hilles, chairman of the English Department at Yale, has edited them and I have the typescript before me. I have read half of it and am sure it is going to be quite a nice little book. I should go on now and finish it. But at noon today your letter came, so I am writing to you instead of doing my work, and that seems to me a good thing.

Why is it that we both feel a need to talk and write about Charlie

Scribner? We can neither add to nor subtract from the frustration and tragedy of his life. Yet, somehow, it seems important to get certain things said. The effort of sorting one's memories and committing them to paper is, I suppose, a way of holding onto them a little better. I felt this need most strongly the night of Charlie's death, and that is why I telephoned you. I simply had to talk to someone, and you were the best possible person. But that conversation did not dissipate the need. Immediately afterwards a telegram came from Whitney Darrow, such as he had sent to you, and apparently to hundreds. So, almost without reflecting how useless it was bound to be, I also called Whitney.

I wish I had Tom's gifts of sensitivity, perception, and evocative expression. The overtones of life often seem more important and meaningful than the major chords, but they are elusive and hard to capture. So it was in my talk with Whitney. He had been through as tough an experience that day as a man can go through. He had been called upon to accept the sudden death of perhaps his oldest friend. That was in my mind when I rang his number, and since I have lunched with Whitney several times in recent years, I felt like reaching out a hand to try, through touch if in no other way, to communicate a little of the inexpressible. But as I might have known, it was impossible with Whitney. My first faltering attempt to voice the sympathy of one human being for another was cut off short, in mid-sentence, and he began in that breathless way of his to tell me all about it – the facts – and how, after the supreme fact, he had notified the family, sent out telegrams to friends, and had already turned his back on Death and was thinking of the future, of Charlie's son, and how they would go about getting him out of the navy to come home and head things up. Oh, it was all very proper, and very efficient, and as cold as ice. The day had been hard, and now it was night, and he had done all the right things and was ready for bed. I could certainly understand – and could understand, too, what was lacking.

After listening to this spate of words from Whitney, I needed more than ever to talk myself and phoned Aline Bernstein. Another mistake. I assumed she knew Charlie at least as well as I did, but she knew him hardly at all. It was Max she knew. As for Charlie, well that was too bad – spoken cheerfully. It was almost as if she found the news somehow strangely comforting. And then she told me that her husband had just had a heart attack and was in bed and had come through it. What had happened that day might have happened to him, but fortunately it had only happened to Charlie Scribner whom she hardly knew, and wasn't life strange?

Then, feeling disconsolate, I phoned Frank MacGregor, president of

109

Harper's. I did it blindly and couldn't have said why, but now I know. It was Frank MacGregor who had brought me the news of Max's death. I remember how he suddenly appeared in the doorway of my office that day with a look on his face that told me something terrible had happened, and I said, "What is it?" – and he said, "Max Perkins died this morning." It hit me like a bullet, and I broke down and wept, and MacGregor came over and patted me clumsily on the shoulder and made comforting noises. That is surely why I phoned him that night, the first time I had called him at his home since leaving Harper's. But he was giving a dinner party and I had to argue with the butler to get him summoned to the phone, and when he came it turned out he didn't know Charlie at all, had never met him, though I assumed they must have been associates at the Grosset & Dunlap meetings; but this was wrong, for it was Cass Canfield [president of Harper's] who went to those meetings and knew Charlie, and Cass had just had a minor operation to remove a varicose vein in his leg and was getting along fine, and it really was too bad about Charlie Scribner.

Why do I tell you all this? I don't know. Perhaps because the last time I saw Charlie he talked of you. It was less than a week before he died, the night of the National Book Awards. Charlie was there because James Jones got the award in fiction, and Jones, appearing smaller than I had expected from his pictures and very much like a slightly undersized gorilla, made a bad speech, and Charlie sat through it looking bored and uncomfortable. After the formalities were over I went up and congratulated him. He stuttered a bit and made some appropriate remark, then switched the subject quickly and said: "I've been trying to pacify your girl friend, Liddy. She's still worried about libel, and I wrote her she had nothing to worry about." I told Charlie I had also had a letter from you about the libel business and that I had written you to the same effect. Charlie seemed pleased that we had both done what we could to keep you from worrying. That was the last time I saw him, and those were the last words I had with him.

He was very fond of you and liked to talk about you. I think I never saw him that he didn't talk about you. Once he told me how, early in your connection with Scribner's, you would barge into his office and perch on the corner of his desk and spill over to him about all sorts of things you had observed in connection with the business and the people in the office. He said that in anybody else this would have been intolerable, but that in you it was somehow all right. One thing he told me may seem a little improper, but it wasn't improper as Charlie told it. He said that one day soon after you came to Scribner's he went out to lunch just as you were coming back from lunch. He was walking down the street and saw you approaching him from the opposite direction, and it was a very windy day, and suddenly the wind caught your skirt and blew it up over your head, and – "God!" said Charlie, "she didn't have on anything under the dress, and she was the loveliest thing I ever saw, and I couldn't work all afternoon for thinking about her."

You may not remember the event, but it obviously made a deep impression on Charlie. I thought he seemed a little wistful as he told me about it. Your speaking of his wife made me remember it. I never met her, and Charlie never mentioned her to me. But he talked of you all the time. Perhaps the windy accident was one of those revealing little things which are sometimes more important than the big things. Thinking about it as Charlie told it, and thinking, too, about the wife as you describe her, I have a notion that that day on the street you became for him, and always remained thereafter, the symbol of beauty, of naturalness, of spontaneous warmth, of everything he had wanted all his life and had somehow missed. I think that's the way it was, and that's why I tell you of it.

Ed

*

March 11, 1952

Dear Liddy:

So far as I know, Mr. Bernstein has not died. At least I haven't seen any notice in the obituary columns, and I usually glance at them. If I hear anything I will surely let you know.

I agree with you that Helen Harding and Marjorie Fairbanks should not be identified, either by name or in any other way if it can be avoided.

Mrs. Bernstein presents a different kind of problem. While I would think it inadvisable to tell chapter and verse of everything that happened or to spell out the exact relationship between her and Tom, you have certainly got to talk about their friendship, and I think you will have to name her. I could be wrong in this, but I think she would be hurt if you did not name her. But will it be necessary to say or imply that she and Esther Jack were the same person? Of course, it's no secret, but my present hunch would be not to quote anything Tom wrote about Esther Jack in describing Mrs. Bernstein. It seems to me safer in many cases to carry on Tom's fiction, that the characters in his books were inventions (and certainly some things about them were), and not link them with people in real life.

The only thing you can do in wrestling with this problem is to think it through along the lines I have indicated, if you agree, and leave it to Cane and me to see whether it is dangerous when we read the script. As far as Mrs. Bernstein is concerned, I wouldn't mind showing her what you write about her when the time comes, and get her approval in advance.

My best as always,
Ed

*

March 13, 1952.

Dear Ed:

. . . I have a couple of letters here from you, and thank you verry much. I'll try avoiding saying that AB is Esther Jack, but I do agree with you that it would be nice to show whatever I say to Mrs B and see if she approves. Certainly anything she would <u>dis</u>approve would be unintentional. And I agree with you that she would be offended if, through caution, I slighted her relationship with Tom. I even think we can get to use that passage at the very end of Of Time and the River. Because <u>that</u> book makes no mention of Esther Jack — not till the Harper novels does she appear. I also have a vague idea that Tom may have quoted that passage to Mrs B somewhere, maybe on the fly-leaf of the copy of Of Time he sent her. Anyway, if I do put it in, I'll fix it so it can come out without leaving any sort of gap.

As for your other letter, of course the part that fascinated me was the last part, and of course I whooped just like my mama, (though with less volume). I am quite positive that I never never went to work without at least some kind of underpinning, and that if I ever had been caught in that predicament on the corner of 5th Ave and 48th or 49th, I would have a vivid memory of same. Nor was I ever a desk-percher. Georgie, his nephew always did that and it annoyed me so that I would never never. . . . But this whole picture sounds to me like the kind of thing a frustrated person would dream up. Which brings us back to the original remark, "Poor guy". Ed, does this sound too flippant and hardboiled? I didnt mean it that way, but the whole interpretation was so different from mine. There was certainly a lot of affection there between us, but — oh well — you see what I mean.

Jack says my Harvard chapter is "excellent" except for some very slight changes in sentence structure and such: many of which I think he's wrong about, but have fixed or argued against, so that portion is all done. Hope to tackle the beginning of the next, and toughest, one to-night, or some time before Monday.

Love,
E.P.

*

September 6, 1952.

Dear Ed:

. . . Well now, are you still hoping to persuade me to do a biography of Tom some day, as you had vague ideas of doing a few years ago? Because it looks as if maybe I have been persuaded, willy nilly and somewhat against my better judgment. I have just finished the fourth chapter of the expository material, or whatever you want to call it. And the total of these first four chapters is 40,000 words! And there have to be 17 chapters, one for each section of the letters. And that means that the Expository Material alone will come out about 160,000 words!! And it seems just plain impossible to try to jam that much into the already-too-long Letters Proper: The Letters are 400,000 words, which was the limit Charlie gave me. With 160,000 added, the thing would be 560,000. Holy Smoke!!!

I have now sent Chapter IV to Jack and have written him saying that I think its time we faced this fact before I write my guts out for another year, and have asked him if they do or do not want to give me a contract for "A Short Biography". . . . If they say yes, you and they and I will have to hash it out. I'll have to get Eddie Colton out of moth-balls, I suppose, because I can afford neither the time, nor the money, nor the new fall bonnet that would be required to come to N.Y.C. (The entire population of Padanaram, Mass, dispensed with hats long long ago: the goddamned things blow off, for one thing.)

If they say No, I will then at least have fulfilled my obligation of loyalty etc. etc. to CSS, which of course is greatly diminished now anyway since Charlie died, and can ask you if McG Hill would be interested. . . .

Goombye, I will let you know about this contract business whether it comes to anything or not. But I wish it would. As the guy in Thar She Blows didn't say "I'd like some plain ordinary everyday Encouragement, and goddamned little of that."

Love,
Liddy

*

Monday, Sept 7 ? 1952

Dear Ed:

Written in great haste. George McCoy [editor of *The Asheville Citizen*] has just written me saying that he has been asked to speak in early December before the annual meeting of the State Literary and Historical Association in Raleigh, and has chosen as his subject "Asheville and Thomas Wolfe." And of course he wants me to help him. Says "I expect to get much information right here in Asheville, but I did think that you perhaps

113

have certain facts (as contained in letters) that are not available elsewhere."

Well, here we go again. Of course I have any number of facts and many long or short quotations about Asheville both in the letters, the notebooks, the Purdue speech, etc. etc. It'll be a big job for me to winnow and copy them all out for McCoy, IF you think it is all right to do so. Of course I am miserly in a way, and hate to give McCoy the things I had discovered for myself and was going to use. But he is a terribly nice guy, and Tom was devoted to him, and he helped me a lot when I began the letters, not only in giving me copies of his own but helping identify and track down other people for me. So, as far as I personally, go, I think I ought to do it for him even if it guts my own material and takes me weeks. BUT I have no right to unless you give your (the Estate's) consent. . . .

Also, if you can, maybe drop me a line now, telling me whether to go the whole hog, or to answer him with caution. Which is very hard to do, but, well, give me your general reaction to this, and I can then proceed accordingly.

Gotta make fish chowder now. In haste,

Liddy

*

September 9, 1952

Dear Liddy:

If you hadn't written me, I was going to write you, for I was beginning to wonder how things were with you. Now I see.

So you have at last come around to my idea that you ought to write a biography of Tom. Of course at the time I proposed it, I was thinking of it as a book for McGraw-Hill to publish, but I shan't stand in the way if Scribner's say they want it. On receiving your letter, my first thought was to call up Jack Wheelock and see what his views were, but then it occurred to me that you would only just have put the proposal to him, so it seemed to me only fair to allow him time to think about it. It will probably be much better anyhow for Jack to call me when he is ready to talk, as he undoubtedly will if he is interested. I can tell you right now that if Scribner's turns out not to be interested, I very definitely am, and am prepared to give you a contract the moment you want it. . . .

As I indicated earlier, I will make no approach to Scribner's about the biography but will wait until I hear either from them or from you. I shall, of course, be very much interested in their reaction.

Cordially,

Ed

*

114

September 10, 1952

Dear Liddy:

A letter from George W. McCoy came in the same mail with yours of September 7. He wanted me to give permission for him to see some of the restricted material in the Wolfe Collection of the University of North Carolina, and I have given him this permission for purposes of his address only, though he mentioned the possibility of publishing the speech in a magazine afterward. I have written him that we shall have to deal with that as a separate matter when, as, and if the time comes.

I strongly urge you not to spend a great deal of time winnowing out and copying all the material you have for McCoy's use. For one thing, it would be unfair to your book, and for another, it would be unfair to you to spend a great deal of your time in that way. McCoy tells me that the subject of his address is to be "Asheville and Thomas Wolfe." Can't you pick out just a few things bearing on this subject and let McCoy have them? After all, he is not planning a piece of exhaustive research.

I agree with your suggestion about procedure. In other words, why not send me whatever it is you select for McCoy's use, and I in turn, after reading it, will send it on to McCoy, giving him permission to use it in his speech but again reserving the publishing rights as a subject to be dealt with separately.

I have suggested to McCoy that he show me his speech and also told him that I should like you to see it before it is delivered.

Cordially,

Ed

*

DON'T FORGET TO WRITE MABEL ON OR BEFORE TOM'S BIRTHDAY OR SHE'LL SPIT IN YOUR EYE. Or is it fresh of me to remind you of this. I have it down in Grandmaw's Phillips Brooks calendar, which is why it occurred to me.

September 11, 1952.

Dear Ed,

You really are a sweetie pie. I mean, of course, bout the contract for a B-------y, if any, and all the rest of it. And if CSS shouldn't want to give me one, I'd take you up in just about 60 seconds, but as long as it started by going with the letters and Jack has helped me with criticism so far, and everything — oh well, you understand, as your very swell letter shows, and bless you for so doing. Also, bless you for flattering me so in thinking I could do it. When you first suggested it four years ago I thought I never could, and even when I began sneaking up on it I wasn't sure. But I guess now that I can pull it off, tho its a long, slow, nerve-wracking job. . . .

Of course if I do get to do it, either for them or you, I'd prefer to keep the news that I am working on it a secret, especially from Terry. And I think you would prefer that too, so he can't try to stir up Fred and Mabel against me, etc. etc. . . .

Well to-day I got your note about McCoy and agree with you absolutely. Will write him just a short note now saying I will help him, and will send you the long document when I get same done. I think I'll have to tell him everything I know, but maybe I can save myself by trying not to copy out any actual long quotes, simply giving him the source of same instead.

And so it goes. Wheels within wheels. But maybe it will all get us and Tom somewhere some day. God only knows, and God knows I hope so, and meanwhile

Love and <u>thanks</u> from
Mme. P.

Some babe in Abilene, Texas, is trying to do a thesis on You Cant Go Home Again and wrote me as Mrs Elizabeth Nowell Scribner, care of Scribners. I told her that she flattered me, but that she'd have to consult you about research into Tom's stuff, etc. I dont think she's much good. E.H.P.

*

September 15, 1952

Dear Ed:

Well, here is this damn thing for Geo. McCoy. If you see anything in it that I should not have said, just cross it out and send it back and I will type it over. I think it may get a little hasty toward the end, but that was when I entered into the <u>period of sturm und drang</u> with C.S. IV or whatever his right numeral may be.[1]

. . . . but I am not going to let him rush me through. I've about decided that he is not a true Scribner but a domineering Bloodgood, like his mother, the lady with the ramrod up her back. I thought her extreme impatience and temper outbursts came from her impatience with poor Charlie — that it was simply sexual and marital. But maybe it is inherited in that family. Or maybe I'm just being bitter now, because I am so mad. . . .

Aw nuts.

Love
Liddy

---

[1] Nowell had written Charles Scribner, Jr., (whom she calls Charles Scribner IV) to ask

if Scribner's would be interested in publishing a biography of Thomas Wolfe, separate from the letters. Charles Scribner, Jr., whom Nowell describes as "an imperious youth," declined her suggestion, and so Wheelock wrote Nowell to summarize what he called "the consensus of opinion here":

(1) Scribners wishes to defer consideration of the biography until the letters are in "complete and final form, either under the title, *The Life of Thomas Wolfe as Shown in His Letters,* and containing explanatory commentary not to exceed 80,000 words; or under the title, *The Letters of Thomas Wolfe,* and containing the minimum commentary necessary to an intelligent reading of the Letters. The latter is what you are under contract to do for us; the former was an idea volunteered by yourself.

(2) Upon delivery of the complete manuscript of the Letters, we shall take up the question of the Biography as a separate work to be published at some time later than the Letters.

(3) We want to publish the Letters as soon as possible. The deadline for delivery of the finished manuscript is May 1, 1953. That surely will give you time to finish the work, either with the minimum amount of commentary, or the 80,000 word commentary, as you may elect. We shall have to regard failure to meet this deadline as a default.

The word limit, the apparent rejection of her biography proposal, the deadline, and the manner of "young Charlie's" reply all caused Nowell to term this her "period of *sturm und drang* with C.S. IV, or whatever his right numeral may be."

*

September 24, 1952.

Dear Ed:

Please find enclosed, in one easy lesson, a sheaf of correspondence entitled How Not to Conduct a Publishing House. In other words, the letter of Sept 11 written by Jack after consultation with young Charlie, the letter of September 17 in which he retracts what he said in the letter of September 11. And my own reply of September 24 in which I tell 'em off. I think this will be the end of it, but if it isn't, I am going to ask you how much you think it would set me back to hire Ernst (not Cane, who is Scribners lawyer too) to go and call on "Mr. Scribner" for me. But no sense worrying about that. They have retracted that "default" business, and they couldn't put it through anyway unless there had been a deadline given in the contract. And if there had been one, neither you nor I would ever have signed the goddamned thing, so what the hell. . . .

Of course this leaves me stuck with writing the whole biography too fast, and with no advance to see me through. But it is much better that-a-way. It will at least give me time to write it, and will also give us all time to see what young CS is really like, etcetera, etcetera, etcetera. Also, if I do decide to leave them, I'll have to do it very gently. Because if this Biography is going to be fair about the Tom-leaving-Scribners business, it has got to quote a lot from Perkins and CS's own letters. And also it quotes a lot from Scribner-published books. And we'd have to get permission from them to use this stuff. . . .

SO, all in all, I hope you'll read the goddamned thing anyway, even tho Jack probably will read it too. If and when I get it finished and have to decide who to submit it to, the two chief aspirants will then be neck and neck, as far as having read it is concerned. Mebbe I'll have to get myself an agent (hah) to help me thrash it out. But the main thing is to <u>write</u> it first. Amen, and

Love from Liddy

*

January 23, 1953.

Ed dearie: Thanks loads for your letter. It is what I thought, but I'm glad you are getting it in shape with her (Aline Bernstein) at any rate. There are so many things that only she would know, and she'll tell you everything as she would few other people.

There is one thing that only she would know, that I sort of need to know. . . .

What it is, is I think she must have made two suicide attempts round 1931 or 32. There is the one she describes in The Journey Down, which I think was in March, 31 . . .

But Tom told me of an attempt which he and Perkins thwarted. He was in a terrible state about it and poured it all out to me, I think when I was working on Scribners Magazine, but I'm not sure now. What he told me was that he and Perkins were at the Chatham bar, and he kept glancing toward a woman who was sitting there, because she had on a beautiful print dress, and he thought vaguely that it was like the sort of print that Mrs. B used to wear. He said she had a big hat on, and her head down, and he didnt see her face, but that finally Perkins whispered to him that the woman was watching him. He realized then that it was Mrs B, went over to talk to her, introduced Perkins to her, wanted to talk with her more privately, and so she and he and Perkins walked to Scribners and went up to the 5th floor. (It was at night, the place was empty except for Mr Hinkson, the night watchman.) That he was terribly upset and wanted to talk alone to Perkins. I think he wanted to try to pay her back some of the money she had given him, and wanted to confer with Perkins about that, but I cant be sure now. He and Perkins went inside the glass partition to P's office, asking Mrs B to wait a minute in the railed-off enclosure just by elevators. When he and Perkins came back out to her, he saw her put a bottle of pills up to her mouth. He rushed up and struck them out of her hand, and she half-collapsed in his arms. He and Perkins were terrified that she had actually swallowed some, and might die then and there on their hands. I think they got hold of Perkins son-in-law, Dr Frothingham, but am not sure. Anyway, I think Tom told me they took her to the hospital, but that she was all right.

But Maybe she wasnt all right. Maybe that was when she actually took the pills. Or maybe she went home and tried again later, and that time swallowed them without Tom's or Perkins interference. I think the latter. Because as I remember, Tom's letter to her in the hospital in March, 1931, began by saying he didnt know that she was sick until Abe Smith [Wolfe's loyal former NYU student and typist] told him, or somesuch. And in The Journey Down, she mentions coming out of her coma and remembering having looked at the pieces of pills on her tongue in the bathroom mirror. Which would imply that she had taken them at home in Croton or somesuch place, not at 597 5th Ave.

In The Journey Down, the description of her seeing Tom at the Chatham comes in the chapter right before the hospital chapter. SO, all in all, I guess she met Tom at the Chatham, tried to swallow the pills at Scribners that same night. Was foiled in her attempt. Went home, and later tried again with such success that she was hospitalized for some days.

Well, this is a hell of a mess to expect you to wade through. . . .

I am up to 1930 on the "expository material." and now busily engaged trying to explain in one brief paragraph why Tom didnt like Scott Fitzgerald, with justice to all and malice toward none. Hell, you could write a whole book on why he didnt. But never mind.[1]

Love,

Liddy

[1] Nowell's expository material contains a letter from Scott Fitzgerald, written July 19, 1937, which urged Wolfe to cultivate an alter ego, "a more conscious artist in you." Fitzgerald suggested that Wolfe needed to be more selective, like Flaubert, and less like Zola. The letter prompted Wolfe's famous reply, "Flaubert me no Flauberts, Bovary me no Bovarys, Zola me no Zolas, and exuberance me no exuberances" (*Letters,* p. 644).

*

February 27, 1953

Dear Liddy:

I am returning the copy of your letter to Professor Cargill [Oscar Cargill, a colleague of Wolfe at NYU and head of the English department], and I am grateful to you for showing it to me. It seems to me a remarkably perceptive and diplomatic document, and I agree with everything you say. I do hope Cargill won't make the mistake of identifying Tom's characters with people in real life. It could be very dangerous. It is also quite wrong to imply, as any such identification would imply, that Tom was just a sort of "super duper" newspaper reporter. It takes no account of the operations of the creative imagination.

What should I do to set Cargill straight about this?[1] Since I can't tell him you have shown me your letter, I am at something of a loss. Perhaps the best thing would be for you to write him and say something to the effect that you mentioned the matter to me since it affects the interests of the Wolfe Estate, and then you can quote to him whatever you think wise from the paragraph above.

Cordially yours,
Ed

P.S. As an afterthought I am enclosing a copy of a letter to Cargill answering one from him. Maybe this will do it.

[1] Professor Oscar Cargill, chairman of the English department at NYU when Wolfe was an instructor there, had written Nowell asking her to read his introduction to *The Correspondence of Thomas Wolfe and Homer Andrew Watt* that NYU Press would publish (1954). She thought Cargill seemed "a very nice guy" but worried she might have to spend her own time "checking things" Cargill had written. Aswell's reaction was stronger. In his view, the introduction was "insane" and "ungrateful," since its negative comments about Wolfe ostensibly would work against a scholarship established in Wolfe's memory. He sent Nowell a draft of his retort to Cargill. Reading between the lines, she saw that the real reason Aswell was so angered was that Wolfe's image was threatened.

*

March 19, 1953.

Dear Ed:

I guess it's more or less a question of how much each of us admired Tom, and I think that maybe the degree of unconditioned admiration may depend upon what stage of his life we knew him in. I think that you admire him more than I did, and that my lesser degree of admiration comes from the fact that I knew him when he still was in the Eugene Gant-y stage. (Though of course what I'm trying to talk about is admiration of him as an individual — admiration of him as a writer isn't influenced by this.) I do know, though, that in the last couple of years of his life I was constantly delighted and impressed by how tremendously he had improved in his relationships with other people, his general viewpoint, and all other later characteristics that you know.

BUT, by this same token, I think the people who knew him in the

NYU period admired him much less: in fact disliked him. From all the letters and other evidence I can put together, he was pretty un-likeable in those days. He says so himself in his Purdue Speech, BUT he explains very clearly why he was like that. Because he was so unsure of himself, because he had failed in his great ambition to write plays, etc. etc. etc. Some of them did like him: for instance, I think both Watt and Munn. But not his fellow-instructors, his equals. Though I think some of them began to like him better around 1928: for instance, Volkening, Vardis, and Desmond Powell.

Well, what is there to do about it? We can't dun into Cargill our own interpretation. But I dont think you really need to. And, honestly, Ed, although I think this is a fine letter, I think it is written at too white-hot heat. And I think that you would too, if you could either talk to Cargill, or could get him to answer you without making him mad as a wet hen first. You read the long letter I wrote to him. I didn't send you his reply which was really very swell and meek and well-intentioned. He said that he, personally, always liked Tom, that he thought of him as a nice big noisy big-hearted enthusiastic person. I think I had suggested that he might have got his bitterness from Dow [Robert Bruce Dow], and he replied that he thought he might have got it from Tindall [William Y. Tindall]. Then he said that he would go over it very carefully to "check the slanting", and I wrote back that I agreed he couldnt omit the bitterness against Tom which was so generally felt by his associates at NYU, but that I thought that he, Cargill, ought to be like God and make it clear that he, personally, did not subscribe to the bitter things that had been said about him. He also wrote me a short note later, saying that he had sent copies for reading to both you and Dick Kennedy. I should think that Dick's reaction would be somewhat the same as yours and mine, and if so, so much the better.

Does all of this prove anything? I guess the only important thing is that I think a gentle, even tho firm, hand would get better results from Cargill now that you've got the first shock and indignation off your chest. Whether you and he can finally hash out a piece that will be acceptable to both of you, God only knows.[1] I think Cargill undertook the job unwillingly, and with too little time and knowledge. I think he was over-conscientious in trying to write almost a brief biography, and has got in way over his head, although with the best intentions in the world. In other words, I think his errors come from ignorance, not malevolence, but I also think that he (like you) is terribly overworked and pretty much fed up with the whole thing. It might be better to try to persuade him to write just a brief, vague introduction — just a few general paragraphs.

But that will be up to you to hash out with him. And my heart bleeds for you, having to do this on top of everything else.

But I do most certainly agree with you that for the reasons which both you and I pounced on, the introduction as it stands can't be published with the Wolfe Estate as a co-author. If Cargill wants to publish it elsewhere himself, and you want to retort to it — oh God. Poor Ed!

And I do want to say that I am both glad and sorry that I sicked you on to this. I mean glad because you agree so intensely with me that all is not well with it. And sorry because it is just another awful chore for you.

God! Ed! The thought occurred to me that you might object with the same devoted (Bless you) heat to some of the things I am having to say about Tom in my own "commentary". There are things, like some details of Tom's behavior to M.E.P. and Mrs. B. which I cant whitewash. But I've tried hard in every instance to <u>explain</u> why Tom did them — why he was <u>impelled</u> to do them. And wherever possible, I've tried to use Tom's own words as explanation and justification of them. But no sense worrying about that now. Sufficient unto the day the evil thereof.

And love and luck, but <u>do</u> be gentle with him. (Cargill)

Liddy

[1] A subsequent agreement with the estate led to the publication of the Wolfe-Watt correspondence in one volume and the Cargill comments in another volume having to do with "memorabilia" of Wolfe's NYU days. Cargill referred to this agreement in his introduction to *Thomas Wolfe at Washington Square* (ed. Thomas Clark Pollock and Oscar Cargill [New York: New York University Press, 1954]): "A number of practical considerations in relation to permissions made the present form of publication the only practicable one" (p. viii).

*

March 25, 1953

Dear Liddy:

Thank you for your good letter of March 19. You are quite right in saying that the letter I drafted to Professor Cargill was written in white-hot heat, and I am now quite glad that I did not send it. Instead, acting on Melville Cane's advice, I wrote a different kind of letter to Dean Pollock, since he was the one who signed the contract with the Wolfe Estate, calling his attention to the fact that the project has taken a completely different turn from anything that was envisaged at the time the contract was signed. This will, I hope, result in a conference with Dean Pollock and probably Professor Cargill. Perhaps Cargill's introduction can be put back on the right track. If not, Cane thinks I have good grounds for canceling the contract and withdrawing from the whole thing. What I say here is, of course, confidential. We'll see what we'll see.

I think I have wasted far too much time and energy over this matter, but it has caused me great concern, for I think I have never been put in quite so uncomfortable and untenable a position.

Please don't think that I fail to understand that the Tom Wolfe I knew was a very different person from the Tom Wolfe of the early days. Of course in your book you are going to have to deal with the man in all his phases. That is not only legitimate but necessary. The New York University project is a wholly different thing since it was conceived by Watt as a memorial to Tom and has taken the unexpected direction of a very nasty attack on him. . . .

Cordially,
Ed

*

April 3, 1953

Dear Liddy,

Yesterday I had lunch with Dean Pollock and Professor Cargill of New York University, and I took Melville Cane along for moral and legal support. The discussion went better than I anticipated, Cargill admitting that his introduction went considerably beyond anything that was originally intended. To make a long story short, I proposed and they accepted the idea of making two books out of one. The first will contain the Wolfe-Watt letters and a very brief note of introduction. The second will contain Cargill's long introduction, very much revised, together with certain other material he wants to use. This device will relieve me of my twin embarrassments of being a party to what seems to me a biased and rather hostile interpretation of Tom and of being put in the position of having to censor Cargill's views. In other words, I shall be associated with one volume but not with the other. Dean Pollock will have to present this plan to the board of New York University Press and obtain their approval, but it seems apparent that this will be a mere formality.

All my best,
Ed

*

123

June 10, 1953, My 49th (!) birthday

Dear Ed:

. . .[1] I realize that I am asking an awful lot of you, but, to quote from the letters of T.W., "I am in terrible trouble, and I need a friend." You pretty much persuaded me to undertake this damned biography, and if it is ever going to come to anything, we are going to have to "pull together" (again I quote T.W.). If neither Scribners nor McGraw Hill wants it, I thought of trying the Harvard University Press. But you, as the Administrator of the Wolfe estate, would have to read it and approve or disapprove of it at any rate. So how about it?

Next thing I write is going to be By Myself, About Myself, and Purely Fictitious. IF I ever get through this biography mess and am still alive.

Love,
Liddy.

I didn't make clear how much there would be for you to read, because it would depend on how much I had got finished by the time you took your so-called vacation. I have finished 7 chapters, amounting to about 80,000 words. Jack has read 6 of these, and I have his word for it that nothing could, or should be cut from same. I am now doing Chapter VIII. I think maybe I can wind the whole thing up in 10 chapters, but I can't be positive till I write 'em and see how they come out. At any rate, there is surely enough for you to get a good general idea of the whole thing.

[1] The letter opens with Nowell's concern over Scribner's and future contract arrangements. She explained that she had "only 2–3 more chapters to do on the biography, and the nearer I get to the end, the more I dread the prospect of having to discuss it with that wild and unpredictable young man, Charles Scribner IV." Nowell had decided definitely that the biography should be separate from the letters, and she told Aswell, "I desperately need to know how you stand on the biography *before* I get involved in any further arguments with young Charles Scribner."

*

June 29, 1953

Dear Liddy:

Last night on returning from my vacation I found your letter of June 10 awaiting me. . . .

Your change of plan — that is your decision not to incorporate what you most recently have been writing in the Volume of Letters, is news to me. The decision seems right. So let me say immediately that I am tremendously interested in publishing your biography of Tom. You will recall our last talk in Boston when I urged this project upon you. Ever since I became Administrator of the Wolfe Estate, I have been trying to find the right person to do the job, and many names were considered from time to time. But there always seemed to be some reason why each of them wasn't quite right for it. It was through this process of elimination that I finally concluded you were the right person and that is why I asked you to meet me in Boston.

Your situation with Scribner's appears to be rather complicated and I am not sure that I wholly understand it, for you seem to have offered them first chance at the biography as a separate book, at the same time, reserving to yourself the right to decline their offer if they make one. I gather this means that you are so unsure of the new regime there that you would no longer feel entirely happy if perhaps Scribner's published the book. It seems to me, therefore, that the first thing you need to do is to clear your lines with Scribner's. As you say, I shall need to read your manuscript in any event. So why not send on to me the completed portion of it, and I'll read it as soon as I can. In the meantime perhaps you can clear up things with Scribner's. I am afraid I can give you no help in that connection because I have still not had the pleasure of meeting young Charles Scribner. Since his father died, there have been very few matters affecting the Wolfe Estate that I had to take up with Scribner's, and these I managed through Jack Wheelock.

Just for your information, I have been sitting on young Kennedy's project for a God-awful long time. I hate to be put in the position of discouraging any legitimate scholarly project, yet I feel that Kennedy is much too young and immature to write a biography of Tom. One reason I have delayed writing him is that I continue to entertain the hope that you might eventually do the book. Certainly it would be a mistake to authorize Kennedy to go ahead and thus perhaps be the first person to skim the immensely rich cream off the top of the jug of Wolfe papers.

Under no circumstances, I think, should you consider letting the Harvard University Press publish your book. They do not have the selling organization to push it properly. There are a number of Wolfe enthusiasts here at McGraw-Hill aside from myself, and I think I am honest in saying that our sales and promotion set-up is one of the best in the business. As you can see, I am immensely enthusiastic, but I shall feel much happier when you have come to some sort of understanding with Scribner's.

All my best,
Ed

*

125

July 7, 1953

Dear Ed:

. . . Just between you and me, my decision to publish the biographical material (if possible) as a separate biography is no sudden "change of decision," as you thought. I had pretty much decided to do so last September when I asked Scribners for a contract for a biography and got a kick in the teeth from C.S. IV instead. But since I did get the kick in the teeth, and since I could not be sure till I had written the thing that it would be over the 80,000 word limit for possible inclusion with the Letters, and since I had every legal and ethical right to defer my definite decision till I'd written the biographical material and found out how long it would be, I decided to defer same instead of going off half-cocked. . . .

I suppose you know, Ed, that the time last September when I was maddest at young Charlie and called you up in Chappaqua, I did so with the intention of asking you, as editor of McGraw-Hill, for a contract. . . . But because of those very confidential things which we discussed on the phone, I didn't ask you for one. And I know now that it was a good thing that I didn't, because it would have been going off half-cocked.

I mean, Ed, that neither you as Administrator of the Wolfe Estate nor I as editor of the Letters and author of a biography, can afford to get in an out-and-out row with C.S. IV. Because we need his good will for the publication of the Letters. And because we also need his consent to the quotation in the biography of a great many things which he controls. . . .

Now maybe I have quoted too heavily from these sources. But it would seem ridiculous, when Tom has described so many things about himself so fully, for me to paraphrase his descriptions in my own vastly inferior prose. . . .

Also, I am constantly haunted by a vision of Tom and Perkins sitting in a celestial counterpart of Chatham Walk, and shaking their heads over their seventh ambrosia-martinis, and saying: "It's too bad: Miss Nowell means well, but she didn't get us right!" Therefore, I have tried to give them a chance to get themselves right, in their own words, wherever possible.

. . . Moreover,[1] I am certainly indebted to you for the same things which make me so in debt to Jack. You and I have been damn close friends on all this Wolfe business now for 15 — count 'em — years. And when Tom went to you, and later when Perkins died and I wrote Fred and Mabel suggesting that Tom would have wanted you as his next executor, I certainly meant to support you with my whole heart. Moreover, it was you, and nobody but you, who convinced me that I could actually write a biography. It took you a long time to do it, but if you hadn't planted the idea in my head, and watered it and given it Vigoro at intervals, I never would have dreamed of attempting same. Therefore for that reason, as well as all the more general, harder-to-express reasons, the damn thing really ought to go to you if you decide you want it. And I can see no reason why I shouldn't say as much to Jack and C.S. IV.

. . .[2] Ed, I do hope that I won't be the reason for your discouraging poor little Kennedy, if he has to be discouraged. I would hate like hell to stab him in the back, or even to have him think that I had done so. But I realize that you have to do whatever you think best about his book, regardless of him, or me, or what he might or might not think. . . .

Love,
from
Liddy.

[1] Nowell gave, as another reason for dreading "getting in a row with Scribner's," her indebtedness to Jack Wheelock, "who has nursed me all through the writing of this time with the most tender solicitude and sympathy and encouragement. If I could have done it without his help, I wouldn't feel so like a heel." In recognition of this sentiment, she dedicated the biography to John Hall Wheelock.

[2] In the next five paragraphs, she discusses the original three-way arrangement with the letters, which was ideal for her when Charles Scribner III was alive but totally different "when young Charlie gave me the kick in the teeth" about the biography. She then suggests ways she might get Scribner's to decline a contract for the biography. Nowell's *Thomas Wolfe: A Biography* was eventually published by neither Scribner's nor McGraw-Hill but by Aswell's last firm, Doubleday, in 1960 — two years after both Nowell and Aswell had died.

Chapter Five

"The Terry business becomes more shocking and more complicated all the time."

ASWELL, SEPTEMBER 29, 1953

*

JOHN S. TERRY died in his Brooklyn apartment, creating problems for Aswell and Nowell, who had long suspected that he was not working on the biography of Wolfe sanctioned by Maxwell Perkins. Once Terry's executors gained access to his apartment, it became apparent that Terry's biography was nonexistent. Instead, the executors discovered numerous letters about Wolfe, including responses from Perkins to questions Terry had asked him. Aswell inspected the apartment, then expressed revulsion at the chaotic state of "the Terry business," which included mounds of unopened Wolfe material "strewn on the floor and trampled upon over the years."

The situation became even more shocking to Aswell when he read the letters Perkins had written to Terry. In a state of high emotion, Aswell turned to the typewriter. He wrote from his home, pouring out his "night thoughts" in a ten-page, single-spaced letter. Uncharacteristically, he wrote hastily, full of heat and feeling, showing the extent to which he had been — all along — shadowed by giants. He who had earlier accused Nowell of "looking around corners" here confessed to being an inveterate "looker-around-corners" himself. He speculated on Terry's motives in questioning Perkins and, more especially, on Perkins's replies. He wondered why Perkins had selected Terry as the official biographer of Wolfe. Could it be that Perkins had chosen a biographer who would vindicate Scribner's but vilify Wolfe; that Perkins had betrayed Wolfe; that Wolfe's unflattering portrait of Perkins as Foxhall Edwards, The Fox, had been uncannily true? In his partiality to Wolfe, Aswell wrote as if there could be no degrees of truth.

"All the separate colors of the spectrum," he said, "add up to what we call light."

Nowell replied with a thirty-two page letter. Usually the one to write with emotion, now she dealt rationally with Aswell's outburst, saying she found no "deliberate Machiavellism" in Perkins's letters. She separated Wolfe's fictionalized account of Perkins, sly as a fox, from the Perkins she had known and thought of "almost as a father." Through this exchange, it becomes apparent once again that Nowell and Aswell saw truth differently when it came to Wolfe.

The issue was of utmost importance to Nowell, now that Terry's death had cleared the way for her biography of Wolfe. Because of Aswell's strong reactions to the Perkins-Terry letters, she worried that he would object to her biography, which presented a different version of the truth from his. She asked if he would accept what she had already written and sent to him or if she must begin the search for a publisher on her own. Aswell replied, "I stand before you in awe and admiration" and promised to do everything in his power to get her biography published "no matter who publishes it."

July 9, 1953

Dear Ed:

It would be hypocritical of me not to admit that my first flash of feeling about Terry's death was one of relief.[1] I think you must have felt that way too, all things considered. It wasn't till later that I began to feel sorry for him, dying all alone that way, and in Brooklyn of all places, instead of in Carolina where he really did belong. Today I got two reports from Miss Stark [identity unknown] to Jack and me, and I gather that you are busy as a bird-dog. But, as you say, there's nothing to be done till Terry's executor has been appointed, and I certainly do hope for your sake that even then there will be very little to be done.

Miss Starks second report says that there was "a great mass of papers concerning Thomas Wolfe" which the police put in a suitcase. Well, cheer up, a suitcase full is no "great mass": if I should drop dead tomorrow, Chief Hervey of the Dartmouth Police would need at least two trunks. I may be all dead wrong about this, but I bet you'll find what you suspected all along: that Terry had done very little about an actual biography. And I even bet that the great mass of valuable letters from Tom to Mabel and Mama which Mabel talked about at first, is either non-existent or almost so. You told me once that you had the Letters to His Mother unopened in your safe,[2] and Mabel has never mentioned any Terry-hoard of her letters since she found the batch in Washington which she gave to Chapel Hill. Of course, if Terry did have any important letters of Tom's which covered subjects not covered in the present manuscript, I would have to rip that up to put them in and cut others out to make room for same. But I don't think there'll be much, if any.

Ed, I do not want to add to your headaches, but to help you all I can, and if you want me to go through any of the Terry stuff, I'll gladly do so. But, unless it is imperative for the sake of the Wolfe Estate, I do not want to finish any biography of Terry's, nor to incorporate much, if anything, of his in my own work, nor to be co-author with him on a biography or any such. His way of thinking and mine don't mix, and that applies to our respective ways of thinking about and writing about Tom. Moreover, I may be conceited, but I doubt if Terry's suitcasefull of material contains any major information about Tom's life which Tom himself did not mention in his letters to people, or in his books, or in his pocket notebooks, or verbally to you, me, Jack, Perkins, and other close friends of his. I think I have all the main facts about Tom either written down or "straight as a string in my head" as he used to say. And at this late date, I would hate to have to stop and have indigestion trying to assimilate any great mass of stuff of Terry's unless you should insist on same for

Tom's own sake.

There is one thing that you may run across and want to be forewarned about in Terry's papers. Kennedy once asked me if I thought Tom could ever have murdered an old lady in a Budapest junk-and-antique shop, and then he and I both laughed and said no. But Dick said that once when he saw Terry, Terry asked him if he had ever found any information about same. Seems that Tom once told Terry a tall tale about his having murdered this old lady, and Terry even considered looking in old Budapest papers for the right date (it was in 1923 that Tom was in Budapest), to see if any old junkshop lady had been murdered. There was such an old lady and such a shop: Tom mentions it briefly in a letter to Mrs B, and other places. But you know as well as I do that he no more murdered her than we did. In one notebook later he has one sentence "How I murdered the old lady in the _____ (French word for antique shop)," but this was to me quite obviously an idea for a short story. It was not in Tom's nature to murder dear old ladies, and it also was not in his nature to murder dear old ladies without talking about it at great length afterwards to all of his close confidantes. But it was very much in his nature to tell tall tales just to pull John Terry's leg, and he must have had a fine time doing same.

Goombye, don't answer. Just remember that I want to keep as clear of entangling alliances with Terry's ghost as I wanted to with Terry-living. But I will help you all I can, short of a ludicrously incompatible literary marriage of that sort.

And love and luck
from
Liddy

---

[1] Seven months after John Terry died, his papers were shipped to Houghton Library, where Nowell in 1953 began the time-consuming task of going through them for Wolfe letters, adding the new material to her letters manuscript, now five years in the making.

[2] There are two editions of letters to Wolfe's mother. The one Nowell was referring to, of course, was the Terry edition of 1943.

*

July 9, 1953

Dear Liddy:

For your information, I have a date for luncheon next Wednesday with young Mr. Charles Scribner. It came as a result of John Terry's death.

I have heard conflicting reports from several people who knew Terry well about the status of the project on which he was working. Some say he had made considerable progress in the actual writing of the manuscript, and one person who claims to have been a very close friend reports that Terry told him shortly before his death that the manuscript had been completed. This I cannot believe.

It is now fairly well established that Terry left no will. He has a sister and brother surviving, and I am told that they have executed a petition to the Surrogate's Court in New York asking that three people, two of whom I know and am in touch with, be named administrators of Terry's estate. [1] The legal moves in connection with a matter of this sort are simple, so I imagine that within the next week or ten days the administrators will be officially appointed by the court, and will then be given access to Terry's papers. After that it will soon be possible to determine just what the facts in the matter are. I shall let you know more when I know more myself. Meanwhile, keep all this under your bonnet.

Cordially yours,

Ed

P.S. Since the above was dictated, your very good letter of July 7 has come. You are right, I think, to want to hold everything as is for the moment and not precipitate any sort of issue with Scribner's. I greatly appreciate everything you say about my so-called right to your book — a right which, if it exists, I never would have pressed — the main thing for the moment as you say is for me to read the present chapters and the others as they come along, and then we'll decide what to do. Meanwhile, this Terry business raises certain questions and creates certain problems. If it is true that he had actually completed before his death any considerable part of his biography of Tom, and if it is in publishable form, it will be offered first to Scribner's since it was Max Perkins who set John Terry going on the project. Terry never had a contract but the moral obligation to give Scribner's first chance at that book, if it turns out to be a book, is clear. On the other hand, if anything publishable is found among Terry's papers, I find it extremely difficult to believe that it will be the book I think should have been written. It is no secret to you that I had a low opinion of Terry because, though he knew Tom for years, I could never discover that he really understood him or had any insight into Tom's writings. Terry's introduction to THOMAS WOLFE'S LETTERS TO HIS MOTHER proves that, even if no other evidence were available. Moreover, Tom had stopped seeing Terry in his later phase and Terry resented this. Even more, Terry was very embittered against Tom when the character sketch of Jerry Alsop was published. [2] I rather suspect therefore that if there is a manuscript of Terry's, there will be a good deal of venom in it

133

directed against Tom. For example, I am told by one of Terry's friends that he thought Tom had treated Scribner's shamefully in leaving them, and he was going to see to it that the true story was told.[3] Well, you and I know practically all there was to know about that particular episode and I think Terry knew very little. I suspect, for example, that he subscribed to the Struthers Burt theory.[4] At any rate he was one of the few people who was supposed to be a close friend of Tom's who did not write and thank me for setting the record straight. All this is just thinking off the top of the head and may turn out to be quite wrong. Anyway we will know what the truth is before very long.

By the way, in the telephone conversation with young Charles Scribner this morning he was almost excessively cordial. Maybe you know what that means, I don't. He spoke of his father's "affection" for me and of his desire to meet me, so maybe he knows more about what happened than I thought.

[1] The three executors of the Terry Estate were two of Wolfe's friends, Kitty and Clayton Hoagland, and one of Terry's students, a lawyer. See Clayton and Kathleen Hoagland, *Thomas Wolfe Our Friend 1933–1938,* ed. Aldo P. Magi and Richard Walser (Athens, Ohio: Croissant & Company, 1979), and "Terry, Wolfe, and the Biography That Never Was," *Thomas Wolfe Newsletter* 1, no. 2 (Fall 1977): 9–14.

[2] The portrait of Jerry Alsop appears in the "City of Patriots" section of *The Web and the Rock:* "Alsop was a man who had to live through others. He was an enormous Ear, Eye, Nose, Throat, an absorptive sponge of gluttonous humanity — he was not a thrust or arm — and in such a way as this, and so perfectly, so completely, the city was his oyster" (p. 235).

[3] Terry, writing as Wolfe's "official biographer" ("Two Interpretations of Thomas Wolfe: En Route to a Legend," *Saturday Review,* November 27, 1948, pp. 7–9), advanced the argument that false beliefs and innuendos "may have had something to do with Wolfe's leaving Scribner's in 1938." Aswell responded in the same issue, claiming that Wolfe's judgment of human character, abilities as a writer, and hatred of lies was so great, Godlike even, that he could not possibly have left Scribner's under the conditions Terry cited. Aswell's comments were subsequently published as the introduction to Wolfe's *The Adventures of Young Gant* (New York: New American Library, 1948).

[4] Struthers Burt's theory was that Thomas Wolfe killed Maxwell Perkins — caused his death, that is. See n. 1, July 23, 1951, chapter 3.

*

July 14, 1953

Dear Liddy:

. . . I am informed that Terry had in his possession a great mass of letters Tom wrote to him over the years. They of course have not been made available to you. I have already registered the fact with the proper people that when these letters are found I should like it if they will permit me to have them photostated before they are sold as I assume they will be.

I am told too that from time to time Terry bought various Thomas Wolfe documents from people who had them. Presumably most of these were also letters, and I have made the same proposal concerning them.

When I know more I will let you know.

Cordially yours,
Edward C. Aswell
mg

P.S. Here is something you will appreciate. Last Monday I telegraphed both Mabel and Fred to let them know of Terry's death and the plans for his funeral in Rockingham, North Carolina. Knowing that they had always liked Terry, and knowing too the Wolfe fondness for a good funeral, I assumed they would want to attend. Mabel telephoned me at home the night she received the telegram and wanted to know all the bloody details, which I gave her. I also told her that the body had already been cremated and that the ashes were being shipped to Rockingham. At this point Mabel said, and I quote her words exactly for I am not likely ever to forget them: "That spoils the fun for me. I always like to see the body."

*

September 4, 1953

Dear Liddy:

Day by day I get more deeply involved in the Terry business. His administrators have now been appointed and have taken possession of the apartment, and have begun the seemingly hopeless task of trying to sort out his papers and find out what is there. I was asked to visit the apartment the day after they obtained access to it and I did. You can form no idea of the task that lies ahead without seeing the place as I did. I am sure the confusion was bad enough while Terry was alive, but the police literally wrecked the place, tearing pictures from the walls, dumping books out of the shelves onto the floor, scattering Terry's pitiful possessions all over the place, and messing up the papers and documents as though they were animated by the most savage and demoniac destructiveness. There was not a foot of space on which you could walk without climbing over mounds of scattered documents, old clothes, dirty dishes, half empty whisky bottles, and everything else you could possibly think of, and to cap it all, the sickly stench of death hung in the fetid air.

Up to now, the administrators have just barely begun clearing out one corner of one room, but they have made an exciting discovery. They have found a series of letters from Max Perkins to Terry, in which Max, writing from day to day as he could find the time, set down pretty much the whole record of his relations with Tom beginning with their first meeting. I have not seen these letters myself, but Kitty Hoagland gave me a brief description of them. Everyone thought it was such a pity that Max never wrote anything about Tom except that little article in the Harvard Library Bulletin. Well, it seems that he told all. But isn't it strange that none of us and apparently no one at Scribner's knew Max had done this.

More later. Meanwhile,

All my best,
Edward C. Aswell
mg

*

September 29, 1953

Dear Liddy:

. . . The Terry business becomes more shocking and more complicated all the time. Kitty Hoagland reports to me almost daily, and new things are constantly turning up. She said this morning that she has now packed away, for eventual delivery to me, four large fiber containers of Wolfe documents of various kinds. Most of them were lent to Terry by Perkins or by members of the Wolfe family.

Have I told you what to me is one of the most shocking revelations? When Terry approached Perkins about writing the biography he stated that he was Tom's oldest and best friend, and that he had in his possession a very large collection of letters Tom had written to him over the years, covering almost every aspect of Tom's adult life, and that these letters would be source material of the greatest value for a biography and that he, Terry, would not permit anyone else to have access to them. Max discussed this with me at the time, when, as you know, I thought Henry Volkening was the one who should do the book. In the end, Terry's statement about his large collection of letters from Tom — statements which Terry later repeated to me — had a lot to do — that, plus Mrs. Wolfe's preference — with Max's decision to let Terry do it, and to give Terry all the help he could. Well, it turns out that there are only five written communications in existence from Tom to Terry. At least two of these are postcards, two others are brief notes of no importance, and the one letter of consequence is an eight page letter Tom wrote from London about the remarks Sinclair Lewis made when he received the Nobel Prize.

Another shocking thing is that some of Tom's letters to various people, which have turned up in Terry's apartment, are marked in Terry's handwriting, "To be destroyed." The correspondence with Claire [Claire Turner Zyve, one of Wolfe's short-lived love interests] was so marked. Whether Terry ever did destroy anything no one can tell. But his intention is clear enough.

There also seems to be evidence that Terry may have sold some of the Wolfe documents that did not belong to him.

There is no point in citing instance after instance. Some of the particulars would be too revolting to put in a letter. One thing that has become abundantly clear is that Terry was a psychopathic case.

My best to you as always,
Ed

The portrait of Jerry Alsop makes fascinating reading in the light of all this.

*

October 6, 1953

Dear Liddy:

. . . As for Terry's death and the need of appointing a new "official biographer" — well, my dear, you are already it, only let us never, never refer to the book as an official biography. I am against erecting monuments to the dead and so are you. The important thing is to bring the dead to life again in a book that will be accurate and reasonably complete.

What you say about Terry's use of the term "official biographer" echoes my feelings exactly. And have you ever thought that he never came forward with that claim until both Mrs. Wolfe and Perkins were dead? Perkins would never have appointed an "official biographer." He encouraged Terry and, as we now know, helped him more than any of us realized. But Max always had reservations about Terry as is indicated by the fact that he never gave him a contract; and toward the end of his life, Max lost what faith he had ever had and told me he did not believe Terry would ever finish the book. Apparently it did not occur to him that he would not ever begin it, or that he would not care enough to open and read two of Max's long letters of reminiscences about Tom.

Thank God for Kitty Hoagland. She has genuine admiration for Tom as a writer, and is determined to do the right thing about restoring all the papers that did not belong to Terry to their rightful owners. She has now completed her examination of every scrap of paper found in Terry's apartment and there is positively no biography, nor even an outline of one. Terry had many of the original documents typed. Most of them were found in sealed envelopes as they came to him from the typists, with the copies clipped to the originals.

It is clear now that Terry, after Max's death, considered all the Wolfe documents Max lent him as his own property. Again and again, he refused to return them to Randall [David A. Randall of Scribner's Rare Book department].[1] Fortunately, there are letters both by Max and Randall, requesting Terry again and again to return the documents. I say fortunately because Terry's heirs, having been lied to as everyone else was lied to by Terry, believe these documents all belong to them. Tomorrow Terry's brother, Harvey, arrives in New York in a truck, accompanied by what he calls "a little nigger boy." His announced purpose is to take all the documents back to North Carolina. Kitty Hoagland's Irish is up. She has all the documents at her house in Rutherford, New Jersey, and she says Harvey Terry can look at them if he wants to, but that he will not be permitted to take a single piece of paper out of her house. If Harvey presses his demands, she is prepared to turn all the contested documents over to the Surrogate's Court. And in that event, I shall have to make some quick legal moves to put in a claim for them. I hope it will not come to that, but the next few days shall tell.

The Terry family is also saying that it will be up to them to appoint a biographer of Thomas Wolfe. This, of course, is ridiculous. Anybody can write a biography of Tom who wants to, but he cannot quote any written word of Tom's without my written permission.

The contested documents are, I gather from what Kitty Hoagland has told me, rather important ones. This was inevitably so since Max Perkins selected them out of the mass of Wolfe's papers at the various times he lent them to Terry. Max would not have picked trivia. When I can gain possession of them, I shall want to go through them as quickly as I can, and then make them available to you. Some will be useful in connection with your volumes of Tom's letters and others will be useful in connection with the biography. It is my present thought that in due course you should go over the biography and see how much you may want to add to it since you now know that it will be the real thing and will not have to compete with any other.

I still do not dare to put into a letter the revolting details of some of the things that turned up in Terry's apartment, but I will tell you when I see you. They prove Terry to have been not merely a monumental procrastinator as Jack Wheelock thinks, but a psychopathic case. The Terry thing has been a continuous horror story, and has rather preyed on my mind as new details were revealed day by day. I gather though that the worst is now over and that there is not much more that can be added.

My best to you as always,

Ed

P.S. I knew that Terry had had Mrs. Wolfe talk into a recording device, giving her reminiscences of Tom's early life. These records have all been found and I think that as physical property, they belong to the Terry Estate since Terry rented the machine and paid for the recordings. But in addition to that, a piece of paper turns up showing that Terry had persuaded Mrs. Wolfe to grant him all the literary rights in these recordings. This and other matters too numerous to itemize suggest to me that if the Terry heirs are at all reasonable, it may be wise for me, on behalf of the Wolfe Estate, to buy certain things like these recordings from the Terry Estate. They may prove valuable for your biography.

[1] David A. Randall, author of *Dukedom Large Enough* (New York: Random House, 1969), was manager of the Rare Book department at Scribner's in 1935, a position he held until 1956. In his book, Randall described the Terry affair:

"Other Wolfeian episodes included a sad one with John S. Terry, who had graduated from the University of North Carolina in 1918 and become an English professor at New York University. He was editor of *Thomas Wolfe's Letters to His Mother* (Scribner's 1943) and aspired to be his official biographer. He was a cripple, dragging himself around on crutches with the help of a sort of a major-domo chauffeur, when he left his Brooklyn home at all. Perkins allowed him to borrow some of Scribner's (and Wisdom's) Wolfe material, and when I tried to get it back several years later, Terry denied ever having had it. This entailed police-protected visits to his Brooklyn home where he existed in incredible squalor — he had threatened to cane Perkins and brain me — and eventually we got our manuscripts back" (p. 252).

*

1177 Hardscrabble Road
Chappaqua, New York
October 29, 1953

Dear Liddy:

I am typing this hastily and it will be full of scrambled letters (for my typing does not improve with the years), but there are some things I want to say while they are fresh in my mind.

Today, Kitty Hoagland came to my office and turned over to me all of the letters about Tom which Max Perkins wrote to Terry. They number 15 and not 8, as Kitty earlier reported. These letters are the undisputed property of the John Terry Estate, but Kitty wanted me to read them, and she gave me permission to have them photostated. I brought the originals home tonight and have just finished reading them.

They contain matter of the first importance to you and the biography, but they are not what I was earlier given to understand them to be. They do not constitute Max's reminiscences of Tom. I do not know how Kitty could ever have thought so. . . .

What have we here, then, if not Max's reminiscences of Tom? It is quite clear what it is. Terry had sent Max a lot of numbered cards on which Terry had written down questions; and Max, without quoting the questions, gives the answers. This was obvious enough from the very first letter; and then, to prove it conclusively, with one of the later letters there is one of Terry's cards with the question on it. In other words, Max did not write his reminiscences at all. He tried to answer Terry's questions; and the only debt we owe Terry is that he did ask the questions (some of them obviously foolish), and if he had not done so, Max wouldn't have written anything. Terry told me more than once that he was going to send me cards with questions about the last phases of Tom's life, but he never did.

What we have, then, is not reminiscences, nor is it really letters, but a series of replies to questions, usually several in a single envelope. All the original envelopes are here, showing the postmarks. The first is postmarked Oct. 25, 10PM, 1945. The second in the series bears the same date, but the hour in the postmark is 8PM. What happened? Did Irma take the first out to mail and forget it till later in the evening, while Max himself mailed the second one earlier the same evening? Who knows? Somehow I think all of these answers to Terry's questions must have been dictated late in the day or at night. One envelope is postmarked 6:30AM. One reason I think so is that the typed answers (and they are all typed) contain a number of corrections in Max's hand, but it is a very shaky hand, not like his usual writing at all, and I suspect Max was drunk. This may possibly account for a number of errors that occur in Max's answers. In other words, I think you will have to be critical of what Max writes, for even when he seems most sure of himself, he is sometimes completely wrong. I shall cite instances later.

But first, let me quote you the notations that appear in Kitty Hoagland's handwriting on the large manila envelope that contained all these letters when she presented them to me:

"Max Perkins' reminiscences of T. Wolfe found in a pile of junk 8/31/53. K. Hoagland. Placed in the env. by me. Some had never been opened by John. I leave one still closed. Very important material for biography."

The one she refered to as "still closed" was sealed when she handed the material to me. She said: "I thought you might get a kick out of opening it." So, with her permission, I opened the envelope, carefully lifting the flap without slitting it. I remember it particularly because it contained Max's answer to some question Terry had asked about you, in which Max said that he thought your influence on Tom had been good. Looker-around-corners that I am, I suspect Terry hoped for a different answer, and it seems too bad that he was too lazy to open the envelope and read what Max wrote.

One question that bothers me is how to proceed with the photostating. The original envelopes may or may not be important, but I think they should all be photostated so you can read the postmarks. The envelopes are all those of Charles Scribner's Sons. For identification, I have marked above the Scribner imprint on each envelope, in Roman numerals, the order of the series from I to XV. And for further identification, I have marked the pages contained in each envelope, in the upper left-hand corner, I1, I2, I3, etc. (Irma's pagination, like her typing, was sometimes erratic.)

Now let me summarize briefly the contents in these envelopes. I shall add my comments whenever I have anything pertinent to say.

I. Tom and Madeleine Boyd [Wolfe's first agent] and Aline Bernstein, and how and why the first 100 pages of the Angel were cut out. These pages are accompanied by a letter from Max to Terry: "Just to show you that I have at last got around to answering your questions, I am sending you a first installment of replies."

II. The contract for Angel, and the work with Tom in cutting and making it ready for publication, together with a note from Max: "I succeeded in doing a little more, which I enclose."

III. First quarrel with Tom, over royalties on The Story of a Novel, and work with him on Of Time and the River.

IV. Max's full account of his meeting Tom at the boat and the evening that followed. Important because this was the event Tom referred to in his last letter to Perkins from Seattle: "I have met the dark man, etc."

V-1. Max's statement that nothing was ever cut from Tom's manuscripts to save the feelings in Scribner's. He refers particularly to the chapter in one of the posthumous books, "The Lion at Dawn," about Charles Scribner, Sr. My recollection of what happened is quite different from Max's. He has it certain things had to be changed to protect the widow of Charles Scribner, Sr. But, by God, I never heard that until I read it in this thing Max wrote to Terry. Max never mentioned to me the widow of Charles Scribner, Sr., and I never willingly agreed to change anything in that chapter. Max said to me: "You'll have to change this or I'll have to resign, because Tom did not know old Mr. Scribner very well, and what he has in there is what I told him."

V-2. Max says no one at Scribner's but he was worried when Tom reached the point of writing about his experience with Scribner's. This is simply not true. They were all worried, especially Charlie Scribner. Tom showed me a letter from Charlie to that effect, saying bluntly, "You can't write about Scribner's." It was one of the real causes of the break that Scribner's took the position that they were like a church, which could not be examined on human and moral lines — and Tom said, in effect: "To hell with that. You have published my books, knowing what kind of books they were, in which I have used my experience and have tried to find out what it meant. Part of my experience has had to do with Scribner's, and it has been like all the rest. You can't rob me of it. I shall write about it as I have written about all the rest of my experience, and if you don't like it — the hell with you." In other words, Max was being something less than honest when he wrote as he did to Terry.

V-3. This accords with my recollection of what I did after Tom signed with Harper's, my going to Perkins to tell him of it.

V-4. This is of some importance. Terry was obviously fishing for something bad in Tom's going with Harper's, and Max set him straight.

V-5. Tom and the Chelsea Hotel. Not important.

V-6. Max's first comment on the Dooher case. [1]

VI-1. Max setting Terry straight about something Terry had obviously been stupid about, but Terry's stupidity brings out a cold anecdote.

VI-2. Max's opinion of Elizabeth Nowell. Blush prettily when you read it.

VI-3 to 5. Max's visit to Johns Hopkins when Tom was dying. Max states I was not there the day he was there, and that I came the day after. True enough as stated, but Max did not know that I was there several days before he arrived, and the day after, and until after Tom died, and that the reason I was not there the day he was there was because of something you said. Do you remember? You said it would be like the meeting of the new wife and the divorced wife, and I agreed with you, so I disappeared for a day to let Max have his day with Tom alone. But Max says he never saw Tom, which I somehow knew. Perhaps you told me. Also Max doesn't mention that he argued Aline Bernstein out of going down with him. What fireworks with Mama Wolfe there would have been if Aline had turned up at Hopkins.

VI-6 to 11. The dinner with Countess Eleanor Palffy — something wholly new to me, and I don't doubt its accuracy. [2]

VI-9. Dinner at Cherio's with Jonathan Daniels [a University of North Carolina classmate of Wolfe]. The unidentified lady was, I think, Noble Cathcart's sister, who Jonathan Daniels married. Years later I lunched with Daniels and his wife at their home in Raleigh, and somehow learned that Cathcart's sister was Daniels' wife. I had known Cathcart slightly.

VII - Tom and Scott Fitzgerald. New and very interesting.

Go back to VI - 3 to 5 on the previous page. I see I have left out the most important thing I wanted to say about that. In connection with his visit to Johns Hopkins, Max writes: "Dr. Dandy said that there had been no way of telling whether there was one tumor or many — that one might have been easily removed — but that when he uncovered the brain there were myriads." Now how could Max have made a mistake like that? In his deafness he could have misunderstood Dandy's word "tubercle" for "tumor." But that really doesn't explain it, for Max and I discussed the cause of Tom's death more than once, and I showed him Dandy's letter to me, now at Houghton, and Max knew it was tuberculosis of the brain. This sort of thing makes me wonder what blunders future scholars may make when they try to sift out the truth about Tom on the basis of documentary evidence alone, without the benefit of any personal know-ledge to serve as a guide and corrective. When the evidence is contradictory, won't they be more likely than not to take Max's word about any point as the final authority? When you get the photostats of these Perkins documents, you will see that they are of great value and importance, but I think you will also be as shocked as I am to discover that they not only contain errors of fact like the above, and things remembered inaccurately (which is human enough), but also a number of important matters quite completely but very subtly distorted, with Scribner's always coming out blameless and lily-white and Tom thus mostly subtly left at fault. Until this moment I never understood Tom's characterization of Perkins as "The Fox." I never saw anything crafty in Max. But there is certainly craftiness of the most polished and innocent-looking kind in these communications to Terry. Was it conscious or unconscious? Damned if I know. Anyway, I now accept "The Fox" as an intuitive and almost uncannily true portrait of a very complex and wonderful man named Maxwell E. Perkins. And isn't it strange how each newly discovered piece of the puzzle somehow fits in and adds up to a new dimension of truth? For example, all this utterly fantastic Terry business in which I have been so deeply involved the past four months, and the proof it provided, if proof were needed, of Tom's deep insights into the hidden sources of human character when he portrayed the young John Terry as Jerry Alsop — that mother-pampered and mother-spoiled glut of oily fat, that psychopathically emasculated male nothing, that human sponge that took all and gave nothing, that embittered hater of Thomas Wolfe who made a mediocre academic career of posing as Tom's best friend and "authorized biographer." Why do I say he hated Tom? Well, I know for a fact that he never forgave Tom for the portrait of Jerry Alsop. That is understandable. But what about his shameless disregard for all the important Wolfe documents Max lent him, which were strewn on the floor and trampled upon over the years, including all these letters Max wrote Terry, some of which had never been opened? And what about the notation on some of these documents, in Terry's hand: "To be destroyed"? And, most conclusive psychopathic fact of all — and I have not told you this before — what of the fact that some of these important Wolfe documents are so soaked and saturated with Terry's urine that you cannot handle them without being nauseated by the stench? Well, make what you can of that. The only thing I can make of it is that here is evidence of an orgiastic, ritualistic, and many-times-repeated peeing on Thomas Wolfe. I have never encountered anything like this before, and it sickens me. But the point is: this is the man Max encouraged to write Tom's biography. Why? Yes, why, why, why? That is the insistent question, and I have been asking it of myself for years. Max consulted me at the time and asked my advice. The choice had narrowed down to two candidates: Terry and Henry Volkening. I urged Max to choose Henry, and in all events not Terry. I had before me, in proof, Tom's characterization of Terry as Jerry Alsop. Max also had the proofs of the as-yet unpublished book and had read them, and had said to me: "I think Tom is a little hard on Terry." And Max asked me to cut out the limp which was one of the important physical characteristics of both Alsop and Terry; so I did cut it out and it does not appear in the published book, but the limp of Jerry Alsop is in the original manuscript at Houghton. Now, at long last, I am beginning to get a glimmer of what may have been Max's subtle reason for choosing Terry to write the biography of Tom. You may think me crazy. And certainly these are night thoughts, prompted by my reading of what Max wrote to Terry. Max was a shrewd judge of human nature. He could not have been taken in by an obvious phoney like Terry. All right. He knew what kind of person Terry was, and somehow he knew, as I now believe, that Terry hated Tom. Such a person would write a biography of Tom which would present him unfavorably and would give Scribner's all the breaks. These communications of Max to Terry prove, to me at least, that that is what Max wanted. But there is something else. Terry was the laziest man that ever lived. One had only to look at the great fat slob to know that. Max was not deceived. Terry would either write the kind of biography of Tom which Max wanted, or he would never write anything at all. Either way it turned out would be quite all right with Max, the second alternative perhaps more preferable than the first. And we now know that this second alternative is the one that really happened. So Max was able to die without ever having to cope with the many problems that would have been presented to him if anyone had attempted to write a reasonably true biography of Thomas Wolfe. Q.E.D.

What I have written here is something I could not have written yesterday. I believe, as I write this, that I may have come close to some segment of the truth. It gives me no pleasure to write it. That is such an understatement that, if I had a gun in the house, I might well go upstairs and blow my brains out. It is not easy to give up one's illusions. I have given up so many. Max was to me a kind of father, certainly a friend, and in instance after instance the model after whom I have consciously patterned myself in my business life. [3] But the truth is here, never meant for my eyes or yours, but only for the eyes of that rascal, Terry. What a combination of good and bad! What a revelation of the unself-conscious deviousness of the human mind!

All of this merely emphasizes to me the supreme importance of writing and publishing a true biography of Thomas Wolfe. And what is a true biography? Merely a book that tells the truth, in so far as we can find out what the truth is. A book that does not defend Tom nor defame him. A book that will honestly try to do for him what he did for others: just get at the facts, whatever they may be, and clothe those facts with the flesh and blood of life. How many years ago was it that I told you that you were the one to write this book? Three, four? I don't remember, and it doesn't matter. The important thing is that you knew Tom better than anyone now living. You know and have absorbed the documentary evidence completely. You also know, admired, and loved all of the people at Scribner's who had anything to do with Tom. You can evaluate all the evidence in the light of this knowledge, as no one else can. Bless you, my dear Liddy. It is a great undertaking, but you are equal to it. Any help I can give you I shall gladly give, but in the truest sense of the word, you are quite beyond my help. Who will publish the book does not seem very important, except in a practical way, to you. You will need financial help. If you can straighten out your troubles with Scribner's, and if they will give you this help, it will make no difference to me — in the sense that I shall still give you every possible assistance at my command. But if you cannot arrange things satisfactorily with Scribner's, or no longer wish to do so, please know that I am still behind you and will give you the contract you want. This thing must be done, before all of us who knew Tom are dead or senile; and I hope this Scribner thing can be straightened out soon, so that both you and I will know where we stand.

VIII-1. Tom and an unidentified girl. A new anecdote to me, but not very important.

VIII-2 to 4. Thomas Wolfe and Marjorie Dorman [who claimed she was libeled in "No Door"]. There is surely much that is wrong in Max's account of this matter. Tom told me this was one of the reasons he had to leave Scribner's, because they settled the suit instead of fighting it. Tom said he had the evidence on which the suit could have been won. Max says the same thing. Yet Scribner's did settle the suit without a fight. The thing that interests me particularly is that Max says Tom "even called in, I think Morris Ernst, as a friend, to ask what he thought." Dismiss Max's "I think." It was Morris Ernst. Morris told me about it. Morris Ernst was Harper's attorney. He was and is my own personal attorney. I have known him for years. When Max says that Morris Ernst came to Scribner's and advised settling the suit out of court, I simply cannot believe a word of it. I know at first hand what Morris' views were and are about this kind of problem. I have heard him say, at least a dozen times, that any publisher who settles a libel suit out of court is an idiot, because in so doing he proclaims that he is an easy mark and a ready victim for the next fellow who wants to bring a libel suit. Morris believes, and so do I on the basis of my publishing experience, that almost every person who brings a suit for libel is not really concerned with what he has to contend is an injustice done to him, but is really and simply concerned about collecting some money from someone, because that is a very easy way to live. What Max reports Morris Ernst as saying is therefore absolutely untrue. But I can add to this. I can recall a conversation with Max about the general publishing problem of libel. He agreed in toto with what I am here reporting as the views of Morris Ernst, yet when it came to the actual case, he disagreed by acting differently.

IX-1 and 2. Very wonderful stuff about Tom's relations with the Perkins daughters; and how Tom combined three of them to create that remarkable little girl to whom The Fox talked at breakfast.[4] In conversations with me, Terry frequently displayed a morbid interest in everything having to do with Tom's relations with women, and Terry seems to have been fishing for something of that sort when he asked Max (one must assume) whether there had ever been any thought or hope that Tom might marry one of the Perkins girls. I can't resist quoting Max's priceless answer: "If Louise had ever thought there was the minutest possibility of Tom's marrying one of her daughters, she would have flown her instantly to the North Pole, but I would have gone so far as to shoot her, for nothing could have been more tragic for any woman."

IX-3. Tom and Hemingway, their one meeting, and what Hemingway thought of Tom, calling him "the Primo Carnera of Writers." All very good.

X-1. How Tom sat for his portrait by Douglas Gorsline, this being, at Max's suggestion, Tom's wedding present to the young couple. Max says of the portrait: "It was sold only a few days ago for $1,500 through

Douglas's gallery. But he does not yet know who the buyer was." Isn't this portrait now at Harvard? Was Wisdom the one who bought it? I don't know. I believe, though Max doesn't mention it, that Gorsline also painted a duplicate of the original portrait and gave it to Mabel, who has now given it either to the Pack Memorial Library in Asheville or to the library at Chapel Hill, I forget which.

X-2. Tom and Belinda Jelliffe. I believe Max is more than a little naive about the nature of their relationship when he writes: "She was a completely disinterested friend to him. She had no designs upon him. . . . There was nothing feminine in her motives." Max had a surer intuition about her when he first met her. He reports he then warned Tom she was "a man-eater." She was, wasn't she?[5]

XI-1 to 4. Tom and Madeleine Boyd. Max tells most of the story, and the facts are accurate, yet you will notice how Max subtly distorts things in the telling so that anyone who knew nothing about the matter except what Max says would come away with the impression that Tom was somehow, or at least partly, to blame for what happened. Max excuses Madeleine for not reporting Tom's German royalties and keeping the money herself, saying: "It was at the very depth of the depression, and she was hard put to it to keep going." But most thieves steal because they need money, don't they? Again Max says: "It was certainly at least technically, dishonest of her." Now why in the world would Max put it that way? He knew she stole the money and that there was no technicality about it. The woman was a crook and was caught at it, so Tom fired her as his agent period. What was Max's reason for turning it and twisting it and trying to make something else of it? Max knew when he wrote this to Terry that Eric Pinker (Pincker?) had been sent to Sing Sing for swindling E. Phillips Oppenheim in exactly the same way Madeleine swindled Tom. Would Max also have called that "technically dishonest"? He even goes so far as to lend credence to Madeleine's cock-and-bull story about some mix-up in bank accounts by saying: "I suppose it may well be true." For myself, I don't believe a word of it, and I'll tell you why before I am done. But, first, consider this: Max ends by quoting a letter Scribner's lawyer drafted and Max signed, addressed to Boyd's lawyer, and Max's concluding words to Terry are these: "Everything in it (the letter) is correct, and it sums up the situation." In other words, that is all there is to tell. But that is not true. Max failed to say anything about the final act of this Boyd episode, and the omission seems to me significant and disillusioning. And it wasn't that Max didn't know about it, for it was he who arranged it. This was an agreement Max had drawn for Tom's and Madeleine's signature, and they both signed it. In it Tom agreed that

Madeleine was to continue to receive her agent's commission on his income from the <u>Angel</u>, and Madeleine agreed that she would have no claim of any kind on any of Tom's later books. But that wasn't all. If my memory is correct (and it has been six years since I last had occasion to read the document), there was another clause in which Tom gave Madeleine a certain sum of money — I think it may have been as much as $500 — and she acknowledged receipt of it. I seem to recall being told, by either Max or Tom himself, that this was an outright gift which Tom insisted on making as a parting gesture, for he did not owe Madeleine a cent. Now why do you suppose Max did not tell Terry about this? Had Max forgotten? If so, what unconscious motives caused him to forget something so revealing about Tom? When you read Max's account to Terry, I shall be much interested to learn whether you get the same impression of it that I get. The chief things I see in it are the picture of Max full of compassion for the wretched woman and ready to forgive her for every-thing, and the picture of Tom as Max paints him, full of outrage and storming at Madeleine in the most violent and vindictive manner. I don't doubt that Tom stormed, nor do I blame him, either. But what Max left out of his account seems to me at least as important as what he put in. He says nothing of the fact that Tom could have sent Madeleine to prison, as Oppenheim sent Pincker, but he didn't. Tom's vindictiveness needs to be balanced by showing this other side of his nature, too; for Max had no monopoly on forgiveness. And Tom's gift of the money: wasn't that evidence of compassion, and of generosity of which few men would have been capable under the circumstances? Maybe I am being unfair to Max, but I don't think so. There is too much subtle distortion in some of the things he wrote about Tom to permit one to overlook it. It was either deliberate or unconscious, probably the latter, but it is certainly there — a form of self-justification, I suppose — and you will have to watch out for it.

L'Affaire Boyd had an epilogue which Max knew nothing about. It happened after his death. It proved conclusively that Tom had a far truer insight into Madeleine's character than Max did, and that Max wasted his tender sympathies on a woman who had the instincts of a common criminal. Very soon after I was appointed administrator of the Thomas Wolfe Estate, I received a letter from Madeleine. She said she had been trying for years to collect the commissions she was entitled to on all of Thomas Wolfe's books; that they now amounted to a large sum; that her patience was exhausted and that she wanted payment made immediately. In writing this, she assumed, of course, that I had never heard of the agreement she and Tom had signed, the one Max failed to mention to

Terry. I then obtained this agreement from the Scribner files, and have kept it ever since in the Wolfe Estate files in my office. It was then that I read it for the first and only time. I answered Madeleine briefly, pointing out that she had been paid scrupulously, directly by Scribner's, every cent of commission she had been entitled to on the Angel, and quoting to her that part of the agreement in which she had disclaimed any right to commission on the other Wolfe books. I never heard another peep out of her.

XII-1 to 5. Copy of a long letter from Tom to Max dated February 2, 1938, in which Tom refreshed Max's memory of the sequence of events in the Dooher case, Max having agreed to appear as a witness for Tom. A carbon of this letter ought to be in Houghton, and you probably know all about it.

XIII-a. Letter from Max to Terry, returning one of Terry's cards, which for identification in the photostats, I have marked XIII-b. The card, in Terry's handwriting, is headed "Celebrities Who Knew Tom." Then follows a list of eleven names, including Clare Luce and Clark Gable, only a few of whom, I think, had any real relationship with or knowledge of Tom. It amuses me that Terry was interested in this celebrity angle, which I would never have thought of, and Max seems to have had something of the same reaction, for on the card he has added in pencil, in a shaky hand, nine more names, all of whom, I gather, probably knew more about Tom than the ones Terry listed. Curiously enough, one of the names Max added was that of Struthers Burt. I assume this must mean that Burt and Tom had known one another, but I had not realized this before. I can't recall that there was anything in Burt's article to indicate a personal relationship. Terry asks Max on the card: "Can you tell me how I can reach these people best?" — and Max, in the letter, tells the ignorant professor to look for their addresses in Who's Who. The final paragraph of Max's letter reads: "I have now answered all of your questions. If you haven't the piece telling of the dinner with Jonathan Daniels let me know, and I'll give you a copy." Well, Terry did have the piece telling about the dinner with Jonathan Daniels and it is number VI-9 of this series, but Terry did not know he had it because this was one of the unopened envelopes he tossed under his bed and never read. But why was Terry so interested in Jonathan Daniels? So far as I know, he never played any important role in Tom's life. I guess it was just the celebrity angle — the same angle that influenced the Wolfe family when they picked Daniels as one of Tom's pallbearers.

XIII-1 and 2. Max writes interestingly, but tells nothing very specific, about how Of Time and the River was put into publishable form to keep

Tom from going insane. Interesting bit: "I swore to myself that I would get it done if it killed me." The Struthers/Burters will fasten on this, I suppose. But, then, what about a letter Tom wrote to Fred soon after Tom came to Harper's, telling something about me and saying, according to Fred, that Tom would repay my confidence by working hard even if it killed him. I have never seen this letter, but Fred has mentioned it several times in a way that suggests to me that Fred half-thinks that I was somehow, quite inadvertently, responsible for Tom's death. Max and I couldn't both have killed Tom, could we? What nonsense! There is a brief account of Cap Pearce's offer to Tom, about which Max writes: "I never knew how much truth there was in all this." But it was true, and you know all about it.

XIII-3 and 4. Just a fragment. Here Max does not seem to be answering a question put to him by Terry. He just rambles along, writing about one of the reasons Tom left Scribner's — his writing about people in Scribner's, specifically, Wallace Meyer. He says he said to you: " 'I'll have to resign when that book is published.' I immediately told Miss Nowell not to repeat this. . . . Miss Nowell did tell Tom what I had said, and that infuriated him." Well, you must know all about that. I can't contribute anything.

XIII-5 and 6. More about Tom's break with Scribner's, some of it particularly interesting to me, and it will be to you, also. For example, "When Miss Nowell told him I said I would have to resign, she also said something that made him think I objected to his writing about me. I never would have questioned his doing that. How could I, when I had for so long worked with him when he was writing about other people? It would have come pretty near to being hoist by my own petard. It would have been contemptible." Concerning this, I want to go on record as saying that Max never objected nor asked me to change anything in what Tom wrote about The Fox. What Max says here is absolutely true. But elsewhere in these memos to Terry, Max is something less than truthful when he says nothing was cut from posthumous books to spare the feelings of Scribner people. Max himself gives it away when he writes here: "He (Tom) had such a gift of ridicule that he might actually have laughed us off the map." What an absurd and ridiculous fear for Max to entertain! But that explains, I think, why Max, quite contrary to what he says elsewhere, forced me to change parts of what Tom wrote about Charles Scribner, Sr. This I have already mentioned. But to document this point further, although Max never refers to it, I should mention that he made me omit from one of the books a fragment about Whitney Darrow: how Whitney (I forget the name Tom gave him) came into Max's office and badgered him about some book, and how Max, trying to escape, kept turning away in his chair until he did a complete circle, while Whitney kept asking: "Yes, I know it is a good book in a literary sort of way, but what I mean is: is it really a good book?" — meaning, "would it sell?" And then I remember vividly my argument with Max over Tom's piece about Robert Bridges, which I wanted to include in The Hills Beyond, but Max absolutely refused to let me print it. I did not understand Max's refusal at the time, and I don't understand it now. True, the piece was libelous and Bridges was then still living. Max based his objections on these undisputed facts. But Max then knew, and so did I somehow, that Bridges was then completely senile, living, I think, with a sister in Pennsylvania, and spending all his few waking hours with his ears glued to a radio, just soaking in whatever blat that came out. He was then wholly incapable of reading or understanding what Tom wrote about him. There was no danger at all that he might bring suit, although Max based his refusal to let publish on those grounds. The mystery of what lay behind Max's attitude was revealed to me, in some measure, later. For, as you know, after Max died and I was appointed administrator of the Thomas Wolfe Estate, one of my early acts was to go to Cambridge and dig out of the files at Houghton this piece Tom had written about Bridges, who was then dead. I offered it to the Atlantic, and the Atlantic published it. [6] And, Oh, what wails went up from 597 Fifth Avenue! They reached my ears. But to this day I have never been able to understand why the Scribner people were disturbed about it. Tom revealed, of course, that Bridges was a complete phoney, a stuffed shirt with nothing under it. Well, that was the truth, and I don't believe there is anyone living now who would come forward to deny it. But at the time of publication, the Scribner people were outraged. This makes no sense at all unless you accept the theory that Scribner's had become a sort of church, removed for the possibility of examination on human grounds; and, if I am even partly right, the chief contributor to this absurd theology was Max himself.

Later in this same piece, Max writes of the telephone calls Tom made from Asheville to various publishers, one of them being Alfred Harcourt. Says Max: "Harcourt came around here and talked to me and Charles Scribner. He asked me what I thought he should do. He said to me that Tom had offered to come to him and asked me whether I thought he should take him. I said I didn't think there was any other possibility, meaning that he was too great a writer to refuse. We explained to Harcourt that we would feel no resentment against him, and that Tom was evidently bent upon leaving us. When he went away, he left me with the impression that that was what he would do. I don't know what came of it." This is interesting, because it does not check at all with what Alfred Harcourt told me. He said Max reported to him that there had been no break with Tom, no final or formal parting; and that is why Alfred Harcourt did nothing about the phone call. This makes more sense, and, I suspect, may be closer to the truth, than what Max tells.

XIV-1. This letter is postmarked Dec. 21, 1945. Three days before on the 18th, Max wrote Terry: "I have now answered all of your questions." Yet now Max is again answering questions. Had Terry submitted a new batch? or had Max found some new cards he had not answered? The latter, I suspect. Sluggish Terry couldn't have stirred himself to any action within three days. Anyhow, XIV-1, very brief, entitled "Tom's Visit to Hollywood," doesn't really tell anything. Max merely says Tom did not talk to him much about Hollywood, and gives his theory — undoubtedly the correct one — that Tom wasn't really interested in the Hollywood offer and just went out because he was curious.

XIV-2. Another very short one, entitled "Tom Wolfe as a Teacher" — a subject about which much could have been written. Max merely wrote that Tom did not like teaching and was through with it.

XV-1 to 3. More about the Dooher case.

XV-4. More about the Boyd case. It reads strangely, though, for Tom is always formally Mr. Wolfe and Madeleine is always formally Mrs. Boyd. My guess is that Terry had asked Max some questions about what Max had written him earlier on Boyd, and that Max was bored with it and told Irma: "Tell him thus and so," and Irma did, putting it all in her own words with the formal Mr. Wolfe and Mrs. Boyd. That is the way it reads. And the story comes out straighter here, without any deviousness, with Tom justified in terminating the agency. But still no mention of the Wolfe-Boyd agreement.

And so, my dear, good night. I began this Thursday evening and it is now Saturday evening, and I am done in and so are you.

Ed

P.S. Looking back over the earlier memos of Max to Terry, I see much in them I might have commented on but didn't — at which remark I can hear you saying fervently: "Thank God!" I did not realize when I started this that I was going to get as deeply involved as I have become. I think the earlier memos are fresher and more interesting than the later ones. One little thing worries me a bit. Like a fool, I have made no copy of this letter. I told Bill Jackson about these Perkins documents when I first learned of their existence and he wants to get the originals for Houghton, and I shall help him do it in any way I can. But shouldn't what I have written here go with them as a corrective? If you think so, return this to me for photostating — that is, after you have received and read the photostats of the Perkins documents. I shall then return this letter to you, and send a photostat of it to Jackson.

No, don't do this. It is enough that I have told you.

P.P.S. Can't I ever stop? I have a set of photographs, taken at my suggestion, showing the state of every room in Terry's apartment when his administrators gained access to it and before they had touched anything. I believed that no one would ever credit a mere description of the place as I saw it the day Kitty Hoagland frantically urged me to come over to Brooklyn and see for myself. If you want to see these pictures, let me know. You will then wonder, as I do, how it was possible to salvage these Perkins documents, together with the great collection of borrowed Wolfe documents you will see later, out of that junk heap.

[1] Muredach Dooher, the brother of Kathleen Hoagland, was a young literary agent whom Wolfe gave some manuscripts to, then dismissed when no sales were forthcoming. Dooher, claiming he was denied his commission, took his grievance to court in February 1938. Wolfe won the case but lost the friendship of the Hoaglands and Terry, as well as a considerable sum in court costs. See David H. Donald, *Look Homeward: A Life of Thomas Wolfe* (Boston: Little Brown and Company, 1987) pp. 367–371.

[2] See Donald, *Look Homeward*, p. 372, for an account of Wolfe's behavior toward the Countess at a Perkins dinner party.

[3] Aswell expressed public admiration for Perkins as "not only the greatest editor of our time, but a very great man," at the conclusion of his article responding to Struthers Burt ("Thomas Wolfe Did Not Kill Maxwell Perkins," p. 46).

[4] Perkins, himself, recounted the incident at the breakfast table, which appears in *You Can't Go Home Again:* "(Foxhall) Edwards's young daughter enters 'as swiftly and silently as a ray of light.' She is very shy and in a hurry to get to school. She tells of a theme she has written on Walt Whitman and what the teacher said of Whitman. When Edwards urges her not to hurry and makes various observations, she says, 'Oh, Daddy, you're so funny!' " Perkins went on to say, "What Tom did was to make one unforgettable little character out of three daughters of Foxhall Edwards" (Reprinted in Field, *Three Decades of Criticism* [New York: New York University Press, 1968] p. 146). The three daughters were Perkins's own.

[5] A monograph details the Wolfe-Jelliffe relationship, Aldo P. Magi and Richard Walser, *Wolfe and Belinda Jelliffe* (Thomas Wolfe Society, 1987).

[6] "Old Man Rivers," by Thomas Wolfe, was published in the *Atlantic,* December 1947.

*

November 20, 1953

Dear Ed:

I have now finished reading the Perkins-to-Terry photostats, and my first and chief reaction to them is disappointment in them — they are so slight, so sketchy, and based only on general, superficial, hazy recollection. I had hoped they'd be as good as his articles in the Harvard Library Bulletin and Carolina Magazine, but they just aren't. To me, they show the evidences of Perkins' age, or complete exhaustion, or disintegration, or whatever it was that came over him in the last months of his life. They seem the hazy reminiscences of an old man, and he sounds <u>tired</u>, as if his mind was only half-functioning. But even in his hey-day, he had a certain haziness and bias: he would seem both physically and mentally deaf when people tried to argue with him or correct him, and would often simply walk away from them if they tried to reason with him. That was why I used to stretch my leg across the narrow exit from the editorial offices of Scribner's Magazine and say: "Godammit, Mr. Perkins, answer yes or no, or I won't let you past."

But, Ed, I cant see any actual foxiness in these, or any deliberate Machiavellism, such as you saw in them. I can see a great deal of Machiavellism in Terry — My God! — and agree with everything you say about him. But I cant see any proof that Perkins was conniving with Terry, or that he deliberately chose Terry as Tom's biographer because, as you think, (a) he knew that Terry's biography would be an attack on Tom and (b) he knew that Terry wouldn't ever write one anyway. For one thing, (a) and (b) seem sort of contradictory, so to me they dont quite make sense as motivation. And for another, it is all so totally unlike Perkins, as both you and I knew him. Surely if he was as shifty and dishonest as this, we would have sensed it? But, as you say yourself, we both idolized him and consciously were guided by his example in our own business lives. Well, I just cant see that there is any proof that Perkins was conniving with Terry, and I think that Terry's Machiavellism was simply smeared on him, Perkins, without his guilt or knowledge.

I admit that Perkins was hurt and bitter when Tom left Scribners, and I admit that these photostats do show some of this bitterness and a good deal of bias. But it doesn't seem fair to judge Perkins on the basis of only one side of the correspondence between him and Terry. Like you, I wish that Terry's questions were still in existence, because I am convinced that the real root of much of the trouble lies in them. If you look at the way many of Perkins' replies begin, you can guess at the tenor of Terry's questions. For instance, take Perkins' #III which begins "Tom never showed any anger at all during our work on the Angel, and in fact he never showed much anger at any time, not even when we were working on Of Time and the River. And I dont think he did drink much then," etc. In other words, Terry evidently wanted confirmation from Perkins that Tom had temper-fits about the Angel and that he drank a lot. In the one about me, I think that Terry advanced a theory that I ridiculed Tom's work or something of the sort. Because Perkins answered "The truth is that . . . she ridiculed his work", as if agreeing with something that Terry'd said, and then went on and said the complimentary part about me his own self. Again, Terry wanted the dirt of several of Tom's most unfortunate evenings: the dinner with the Daniels, and with Countess Palffy, and he dug up that very innocent and very unimportant episode with the little girl from Plainfield who got drunk and sick. Well, there's no sense in listing all of the things which show that Terry was secretly digging for all the dirt he could get on Tom.

However, I think that he also did it in an unscrupulous, deceitful way, by putting words into Tom's mouth which had never actually been there. I have been digging in vain in my back files for the note which Terry wrote to me. Maybe I sent it down to you. Anyway, as I remember it, it began by asking me if I thought Tom had been influenced by the "many political discussions which he told me (Terry) he had had with Maxim Lieber." (My quotes are from rough memory only here.) I think that is probably an example of the way Terry put false words into a dead man's mouth. . . . I am sure that I was present every time Tom ever did see Lieber, and that if they had had any political discussions I'd remember them. And anyway, Tom only saw Lieber four or five times in his life. . . .

Also, and this is a much more flagrant case: do you remember my telling you that Dick Kennedy told me that Terry said that Tom had told him he had murdered an old woman in a secondhand store in Budapest? Terry almost convinced Dick that Tom had really done it, enough so that Dick asked me about it. Terry had suggested looking in Budapest newspapers of the approximate date, to see if there was any mention of such a murder. Of course I pooh-poohed it to Kennedy: I thought that Tom might have told it to Terry as a tall tale, just to get his goat. But now I think Tom never said it — that Terry got the idea from that one line in one of Tom's notebooks which was, obviously, an idea for a short story "How I murdered the old woman in the _____" (Foreign word for secondhand shop, I forget the exact word Tom used). I think that Terry deliberately lied and told Dick Tom had told him about it, in the hopes that he could somehow build it up and give it credence.

Well, I guess you see what I'm driving at: that the general uncomplimentary tone of much of Perkins' replies to Terry came from the questions which Terry asked. Of course it could be argued that Perkins should have caught onto what Terry was up to, but there is always just enough truth in Terry's questions to make them plausible. And Terry took me in, and took Dick in, and God knows how many other people. . . .

155

Ed, have you ever read Perkins' own articles on Tom in the Carolina Magazine and Harvard Library Bulletin?[1] They are written to Tom's great honor, and with warmth and sympathy and love. If Perkins felt as you think he did about discrediting Tom, wouldnt it have showed in his own writing, even if only between the lines? I dont think he could have written as he did about him if he was secretly nursing the ideas you think he was.

In your letter, you say that you were horrified when Perkins told you he had chosen Terry as Tom's biographer. I was too, and I argued with him about it — I think it was one time when Charles' [Nowell's husband] ship was in New York and I had lunch with Mr. Perkins — and he answered somewhat as he did to you, that he thought "John really was all right", that "Tom had been too hard on him in the Alsop portrait", and that <u>Mama</u> and the family were all very anxious to have him do the biography. I think that Mama praised John to the skies and practically rammed him down Perkins' throat, altho Tom had warned Mama about John in a letter which appears in Letters to his Mother, and Mama should have remembered it, in spite of her own vanity. . . .[2]

. . .I know that Tom did see and have interminable talks with Terry all through the Brooklyn years, and right up to the Dooher trouble. And he had known him at Chapel Hill, and evidently, as that early letter which Kitty found, indicates, had seen him at least occasionally during the Harvard years. Mama and Perkins might well have been influenced by this, plus the fact that Terry had edited Tom's letters, plus his outrageous claim that he had countless revealing letters from Tom to him, plus the fact that he could put on a horribly sickeningly sentimental act about "deah old Tom", as in his preface to the Letters, etc. etc.[3]

Somewhere in your letter to me, you said that Perkins was a shrewd judge of character. Well, I dont think he was. He was a shrewd judge of <u>literature</u> and of writers, but he was put upon by all sorts of worthless people too: from . . . the assistant cashier who embezzled I-forget-how-many-hundred-thousand-dollars over a period of years and ended up in the Tombs . . . , to all the would-be writers and drunks and psychopaths and no-good people to whom Perkins lent money from his own personal account. . . . He never would condemn anybody: he would always argue that they were the way they were because of such-and-such a thing, instead of saying that they were sons-of-bitches and to hell with them. The worst he ever said of anybody was that he "didn't think they were much good". . . .

Well, enough of that. Now to read each photostat over and your remarks about each, and to put in my own two-bits.[4] . . . :

VI 3-5. About Tom at Johns Hopkins. Yes, I kept Perkins from seeing

Tom: I made a bargain with him that neither of us should go in to see him, but should not frighten him by having him know we had all come down, and should let him get all the rest and peace he could before his operation. Tom had written me from, I think, Portland, anyway it's in the Letters manuscript. It is the bitterest letter about Perkins of any, and when Perkins first got it from him he answered in denial of some of it. Scribners promised they would not make me suppress it, or any letters that were tough on them. . . .

Ed, you say that Perkins' having neglected or forgotten to mention the outright gift of $150 made by Tom to Mrs. Boyd is proof that he was trying to defame Tom. But I myself had forgotten all about it until I came across mention of it in a letter which Tom wrote to someone, I think, Basso. The thing is that that very generous gesture was like a little grace note at the end of a long, loud, stormy fugue, which went on with intermissions from 1932-1935. Tom made that present to her quietly, almost hastily, just as the conclusion of the whole long row, and it made little impression on me at the time because he did it so quietly, in such an almost offhand manner. When I came across his mention of it in a letter, I realized that I must be sure and say it about him. But Perkins had no letters or such day-by-day documents to remind him — he was tired and sick, and not himself. And I think that his forgetting it was no more deliberate or Machiavellian than my own forgetting of it was.

. . .[5] Perkins wrote me a letter about it which I quote from memory: "I dont think this story can do anyone any harm now, except perhaps Thomas Wolfe. Somehow I dont think it is one of his best." I sent this to Tom and it infuriated him. As he kept saying when he got back to the US, "It may not be the worst [sic] story I ever wrote, but it isn't the worst story either." Perkins insisted that the withdrawn-into-his-shell character of Meyer could not possibly have seen and felt about the river as Tom made his character describe it — that the central character was really Tom and all dead wrong for the character of Meyer. Which, I spose, was true. But I think that Tom was right about this story, and Perkins wrong. We tried to sell the story during 1936 and 37 and right on up to 1938. The Yale Review finally tentatively bought it, with the understanding that before they printed it, Tom would make some revisions on it which they would suggest, as had been done with Chickamauga. But he died before they ever did make the suggestions. Miss McAfee was a fussy old maid, and some of the changes she wanted to make ruined the rhythm of the story. Also some of her requested changes called for some actual new writing. I sent her list of requested changes and the manuscript to Perkins, who was then Tom's executor, and wrote him saying that I had

157

no right to write any actual passages under Tom's name, and what would we do? I thought that he might write the passages in himself. But he answered that "under the circumstances" he thought we would have to call the whole thing off. I think he had a right to do this, but I think he did it with too great alacrity and relief and that it was really wrong. If I'd thought that he would do it, I'd have made a stab at writing the new sentences myself and would have tried to get his approval. But maybe he should have done this for the same reason I was reluctant — that no-one had a right to write in sentences into the body of Tom's work.

About Harcourt. I think Perkins was terribly shocked and surprised when Harcourt came and told him and Charlie that Tom had phoned them. This was his first realization that Tom had actually left. He phoned me, I think, either while Harcourt was still there, or immediately after he had left. He asked me, in a very excited voice, if I had heard from Tom and knew what he was up to. Tom had phoned me and had been, I thought, quite obviously drunk. He didnt explain clearly what he'd done, but kept repeating for me to "keep out of it", over and over. I think he probably said "Well, I've done it now", but he had been phoning me, when he was drunk in the wee small hours, for over a year and had invariably announced in a drunken, lugubrious voice those same words: "Well, I've done it now," but he never actually had, and I had thought he maybe actually never would. I thought it was just another case of this, and I told Perkins so, but Perkins then told me that Harcourt had had a call from him and had come to tell Scribners about it.

Whether Perkins did make the supreme effort and tell Harcourt he should take Tom, I dont know. But if his voice was as shakey and excited as it was when he phoned me, Harcourt must have known what an awful shock it was to him. Certainly Perkins made no effort to make Tom reconsider and come back to the fold. Or if he did, it must have been long distance telephone, and Tom was, I think, at some hotel in Asheville, and probably could not be reached. Moreover, Tom would have told me or said in some letter, if Perkins got hold of him. But Perkins surely knew that it was useless, and so didnt try.

. . .[6] Hi, Ed, are you still with me? I have now finished my detailed comment on the photostats, and your comments on them, and it is 10PM on the evening of December 1st.

Well, what does it all boil down to? That is going to be hard for me to put into words, but the ultimate conclusion of it all is that

I WISH NOW, MORE DESPERATELY THAN EVER, THAT YOU'D READ MY BIOGRAPHICAL MATERIAL AS FAR AS I HAVE GONE.

Ed, now this is what is so hard to say. I think that you, beneath your quiet, calm exterior, are a very whole-hearted and emotional kind of guy. And I know that you were and are 100% devoted to Tom and to his memory. And I think that when you read anything which is not entirely favorable to him, or which deviates in the slightest from his own sincere but somewhat emotional account of his affairs, you get terribly upset, almost as upset as he himself used to do. Please dont think that I am criticizing you for this. I think it wonderful — it is what I thought and hoped you'd be like both times when I put in my small two-bits for you to be, first, Tom's editor and, later, his administrator — and I thank the Lord that there was a guy like you for him and me to trust. But this very same wonderful devotion may make you upset at portions of what I've written, where I deviate even in the slightest from Tom's own account of how things were.

I certainly do not mean by that that I am either deliberately or unconsciously writing a thing which is unfavorable to Tom. I think that if and when I have said anything in the least derogatory, I could either prove it, or could find a passage of Tom's own which said the same thing or worse. But I am trying like all hell to write an <u>impartial</u> biography, and I think that you are very <u>partial</u> to Tom. And after you have read my manuscript you may feel impelled to spend another weary-three-four nights in writing me a whole-heartedly partial rejoinder. Whereupon I would spend another ten-or-so nights trying to thrash the thing all out with you. But whether you and I can finally come to an agreement, God only knows. I am certainly willing to revise; I mean to anyway. And I certainly want to get the frank reaction of people who knew Tom, or anyway of you. But I cannot write a book which says things which I think untrue, or unfair to other people: no writer can do that without becoming a plain ordinary literary whore.

Of course, I've said this sort of thing to you before, and you have answered, as you did in your last long fine letter that what you want is "merely a book that tells the truth. . . . " But, Ed, there is no such thing as pure objective, unalterable, unassailable Truth. Truth is conditioned by the mirror of the personality which reflects it and reacts to it, and unless that personality is an omnipotent God, in whom I do not think that I entirely believe, there is bound to be variance and error.

In other words, there is Tom's truth, and Perkins' truth, and your truth, and my truth. And yea, verily, I suppose that even Burt and DeVoto were writing what seemed the truth to them. Of course I'm trying to sift out what I think is the closest to the truth, but you may not agree with me and we may end up at a complete impasse. Over and over again, as I have worked upon this thing, I've found myself thinking "God, I wonder if I'm wasting these two years of work. If I had any common sense, I'd stop until I found out if Ed does or does not like what I have written so far." But I <u>cant</u> stop — I cant hold up the Letters forever: I have to keep on going while I still have it all in my mind. . . .

At this point, I am starting on the toughest part of all in the biography — the account of the break between Tom and Scribners. I think that you and I see, for the most part, eye-to-eye on this. . . . But Ed, I could no more say that I thought Perkins <u>deliberately</u> appointed Terry as biographer because he knew he hated Tom and also because he knew he wouldnt write a biography, than I could fly. Because it is just not the truth according to my own conviction.

Somewhere in a recent letter to me, you said you had recommended me to Terry's lawyer because I not only knew and loved Tom but also knew and loved the Scribner people. And I think that that was true. But I love the Scribner people too much to agree whole-hog with your idea about the truth of why Tom left them. I knew he had to leave, and I think, I hope, that as Perkins said, I was entirely loyal to him when he did. I also think that Perkins and the other Scribner people showed a good deal of bitterness and bias when he actually did leave, and that they believed blindly in the dogma which you describe so beautifully that Scribners was "a kind of a church". . . .

Also, it may be that I, too, have been unconsciously influenced by the dogma that Scribners is a kind of church. I left there of my own accord in 1933 in a fairly disillusioned state, and as you know, I usually showed my best writers first to Harpers. But I still was fond of Perkins as I have been fond of very few people in my life and made a very satisfactory Father Substitute of him, and I still thought of the whole joint as a kind of home or Alma Mater. Once, when Tom had first begun drinking and brooding over his difficulties with Scribners and phoning me in the middle of the night . . . he said in his best "mountaineer-suspicious" drunken voice: "Of course, for all I know, you may be a tool of the Scribner interests." It was such a funny way to put it that I laughed, and it became a kind of joke between us from then on, but I think the memory of it made me fall over backwards to be completely on his side when he did actually leave. And maybe he was right: maybe I am "a tool of the Scribner interests" unconsciously, through youthful conditioning, and environment, and affection, just as I am a Yankee and a Bryn Mawr girl, and Clara Howland's daughter, and all the other things I am. . . .

I WISH NOW, MORE DESPERATELY THAN EVER, THAT YOU COULD READ MY BIOGRAPHICAL MATERIAL AS FAR AS I HAVE GONE.

I know that you are on the verge of complete exhaustion, and that the Terry mess has consumed and may still consume more extra time and strength than you possess. And I certainly do not want to add to that, nor do I want you <u>ever</u> to sit up till 3 AM because of me. But in your letter you said "Any help I can give you I shall gladly give" and that is the help I so desperately need. So, well, I guess there's nothing else to say, except that lets both of us hope that you can get the time and strength.

[1] Perkins wrote in "Thomas Wolfe," *Harvard Library Bulletin* (Autumn 1947) pp. 269–277 of his sense of foreboding with Wolfe. "We had a Moby Dick to deal with," he said. But he went on to compare Wolfe with Shelley, implying that Wolfe was a great Romantic poet. The article was reprinted in *The World of Thomas Wolfe,* ed. C. Hugh Holman (New York: Scribner's, 1962).

[2] Wolfe wrote his mother that Terry "has sold me out for an occasional dinner" in connection with the Dooher case, and "I therefore do not see how, under the circumstances, I can continue my friendship with him." He continued, "I am sorry to have to tell you these things because I know you were fond of John, as I was too. I have, however, here given you a straight and accurate account of what has happened, and I want to ask you hereafter, if he writes you or you write him, not to say anything about me or what I plan to do" (Holman and Ross, *The Letters of Thomas Wolfe to His Mother,* pp. 274, 275). The same passage occurs in Terry, *Thomas Wolfe's Letters to His Mother,* pp. 322, 324, but this disclaimer appears in a footnote: "The Doohers were unaware of Tom's changed feelings toward them, and still regard him in memory as a dear friend. Tom also never even suggested that Terry give up his friendship with the Doohers nor was there any break in his friendship with Terry" (p. 322).

[3] In his preface, Terry wrote in a style Nowell described as sentimental: "In his novel *Of Time and the River* Thomas Wolfe said that he tried to portray a man's search for his spiritual father, the adventure of a young man seeking an anchor for his faith. His mother he did not have to seek. She was always with him; he had her constantly in mind. . . . He wanted her to believe in him, to sympathize with his ambition as an artist. She responded fully and stood by him in his greatest needs, financially and spiritually" (p. xxxii).

[4] Nowell began a point-by-point reply to Aswell's letter in her letter of thirty-two pages. She explained the context in which she may have ridiculed Wolfe's writing, calling a passage from "No Door" "melodramatic," "self-pitying," and "too-obviously personal," adding "and if that be treason let me hang for it. . . ."

[5] Omitted sections discuss Wolfe's "No More Rivers," about Wallace Meyer, an editor at Scribner's described in the story as a recluse. Perkins's objections to the portrayal of Meyer's character, in July of 1936, precipitated Wolfe's break with Scribner's. As Wolfe's agent, Nowell had put considerable effort into preparing the story for publication, but it was not published until 1983, when Richard S. Kennedy included it in *Beyond Love and Loyalty.*

[6] Omitted sections recount reasons why Harcourt editor Charles Pearce and Alfred Harcourt himself wished to terminate discussions with Wolfe when Wolfe was looking for a new publisher. Chief among the reasons was the possibility that Perkins would sue the new publisher for libel in the Scribner's passages of Wolfe's as-yet-unpublished manuscript.

*

December 9, 1953

Dear Liddy:

Back at the office again today after another bout with my own pet little influenza bug. It must be the accumulated weariness of the past several months which makes it so hard for me to throw the thing off.

I have just finished reading your long and wonderful letter begun on November 20 and finished at eleven p.m. on December 2. Good Lord, if I had ever realized the trouble I would put you to, I would have thrown away that letter I wrote about the Perkins-Terry communications, even though my writing it was some kind of psychological necessity at the time. In many ways, though, I now realize it would have been better if I had waited at least a few days before attempting to comment on the Perkins letters. What I wrote you, as you realize, was written under the first impact of reading them and I can see now that my emotions were very confused, for at this moment, having gained a greater degree of objectivity, I could not possibly advance the theory of Perkins' Machiavellian motives in choosing Terry. Even before your letter came I realized I was off base on this and that the errors and distortions in Perkins' communications to Terry were chiefly the result of a sadness and exhaustion and desperation, and probably also a sense of futility that must have begun to dawn on him then about Terry and what he was supposed to be doing. Bless your heart, your letter cheered me up and I needed cheering. There is a certain brightness about you, as of some inward truth shining through, which always lifts my spirits. This last letter of yours is the finest possible example of what I mean.

Just now I cannot attempt a detailed comment on your comments about my comments. Perhaps we have gone as far as that road leads anyway. The chief reason I want to get this letter off quickly is to assure you that the chapters of your biography are the next thing on my calendar after our semi-annual Sales Conference is over, and it begins today. I promise that it will not be very long now before I can write you and give you my views.

To paraphrase Perkins, I think you have got me a little wrong. Yes, I am partial to Tom and so are you, but that does not mean that neither of us is capable of looking at him dispassionately. He was certainly a strong and wonderful and contradictory and infinitely complex person. In thinking about him I often remind myself of the fable of the seven blind men and the elephant, for I know that many of the people who knew Tom saw him in different lights and it is not that one group was right and the other group wrong. I think the ultimate truth, if it could ever be arrived at, would show that all of the views were right in one way or another, and all of them added up to the real truth about Tom, just as the separate colors in the spectrum add up to what we call light. All I am saying, I guess, is that I am not expecting you to write a partial biography of Tom or one that I should necessarily wholly agree with. There is a lot about Tom that I do not know. Actually, you know a great deal more than I do about many aspects of his life. I do not even want you to write the kind of book which you seem to think I am somehow expecting. So, put your mind to rest on that score. . . .

Richard Kennedy now has a longish letter from me, in which after much agonizing I felt I had to decline both of his requests. One, as you know, was for the right to quote extensively from the unpublished Wolfe documents, the other was for the right of further access to the restricted Wolfe materials, both at Harvard and Chapel Hill, for the purpose of writing his two volume biography. In arriving at what he will, I fear, think a harsh conclusion, I was guided by what Perkins did when he granted Terry unlimited access to everything, while denying it to others. Do not let this be on your conscience. To avoid that I avoided consulting you further after my first confidential inquiry. The decision is mine and mine alone, and I am prepared to take the blame for it. There would be no sense in encouraging the writing of two biographies at the same time. You have the green light, and this means that until your book is out the light will have to be red for all others.

I will come back to your long letter again, but this is all for now.

Cordially,
Ed

P.S. Chapter nine has just arrived. . . .

*

14 December 1953

Dear Liddy:

I have written Bill Jackson that you are to do the biography of Thomas Wolfe and have asked him to give you unlimited access to all the Thomas Wolfe materials at Houghton, and to deny access to all others. In a letter just received from him, he agrees but suggests that a period be placed on this restriction.

I replied, pointing out that there were several future projects in which the Estate is interested, in addition to your biography. These include a volume of selections from the Notebooks, the possible publication of one or more of the plays, and perhaps a miscellaneous volume of selections from Tom's other unpublished writings. I therefore suggested to Bill that I thought it would be reasonable to remove restrictions as far as access is concerned on the various unpublished writings at the time they are published. The restrictions would remain on the still unpublished stuff until the time came to publish it. In other words, you would have unlimited access to everything, but everything you quote in the volume would be made accessible to others as soon as the biography comes out. I assume that this proposal will meet with your approval.

All my best.

Sincerely yours,
Ed

*

December 17, 1953.

Dear Ed:

I guess the only way to keep a letter to you short is to start it on this small-size paper. I just wanted to thank you loads for writing Jackson to give me unlimited access and to deny it to everybody else. That sure is <u>swell</u> and your saying that you "assume that this proposal will meet with my approval" is an understatement of the facts, if I ever saw one.

Nor do I think it will take long. Once I finish up the biography, and give the green light to the letters, that will release a lot of stuff. But I <u>do</u> feel relieved that people cannot nibble and chew at the notebooks till we get those done, because those to me are something very precious and special.

That's all to-night, I guess. I've already wished you a merry Author-less Christmas and a Leisurely — well, anyway <u>comparatively</u> Leisurely New Year. But here's wishing em all over again and

Love from
Liddy

*

1177 Hardscrabble Road
Chappaqua, N. Y.
Tuesday evening, Dec. 29, 1953

Dear Liddy:

Christmas is over, my brothers and their families have come and gone, we had a wonderful time together, and the house is quiet again and shrunk to normal size. [1] What's more I got a little work done — meaning on the biography. I should explain that previously I had read a great deal of it, including Chapter IX, in a very hurried way, just to stake out the boundaries of the forest, so to speak; but now I am going through it more carefully and shall write you a series of letters as I can find time to type them out. This is Number 1.

The first thing I have to say is that I stand before you in awe and admiration. You are doing a wonderful job. The words are hackneyed, but understand them as if nobody had ever used them before and I had just thought them up. Your basic question: Am I really enthusiastic about the book and do I want to publish it? Answer: yes, yes. You can have a contract tomorrow if you want it. But I have said that before.

Go back to your long letter of July 7th. I have just reread it. It was full of the complexities of your relationship with Scribner's. Much has happened since then, and I rather imagine that the new factors have added to these complexities. For example, Jack's saying over the phone: "In connection with the biography of Tom we are to publish, Liddy has suggested —" . . . The fact that Jack has read these chapters one by one as they came along would naturally lead him to assume that it is your intention to offer the book to Scribner's, even though they refused you a contract when you asked for it. Then the fact of my two meetings with the young Mr. Scribner and my reports to you on them. (Incidentally, we can dismiss the idea that once seemed to me a possibility that he would offer me a job at Scribner's.) . . . The point is that the pipe dream "our" Charles Scribner and I once indulged in will not become a reality. In that respect, at least one possible complication is removed. That is, there is absolutely no chance that if you sign a contract with McGraw-Hill, you may eventually find that I have gone to Scribner's. That simply cannot happen. Then, finally, there is the tremendous new fact that now you are to write, not just a brief biography of Tom, but the real thing, the biography no one else can possibly write. That adds to your problems, but also makes the task much more interesting. This, I think, raises the whole problem to a new level, and it takes it out of the category in which Jack is thinking.

One thing in your letter of July 7th struck me particularly when I reread it. Why it didn't hit me the same way the first time I don't know. I guess it was because the letter contained so much meat to chew on that no one bite seemed more important to chew on than the others. You wrote: "It was you, and nobody but you, who convinced me that I could actually write a biography." Then came this dig: "It took you a long time to do it, etc." So let's get that straight. When I became administrator of Tom's estate, I felt myself as much bound by Max's intentions as I was by the contracts he had signed on behalf of the estate. The first instance of that had to do with the Letters you are editing. As you will remember, Scribner's did not want to see me appointed Tom's administrator because, though Max had done a lot of work in collecting letters, he had not signed a contract with anyone to edit them, and Scribner's were afraid I would take the book away from them. After I was appointed, the first thing I did was to go to Charlie Scribner and say I felt bound by Max's intentions and that if he wanted the Letters I would be a party to the contract that would give him the book. So it was done. Similarly, Max had committed himself to Terry for the biography. I had never thought Terry was the right man for this job, but just the same I felt that I should do what I could to see that Max's plans were carried out, even though, as with the Letters, Max had signed no contract. So for years I encouraged Terry and prodded him to get on with his book. God knows how much time I wasted on him. In his later years he gave me such optimistic and, as we now know, such completely false reports about his progress that I was led to believe that there would at least be a book. All right, it would go to Scribner's, as Max had planned. But then a new question arose. I did not believe Terry's book would be a good one. In fact, I believed it would be a very bad one. What then? I thought it my duty to try to set the picture straight by planning another biography to come out as soon as possible after Terry's. That was the time, and these were the considerations, that prompted me to arrange that meeting with you in Boston several years ago when, as you wrote, I planted the idea in your head, and watered it and gave it Vigoro.

But even this is not the whole story. Shortly after Terry died, several of his friends at N.Y.U. reported to me and Kitty Hoagland and others that Terry had told them shortly before his death that his biography of Tom was finished. One of them even wrote young Charles Scribner a letter to this effect, and sent me a copy of it. To me the interesting and ironical part of it was to the effect that it was Terry's dying wish that the book be published by Scribner's. Well, on that, about eighteen months or perhaps two years before Terry's death, I had a long session with him at the Harvard Club. I brought Melville Cane along, and he is my witness to what I am telling you. Terry said his work was almost completed and he promised to show the manuscript to both Jack and me quite soon. But as Terry talked (and drank) he got more and more emotional. He was burned up that Scribner's had not offered him a contract. He said that many publishers had been after him (and that was true), and that he was so fed up with Scribner's that he was going to contract with some other publisher. At this point I became quite angry. I reminded him that it was Max Perkins who had encouraged him to do the biography and had given him great help (much more, as we now know, than I then realized); and that he owed a moral obligation to Scribner's; and that if he dared to offer the book to any publisher but Scribner's, I, acting for the Wolfe estate, would deny him the right to quote any of the Wolfe documents. Terry seemed quite chastized by this challenge, and, so far as I then knew, that ended the matter, and the book was to go to Scribner's. . . .

The only reason for my bothering you with all this is to show that I have done everything within my power to carry out Max's intentions even when I disagreed with them. I think I have discharged my debt to Max. I think I have leaned over backwards to give Scribner's its due. It was not my doing that Terry was ever encouraged to write a biography of Tom. But, knowing of that encouragement, I did everything in my power, when I was misled into believing that there was going to be a book, to see that Scribner's got it. Your biography has a wholly different origin. I have told you before that I shall do everything in my power to help your book along, regardless of who publishes it (and I have already written to both Houghton and the Library of the University of North Carolina to let you have access to everything), but as I see it, Scribner's has no claim on you. On the facts as I know them, Scribner's would have had the Terry biography if he had written one. The fact that Terry was involved was not my doing but Max's. All right. I did everything to follow out Max's intentions. But beyond that, I did something else on my own, and that had to do with you, and Scribner's had no part in it.

This letter may disturb you, but I hope not too much. The decision is yours. You are a completely free agent. You may do what you wish, and you will do what seems right to you. You already have my pledge of complete cooperation, whatever you may decide. You will have to straighten out your own lines with Scribner's. I have done all that I can do there. The rest is simply up to you.

For the New Year, the best of everything,

Ed

What a letter! When I began it I thought I was going to write you a couple of pages about chapter I, and then go from there. But I haven't even started. Nothing to be disturbed about. Just a few suggestions. Well, later.

---

[1] Aswell's two brothers, James and Charles, were eleven and sixteen years younger, respectively, than Edward. A sister, Carrie, three years younger, was not alive at the time of this reunion — the first and last reunion of the Aswell brothers.

Chapter Six

"So maybe I should walk right up to the lion's jaws and say my say."

NOWELL, FEBRUARY 22, 1954

*

In the wake of John Terry's death, Terry's executors shipped four cartons of Wolfe documents to Houghton Library, and for $2.00 an hour plus travel expenses Nowell was paid by the Wolfe Estate to sort this new material. This chore prolonged the completion of her letters book and upset Nowell, who had to compare Terry's letters with what she had already done. However, she was grateful to Aswell for the recompense, which justified the fourteen-hour days she put in at the library and helped keep her checkbook balanced in the black.

In drafting an introduction to the letters, Nowell faced the difficulty of interpreting Wolfe's unpredictable personality, especially the question of his "betrayal" of people close to him such as Maxwell Perkins and Aline Bernstein. Meanwhile Aswell had finally begun reading the biography, making detailed notes, questions, and suggestions to Nowell's text. Nowell, who had immersed herself in Wolfe research for five years, now asked, "who gets the final say?" On the one hand, she wanted to present Wolfe in all the various phases of his development. On the other hand, she worried continually about libel and about the possible financial ruin that could come her way should she, personally, be sued. She also worried that her "say" might not accord with Aswell's.

Nowell anguished over her problems, not the least of which was bidding farewell to Jack Wheelock at Scribner's so as to accept the contract and advance for the biography offered by Aswell and McGraw-Hill. Her decision to leave Scribner's was based on reality: Aswell had been the force behind the biography from the beginning. Scribner's under Charles Scribner, Jr., was a different firm, uncommitted to Wolfe; and, more than anything else, Nowell wanted her book published.

In this chapter we see Aswell's contradictory nature — a tendency to reverse his own strong opinions on one hand and a tendency to stifle Wolfe publications on the other. Predictably, he was protective of the Wolfe Estate, committed only to those whom he personally knew, suspicious of academics. He also refused permission to non-academics like Dan Burne Jones and Marjorie Fairbanks, both of whom sought publication rights. This situation caused William Jackson of the Houghton Library to ask Aswell to soften his stand. Aswell justified his actions by saying, "I have made it clear. . . that the Estate has various plans" for further Wolfe publications. But he did not specify what these plans were, nor did he make it clear that neither he nor Nowell wished her biography to be preempted. Nevertheless, Aswell seemed surprisingly casual about Nowell's concern with libel and suggested that, should she refrain from including certain libelous passages in the biography, she would be "pulling her punches" and not writing a good account of Wolfe.

Aswell at age seven with his sister Carrie, 1907

Freshman portrait at Harvard, 1923, at the time of winning the Mary L. Whitney Scholarship

As assistant editor at Harper and Brothers, when Aswell met Wolfe in 1937

Taken possibly at Pocono Lake Preserve, summer home of Mary Louise Aswell's Quaker father

As vice-president of McGraw-Hill, when Aswell was Administrator of the Wolfe Estate

The Chappaqua house that Wolfe visited, as it appeared in 1937

Elizabeth Nowell, New Bedford,
Massachusetts, circa 1912–1915

Nowell at Bryn Mawr College, 1922–1926

Nowell in New York City, circa 1930

Nowell in her garden at 114 E. 56th Street, New York City (Photograph courtesy of Albert Halper)

Nowell with her daughter Clara, in 1943

Nowell had this photograph taken for use in publicity concerning her edited book, *The Letters of Thomas Wolfe*, 1956

Dear Ed:

I've finished reading your pencil comments on Chapters I-III, and am sure that the thing for you to do is to go right ahead the way you're doing. At first it made me feel a little itchy, but writers (?!) always feel that way, and what the hell. And anyway, its perfectly OK.

Some of the things I disagree with, and occasionally disagree quite strongly and stubbornly. A great many of the things I agree with, and can fix. Some other things I agree with and cant fix, either for lack of documentation and proof, or for fear of libel or somesuch. And some other things I think are swell: for example what Mama said about the last October leaf is falling, about Tom's not being a mountaineer and what he said to you about this and about Koch [Frederick H. Koch, director of the Carolina Playmakers at the University of North Carolina]. Well — if I start commenting on everything, this letter will turn out to be as long as the manuscript itself. If you think necessary, I can take your comments and write you a detailed comment on the same, so you can see what I balk at, what I can fix, what I can't fix, and everything. But I dont believe its necessary now. I think the thing to do is wait until I get the first draft written, then to sit down and revise the whole thing, and to clip on notes to pages where I find that I need to argue with you, or to explain something to you.

There is one general thing that maybe I can say. I dont think we want to get into any detailed arguments or denials of any filth that Terry spread round N.Y.U., or really to pay too much attention to them. But that I have got to try to make my version of Tom's life so real and so convincing that the other stuff will be eclipsed. Certainly Tom was not a fairy, and I dont even think that he knew Terry was, or that Terry ever made a pass at him. I think he just became disillusioned with Terry and saw through him as he says in the Alsop portrait, and that the rift between them was based on the disagreement about Dooher. But not because of any homosexual advances which Tom repulsed. Tom talked to me about John a lot when he felt that he had sided against him for the sake of some good homecooked meals and pleasant company at the Dooher's. If he thought Terry was a real, practicing fairy, I think he would have said so, or at least would have shown that something like that troubled and shocked him.

There is another thing that worries me. In one place you say that he had had love affairs with lots of people and that "There is uncharted country here still to be explored." There sure is — a whole continent of it — but it is all surefire libel, and the girls are almost all very much alive, and several of them have already informed me (when I simply asked if they had any letters) that any mention of them in connection with Tom will make them sue all hell out of the mention-er.

Also, I am not too sure about Mrs. B. I can see how she would talk with perfect frankness to you about Tom, but having somebody else go into too much detail about it now, when both she and Mr B are still alive, is something else again. Nor am I positive that her version of the affair and my version which is based on Tom's entirely agree. I dont mean that she would deliberately lie, any more than he would. But it was a terrible emotional experience for both of them, and each of them had to assimilate it and change its sharpest and most painful aspects. Or so I think. . . .

Well, I guess this is all for now. But, Ed, what if you and I cant make a compromise on some of your suggestions? It is my book and I cant say things under my own name that I think untrue, or, anyway, untrue to me. But the material is yours and I cant use any of it unless you sanction what I say. Who gets the final say? But I dont think we'll come to any great impasse like that.

Love,
Liddy

*

January 28, 1954

Dear Liddy:

Four cartons of Thomas Wolfe documents were delivered to me today by the administrators of the Terry Estate and are now on their way by express to the Houghton Library. At the last minute the fifth carton containing documents that unquestionably belonged to Terry were not turned over to me and I am relieved that they were not. . . .

I have today written to Fred and Mabel telling them of the safe delivery of the four packing cases and I took this occasion also to tell both of them that you are to do the biography of Tom. . . .

Cordially yours,
Ed

P.S. After dictating the above, I received your letter of the 25th. This is not a full answer to it, but as you see, I am already telling Fred and Mabel that you are to do the biography so that complication is out of the way. I have not told either of them that all the documents are being sent to Harvard to be sorted by you. I have merely told them that I have made the necessary arrangements to safeguard and sort them. I did not want to tell them about Harvard because they might be suspicious that Harvard was expropriating for itself things it had no claim to. The arrangements I have made with Bill Jackson and you have been made on my own responsibility and in the end I am the one who will be responsible for seeing that the several groups of documents are restored to their rightful owners. I think the arrangements that have been made are right and proper and so long as the end result is accomplished, I cannot see that it is anybody else's business to question the methods used.

P.P.S. I have now reread your letter of January 25 and shall answer the rest of it. If I were you, I would not say anything to Mabel about Terry in connection with her inquiry about when the Letters will be ready. Just say something to the effect that you are almost through and let it go at that. I have not been able to decipher Mabel's attitude toward the whole Terry mess. As soon as I knew what the situation was I reported it at length to both Mabel and Fred. Fred answered immediately that Terry was a s.o.b. and many other words to the same effect. To this day Mabel has made no comment at all. I think she was terribly hurt. She genuinely liked Terry, gave him her confidence and now probably feels that she was very much taken in, something she hates to admit. This is merely guessing for she has given me no clue at all to her feelings. That is the reason I think you will be wise not to mention Terry to her.

Yes, you are right. Fred and Mabel will both be hurt by the Cargill book. I have sent each of them a copy of the Watt-Wolfe Letters, but have not sent the Cargill volume because I received only one copy. I wrote Pollock last week, ordering four additional copies to be charged to the Wolfe Estate, but have not received them nor heard anything from Pollock. I shall have to send copies to Mabel and Fred when I can get them with, alas, a long letter explaining how it came about. . . .

I have seen no reviews of the New York University volumes anywhere. Like you, I will not be disappointed if they are never reviewed. As you say, "God help us all."

*

February 1, 1954

Dear Liddy:

A man named Dan Burne Jones, who seems to be a wild Thomas Wolfe enthusiast, has asked me for permission to let him publish as a slender little volume that rather inconsequential essay Tom wrote for the <u>Asheville Citizen Times</u> when he went back home for a visit in 1937. I have declined this request on the grounds that the Estate has plans for several further volumes of the writings of Thomas Wolfe and that the publication of

Return as a book would make it appear that we were scraping the barrel and might therefore harm the chances of these volumes in which the Estate is vitally interested. [1]

I am enclosing herewith the typescript of Return, just in case you have not seen it. I remember having read it before somewhere. Maybe there is a copy at Houghton. If not, you might send this along to Bill Jackson. In any event, don't bother to return it to me.

Cordially,
Ed

[1] *Return,* originally published in the May 16, 1937, *Asheville Citizen,* is described in Nowell's *Biography* (p. 382) as Wolfe's "lyrical peace offering" to his home town after seven years' absence. The piece was published as a booklet by The Thomas Wolfe Memorial in 1976, editor Myra Champion.

*

February 9, 1954

Dear Ed:

I was at Houghton again yesterday. . . .

I found a good many valuable letters. There were three and one telegram from Mrs B to Tom. All beautiful with the emotion that is so typical of her. . . .

I also found a letter which I'm sure Tom wrote to her when he first read Three Blue Suits, although there is no salutation on it. I think he probably never mailed it to her, but just wrote it to get a load off his own chest. He begins quite gently and nicely to her, but ends by bawling her out for her description of Eugene[1] and also for having represented Perkins and the people at Scribners as a bunch of snobs. Whether that letter should go in Toms and Mrs B's letters, or the general letters, or where, God knows. Anyway I'll get you a photostat of it too later. . . .

Well, I can see one thing, and that is that I'll have to insert various of these letters of Tom's to various people which I found yesterday into the Letters manuscript. Which'll mean that it'll be longer than 400,000 words, and may have to have other things cut out, and the entire thing revised. It discouraged me horribly yesterday — I could have murdered Terry — it looked as if he had gone through Tom's correspondence and plucked out all the plums, and then sat on them gloatingly for ten entire years. But he didnt pluck out all the plums, and he plucked out an awful lot of worthless junk besides, such as innumerable fan-letters from dumb readers of Of Time and the River, with Tom's carbon copies of his form-letter replies. Well, anyway, I'll just have to finish sorting, then get photo-

174

stats of the things that have to be inserted in the Letters, and then do the whole thing over to get everything in place, and squared away.

I keep thinking that I must write Jack to tell him this, and also to ask them to decline the biography, but I'm so dead tired after the 5 AM to 7:30 PM day going to Harvard, that I havent done it. But I will as soon as I am able to, and will show you a rough copy of my letter first to see if its OK with you. Does he know that you've appointed me to do a full biography, I wonder. I dont think he does, and I don't think that I need tell him — but I will have to say that my own "biographical commentary" is now going to be a full-length book.

Anyway, I got a very generous and swell letter from Mabel, saying she had already written you at length her opinion of me as a biographer of Tom, but then going on to say she thinks it is OK in a very warm-hearted way. I hope to God she said as much to you — I don't think Mabel would say one thing to one person and another to a different one: it doesn't seem like her. . . .

And so to bed,

Love,
Liddy

P.S. Ed, you must think I am a mercenary wretch, but there is going to come a point around the 15th of the month, and another around the end of the month when I wont have any money left to transport myself to Hvd unless I've collected some from you. Have just cashed a check for my last $15 bucks in my checking account till Feb 15th, and that'll cover two-three more days of going there, but after that I'd have to sit home or hitchike or somesuch.

---

[1] "Eugene" is one of three short stories in Aline Bernstein, *Three Blue Suits* (New York: Equinox Cooperative Press, 1933; reprint Athens, Ohio: Ohio University Press, 1988). The main character, Eugene Lyon, resembled Wolfe in nearly every detail, and the story tells Aline's version of her affair with Wolfe.

*

February 9, 1954

Dear Liddy:

Yours of February 5th is here, and I will try to make my comments on it brief because I am pressed for time.

I think all of Tom's manuscript of every nature rightly belongs to Harvard even though some of it, I have no doubt, was in Mrs. Wolfe's possession and was lent by her to Terry. I realize what a terrific job it must be to sort out and try to put together a bunch of separate pages,

175

all scrambled up. For the present I advise you not to try to do this. The immediate job is to determine who owns what. Put all manuscript in one pile without trying to arrange it. Go through all four boxes and simply sort for ownership. You will probably find some things concerning which the ownership may be in doubt. Put all such questionable items in another pile so that when I come up after your preliminary sorting is done, we can go over them together and try to decide who owns them. . . .

I have read Burton Rascoe's review of Cargill's hatchet job and it really is appalling. He sees the book as exactly what it is, a paying off of ancient grudges, but then curiously enough he takes it all for true. Oh well, what the hell!

Sorry to learn that you are considering becoming Vardis Fisher's agent again. I hope you will ponder that one a long time before you let yourself in for it. I am afraid you will find it nothing but a series of headaches. As I see it, Vardis has invented a whole private system of psychoanalysis, partly borrowed from Freud and partly invented by himself. He is its founder and only disciple. The sad thing is, he has moved right out of the everyday world in which you and I live and nothing is what it seems to be.

My best as always,
Ed

*

February 15, 1954

Dear Ed: Here at last is the letter asking Scribners to decline the biography.[1] I havent mailed it to Jack yet — I want you to read it first and tell me what you think of it. If you think it is OK, please tell me so and I will shut my eyes and hold my breath and stick it in the mailbox for poor old Jack. But if you object to anything I've said in it, please send the carbon of it back to me and tell me what it is that you object to, so that I can fix it.

Love,
E.P.

---

[1] Although Nowell continued to do agenting for Scribner's, she wrote to Jack Wheelock, resigning as a Scribner's author.

*

February 17, 1954

Dear Liddy:

The draft of your proposed letter to Jack is just like you, which means that it is honest, straightforward, sensitive, diplomatic, and even humorous. As far as I can see, there is nothing in it that should be changed.

One suggestion only. If you think it right, might it not be well to add a short postscript about how I talked to young Mr. Scribner and explained to him why you had had to examine the whole Wisdom Collection at Houghton and how much labor you often had to undertake just to fix the approximate date of an undated letter? Until then he did not understand your problem at all, and it was then he admitted that he had made a serious error in asking Jack to write you as he did. Perhaps you should also mention that I gave you an immediate report on that meeting, which I gather had the effect of allaying your sense of outrage. The only reason I suggest such a postscript is that I would like all the Scribner people to know that I have not been against them, but with them, and that I have not been up to any sneaky tricks behind their backs.

Cordially,

Ed

*

February 22, 1954

Dear Ed:

. . . .I have been mulling over what to say in the introduction which I'm sposed to write for the Letters. Here is what I want to ask you. Do you think it would or would not be a good idea to enter the discussion of whether Tom did or did not "betray" people, such as Baker, Mrs B, and Perkins. Of course I'd say that he didnt — that it was not "betrayal" but growth, and was completely justified by his compulsion to be the best damned writer he could possibly be. [1] But — well — hell — if I say it, the reviews may be another series of arguments as to whether he did or didnt. And still, the pattern of intense adoration and final disillusionment with one person after another is quite evident from the Letters themselves. So maybe I should walk right up to the lion's jaws and say my say.

If you are undecided about this, too, I'll try to say something, and we can see how it comes out. But if you think it far better just to present the letters as a picture of Tom's life, with no editorial comment on it — well, then I'll present it that-a-way. . . .

Love,

E.P.

---

[1] Nowell and Aswell wanted to present Wolfe's posthumous manuscript as evidence of

177

his growth as a writer, from subjectivity toward greater objectivity. Wolfe had described the process of his creative development in his Purdue speech, calling his work a "chain of clear development" away from talk *about* the artist to real, hard work *as* an artist. As Nowell put it, "Wolfe has been accused of 'turning against' these influential people (George Baker, Aline Bernstein, Max Perkins) in his life, and even, by one somewhat sensational writer, of 'betraying' them. . . . A calmer, more judicious description of what happened would be to say that Wolfe 'turned *away*' from these people, or outgrew them and their dominating influence upon his life" (*Letters*, p. xvi).

*

March 5, 1954.

Dear Ed:

I certainly am an awful nuisance. Or if I'm not, the Wolfe Estate is. . . .

First of all, please see copy of my latest letter from Jack on which I will not comment. And please also see the letter directly to CS IV which I have drafted. Jack seems to recommend that I make no mention of you in this letter. I dont know whether to or not. It's really up to you. I've bracketed two paragraphs in my proposed letter to CS IV, and you can tell me whether you would like this to be in or out. Also, if you want to make any other comment on this letter, go right ahead. It isnt fair to me, because it only hints at why I'm really leaving, but for Jack's sake, I am willing to let it go at this. I rather enjoy this latest effort of mine and think it is full of sweetness and light and tact. But mebbe I am wrong. . . .

Going back to the typed copies which Terry had made of some of Tom's letters. He had copies made of a batch of Mrs Bernstein's own letters to Tom. I think she would object greatly to having these bandied around by Terry's relatives, or made available to the students at Chapel Hill. I dont mean that they are libelous, but that they are intensely personal — repeated expressions of the hurt and grief and resentment that she felt when Tom left her. The originals of these letters will, of course, be locked up at Houghton with Mrs Bernstein's other correspondence. But the copies, legally, belong to Terry's heirs, even if Terry really had no business to have them made. You had better mull this over between now and the time when you come to Harvard.

Got a card to-day from Mabel. Says "I hope to leave here March 15 or 16 for New York on Streamliner which makes trip quickly, and doesnt cost too much. I'll stop on way back at Washington and be home before April 1st. I hope you can come down to New York that week — Wed, Thurs or Friday. I could stop Wash first place and come to New York the next week but its easier on me not changing till I arrive NY. What hotel is decent and nice and near Mr. Aswell? I will be there 2 or 3 nights and have other friends. No one need feel responsible for me. I may be green or strange at first and need a nice spring coat. What <u>store</u> do you suggest. Write me a card anyway and tell me what you can do." Well, it looks as if she really meant to come, and part about "I may be green or strange at first" is really very touching. I will write her about stores, but am damned if I know what hotel to suggest. There surely is none near 330 W 42nd St, and I think M ought to be at a hotel in a quiet, orderly kind of neighborhood in case she comes back to it alone at night or any such.

Ed, I think we ought not to tell Mabel about this Scribner-and-me business. I think she will call Jack up undoubtedly, and might put her foot in it about me, although with the best intentions in the world. But she will probably have so much on her mind about herself and Tom, etc. that we wont get a word in edgewise anyway. I am sorry as all hell if I have been responsible for her coming, but when she asked me if I could meet her if she did — well, I hated to refuse. . . .

Love,
Liddy

*

March 9, 1954.

Dear Liddy:

I am returning quickly the draft of your proposed letter to Mr. Scribner. It seems all right to me. I don't know why Jack thought my name should not be mentioned. If you don't give your reasons fairly fully in your first letter, Mr. Scribner will probably come back and ask you what they are and then you will have to do it anyhow. Jack is probably being too sensitive. But since you and I both know there has been nothing dishonorable on the part of either of us, I think we should just rest on that fact. . . .

It was Max Perkins who had Aline's letters to Tom typed. He told me about it himself after he had done it and I was a little shocked, for he had induced Aline to let him copy the letters on the argument that she could work with them better if she ever planned to publish them if she had typed copies rather than originals to work with. He returned the originals and a set of typed copies to Aline and gave another set of copies to Terry. I gathered that his real reason for asking Aline to let him have the letters copied was in order to let him supply copies to Terry. Since Aline did not know that, and I am sure would never have consented to it, I think I shall have to take the position that the whole thing was more than a little irregular, and that I have no right to pass copies of these letters along to the University of North Carolina or the Terry family. For the present I suggest you ask Mr. Bond to have the typed copies compared with the originals in their possession to make sure that there are no copies of anything of which the originals do not exist. If that fact can be established, before I come up to Cambridge, I shall then take what action seems necessary about disposing of the copies. I shall have to give some thought to this, but at the moment I believe I know what I ought to do.

I have not written to Mable or Fred about your difficulties with Scribner's and I agree with you that there is no reason to tell them. . . .

My best as always,
Ed

*

March 23, 1954

Dear Liddy:

It was very good indeed to get your letter of March 19th, together with a copy of the letter young Mr. Scribner wrote to you on March 16th. His attitude is fine and I hope it has had the effect of removing any psychological hazard that may have been built up.

This week is going to be a perfectly hellish one for me, so I welcome your suggestion that we not try to get together while you are here to see Mabel. We will have Wednesday, March 31st in Cambridge with plenty of time to cover everything that needs to be discussed. Did I ask you to lunch with me that day? If not, consider yourself asked now. I have assumed all along that we would lunch together then.

The Sinclair Lewis biography is to be written, not by Flaccus, but by Mark Schorer. Mr. Bond must have been confused. I am enclosing for your study a copy of the contract with Schorer as well as that with the Sinclair Lewis Estate, since the two documents go together. We shall have to work out a similar three-cornered arrangement for the Wolfe biography. In one respect, however, the contract for the Lewis biography should not be taken as a precedent. . . . It seems to me that the Estate of Thomas Wolfe should not expect to be recompensed out of the earnings of a biography. The Estate's interest is to see that a good biography is written and to make all the documentary evidence available to the biographer. Anybody can write a biography of Tom if he wants to, with or without the Estate's consent. Of course nobody can have access to the papers controlled by the Estate without the Estate's consent.

In other words, it seems to me that the contract for Tom's biography should be drawn more or less like the other contract in so far as the Author's earnings are concerned, that is, I believe all the earnings should go to you. This being so, I am prepared to propose an advance to you of $5,000, payable say $1,000 or perhaps $1,500 on signing, with the remainder to be paid on demand if that is the way you want it. I suggest a royalty scale of 10% on the first 7,500 copies, and 12½% on the next 2,500, and 15% after a sale of 10,000. These are better royalty terms than you got from Scribner's for the <u>Letters</u>, which were 10% to 12,000 and 12½% thereafter. Also, the advance I am proposing is better than the original advance you got from Scribner's although I am under the impression that the late Charles Scribner may have made a further advance to you beyond what the contract called for, though if that was true, I do not know just what the amount of the additional advance was.

The libel problem may be a little bit complicated, but here I think the two agreements covering the Lewis biography set the right precedent, in that together they distribute responsibility where it belongs. To apply this reasoning to the Wolfe biography would mean that you would be held responsible for anything you, yourself, wrote, while the Wolfe Estate would be responsible for anything libelous in the Wolfe writings quoted in the book.

I guess this covers the situation for the moment. I am looking forward very much to seeing you Wednesday week.

Cordially,
Ed

*

April 19, 1954

Dear Ed:

Gee whiz! My God! Well, words fail me! But you are a very lovely guy, as always, and I think I should say right here and now in black and white that any money you send me against the biography royalties before the contract is finally signed are immediately returnable to McGraw-Hill if, for any reason, the contract shouldn't be signed.

But I dont think there'll be any possible reason why it shouldn't be signed, especially now that we have got the foreign rights, etc. business so nicely compromised.

Well, I keep making typing mistakes in my excitement, so I won't write any more tonight. But I <u>do</u> hope you can get out of jury-duty. Ed, why don't you get your family doctor to say you cannot serve: you're carrying too heavy a load for anyone to bear and he could surely find physical evidences of fatigue to justify your getting off?

But I wont fatigue you any more by writing a long letter. Thanks loads, and please do try to let up some on things.

Love,
Liddy

*

May 11, 1954

Dear Ed:

As long as you're so tired and rushed — and God knows this is the time of year when every editor is overwhelmed with Fall List deadlines anyway — I've got an idea about what to do about my contract. I'm sending the McGraw Hill printed form that you sent me to Eddie Colton, together with the letters which you and I have exchanged about it and a brief resume of our short talk at Harvard; and am telling Eddie to make the changes we agreed to in it and send it down to you. But not to bother you with asking for an interview or any such unless there should be some terrific complication — which there isn't.

That way you'll be spared the tedious chore of revising the whole thing. If it isn't right when Eddie revises it in accordance with our discussion of it, you can send it back and tell him what is not all right, so he can fix it. But if it is all right — and I think it will be — you wont have to do anything except skim through it and sign it and send it back to him.

Ed, do you ever have a physical checkup, or is it none of my business. I was thinking that my pal Dr Chickering does that sort of thing for life insurance companies and in general anyway all the time. After I meet you in Boston and see you so chalk-white and tired, I always worry that you might up and drop dead on me like MEP and Charlie. Of course you're younger and dont drink so much, but it would be a good idea to anticipate the time when you will start really getting old?

Excuse it, please.

Love
Liddy

*

May 12, 1954

Dear Liddy:

. . . .P.S. Since dictating the above your letter of May 11th has come. I welcome your suggestion to let Mr. Colton prepare a draft of the agreement and send it to me when he has it ready. If there are any problems, I can take them up with him directly. Perhaps this way of handling the matter may save time for everyone.

P.P.S. It is good of you to be solicitous about my health, but don't worry too much. I do have regular physical check-ups and the doctor has found nothing wrong with me except the normal disintegrating processes which will, if I live long enough, end in senility. I guess I must have been rather chalk-white and tired when you saw me in Cambridge, but that was because I was a fool. I had not seen Henry and Mary Hart in two years so we sat up very late each night I was there just talking and talking and forgetting about the passage of time. [1] The result was that I think I got an average of not more than four or five hours sleep during the nights I was with them and it was loss of sleep rather than anything else that made me so tired that week.

[1] Henry M. Hart, professor at Harvard Law School, had been a classmate of Aswell's at Harvard and after graduation in 1926 had joined Aswell on a five-month cycling trip of Europe. Henry and his wife were among the few close friends invited to Aswell's second marriage to Mary Louise White on January 1, 1935, at Mary Lou's father's home in Penllyn, Pennsylvania. The Harts were also present during Wolfe's Christmas with the Aswells in 1937, just before Wolfe signed his contract with Harper.

*

May 20, 1954

Dear Liddy:

A copy of your letter to Mrs. Fairbanks has caused me to write Paul Brooks a letter, a copy of which is enclosed and which explains itself. I have also sent a copy to Bill Jackson.

My advice to you is to have as little to do with Mrs. Fairbanks as possible. She is a queer and tricky person. When Jackson first told me that they had made a mistake and had allowed her to range freely through the Wolfe files, I was quite shocked. And Bill himself was most apologetic. I think it possible, though here I am only guessing, that she may have enlarged her purpose considerably and that her book may turn out to be a sort of biography. That is the reason I am putting Paul Brooks on notice now. . . .

I have always rather hoped that nothing would ever come of the Fairbanks project. She is so scatterbrained and most of what she may have gleaned from Houghton was obtained at such dubious second hand that I would not be prepared to trust its accuracy even if there were no other reason for holding her to her original limited purpose.

My best as always,
Ed

*

183

May 21, 1954

Dear Liddy:

To my dismay I discovered a letter from you dated February 22nd which I have not answered. This is the one in which you asked my advice about the kind of introduction you should write for the Letters. I am in full agreement with your own thought that you should tackle Tom's so-called betrayal of people and do what you can to set the record straight by showing that it was not betrayal but, as you put it, a process of growth. If reviewers are going to seize on this to argue the question in public — well, they will, it can't be helped. But I think if you point to the evidence in the letters themselves you can make a very strong case. I think it might be a good idea also to indicate that this sort of thing, when it happened to Tom, was really no different in kind to what happens, more or less, to all of us. The difference was one of degree of emotional intensity. Everyone of us, if he looks back over his life, can recall periods when he was seeing a great deal of certain people and regarded them as his closest friends. Then things both known and unknown happened to change the picture and it is really amazing when one stops to think of it how many times it happens that these friends drop away, sometimes over real and clear issues and sometimes for no known cause — they just seem to fade out, so that people to whom one once felt very close have become as strangers. The process of Tom's changing friendships was not wholly unlike that which is part of everyone's experience except perhaps that Tom's intense interest in people of all kinds probably put their friendship on a slightly false basis from the start, thus causing them to feel themselves betrayed when the friendship ended.

Another factor was Tom's intense emotional involvement with people. It was an honest emotion when it was generated and while it lasted. When it ended, Tom seems to have felt honestly impelled in many instances to think out the reasons and then to write them out or to talk them out with the person involved. This gave rise to more crises in such matters than most of us experience as we grow into and out of friendships.

My best as always,
Ed

*

August 4, 1954

Dear Liddy:

To make a long story short, I have consulted with Mr. Leavy and with our attorneys and with my associates here at McGraw-Hill about the libel problem in the Wolfe biography and the limitation of your liability to which you have come to attach supreme importance. The answer is that we will accept the limitation as you want it. I have so informed Mr. Leavy and he will now prepare a revised draft of the agreement so that we can both sign it and put it behind us.

One thing that this means, of course, is that beyond your limited liability, McGraw-Hill will be left holding the bag. Therefore, we think there should be a clause in the agreement providing in suitable wordage that McGraw-Hill (which in this case means me) shall have the final word on what is included in the biography. In other words, if we should think a thing were libelous and you should think it were not, then we should have the right to cut it out. I cannot imagine you not agreeing to this because as I assess your position and mine, I think you are far more scared of the libel problem than I am. In fact, I think you have built it up in your mind so that you have almost knocked yourself out with it. This has given me a certain degree of pause because if you make too much of a bugaboo about it you may pull your punches in writing the book and thus make it a less good book that it ought to be.

My position now is what it has been all along. Namely, that you should tell Tom's story as accurately and as straight as you can, leaving it to me, to Melville Cane, to McGraw-Hill's attorneys, and to Mr. Colton's office, if you wish, to point out the danger spots and keep you out of trouble.

Is all this okay? I hope so.

My best as always,
Ed

*

August 5, 1954

Dear Ed:

Well, now at last we're cooking with gas, and thank you very much. To tell you the truth, I have been away from work on the biography for so long now, and I dread the trip to Asheville so, that I was almost looking forward to discarding the whole thing. But that's all right — once I get the Letters finished, I can moan and groan and get myself wound up to start on the biography again. However, I would like terribly to have the last few chapters back from you before that time, so that I can give myself a running start by going over the chapters written thus far and making the changes which you suggest. I have finished Vol I of the Letters except for the purely mechanical job of transferring the last batch of changes to the carbon copy. Then I'll tackle Vol II which needs less work, so should go a good deal faster.

Now about giving McGraw Hill final word on what is to be included

185

in the biography. . . . I dont honestly think I am going to "pull my punches" about libellous statements. I'm going to say what I can to be fair to Tom within the limits of getting us all involved in a hell of a mess. Which is what I want, you want, Mabel and Fred want, and the various and sundry lawyers want. Amen. . . .

Love
from
Liddy

Chapter Seven

"If I had the command of all Tom's adjectives, I still could not praise you enough."

ASWELL, MARCH 23, 1955

*

THE YEAR was marked by tremendous ups and downs. Professionally, the Wolfe Estate was accumulating income and expanding the types of projects it endorsed. Looking to other media, Aswell sold movie rights for one Wolfe novel and was himself a speaker on NBC's "Biography in Sound" series featuring Thomas Wolfe and hosted by Gene Hamilton. The program recorded the recollections of various Wolfe associates, among them Aswell, whose voice sounds very — and surprisingly — Southern. Nowell was also asked to take part in the series, but illness prevented her from making the trip to the recording studio in New York.

Nowell's year was marked by personal hardship. Her mother underwent a cancer operation in May, and in July Nowell herself was found to have breast cancer. After a summer of hospitalization and x-ray treatments, she was hard pressed for money. Partially out of this new crisis in her life, Nowell asked Aswell about selling serialization rights to a magazine, possibly the *Atlantic Monthly,* which had published some of Wolfe's letters (and where Aswell had been fired from his first editorial position). Aswell rejected the *Atlantic* suggestion probably out of personal pique. But they agreed upon *Life* as a likely publication. Nowell offered to write the article for *Life,* emphasizing the "tragic last chapter in the Wolfe-Perkins story which. . . no one could tell but me." But she said she would go along with whatever Aswell or the selected magazine wanted. Although *Life* selected one of its own writers for the serialization of the Wolfe letters, Nowell's sense of the article was honored.

The only discord between Nowell and Aswell concerned Aline Bernstein. In reading Nowell's final pages of the letters manuscript, Aswell questioned the inclusion of letters by Aline and expressed his own interest in publishing the Bernstein letters through McGraw-Hill. Nowell defended her rights to include some of the Wolfe-Bernstein letters, citing specific instances where Aswell had approved their inclusion. She won her case, but the issue became moot when Aline Bernstein died without ever signing a McGraw-Hill contract for the publication of her letters. Speaking ex officio, Aswell nevertheless claimed that the Bernstein material was his by rights: he could publish it in its entirety "and no one can stop me." It was a claim he would repeat about this and other Wolfe material.

Dear Ed:

Here is a copy of a letter which I have just written to Jack. In spite of all your assurances, I still mistrust the "new Scribners and after lengthy consideration I felt that they might intend to cut the Letters more than would be right, for the sake of publishing them cheaply in one volume and "getting rid" of them. (As somebody — not Jack — told me that young Charlie said about them several years ago.) After all, this would be likely to happen now, since they know that the biography, and probably other books of Tom's own, are going to be published not by them but by McGraw Hill. . . .

But the point is that I think they have to be talked sternly to, to keep them in the path of rectitude, so this time, I decided to talk sternly to Jack ahead of time, rather than run any risk of discovering, too late, that they had forced him to cut the Letters detrimentally. If there is no necessity of conveying the gist of my letter to young Charlie, you can bet your bottom dollar that Jack will not convey it. But if they should try to make him cut the Letters too severely, he will be armed with my advance protest to persuade them not to. In other words, when you take young hounds cub-hunting, you have to crack the whip occasionally and growl "Have a care, there", to keep them with the pack. And Jack cant be the Whipper-in, but you and I and Mr Cane can. [1]

I know you'll think I am making a mountain out of a molehill. Well, all I can say is that I hope I am. But I also know that for Tom's sake you'll stand by me, even though you only have to do so silently unless and until we find that they want to cut the Letters harder than they should be cut.

Yours for the Watch and Ward Society,

Love,

Liddy

I forgot to say what Jack has probably already told you — that I have finished Vol II of the Letters and sent it to Jack, who has now sent it to Mr Cane and is then going to send it down to you. E.P.

[1] In spite of Nowell's protest, the letters were published in a single volume.

*

March 23, 1955

Dear Liddy:

The LETTERS have gone to Jack, complete with Melville's notes and mine. In a work of the scope of this one, it is remarkable that so few questions have been raised by anybody. A tribute, really, to the extraordinary job you have done. If I had the command of all Tom's adjectives, I still could not praise you enough. . . .

Bless you for a fine and devoted piece of work. There is a lot to be said for a New England conscience.

Sincerely,
Ed

P.S. One thing I forgot to say. It is a noble book, very true and moving. Some of it made me want to weep. If the reading public does not recognize Tom's genius and greatness from the overwhelming evidence in these letters, then the public is most surely a consummate and composite ass — and to hell with it!

*

March 30, 1955

Dear Liddy:

Many thanks for your card. I hope both Fred and Mabel will be somewhat reassured by the letter I wrote them about the volume of letters. Both are eager to see the book appear, and both, I think, are more than a little fearful. I think they are chiefly afraid that the book will contain something that will revive memories of the bitter time in Asheville after LOOK HOMEWARD, ANGEL was published. Well, some of it may, but it cannot be helped.

I think, also, that Mabel — and this I say in the utmost confidence — is afraid there may be things in the book that will cause some people in Asheville to say again, as they have said in the past, that the Wolfe family was not altogether respectable. I have frequently observed that Mabel tends to make a fetish of respectability as she defines it, which means acceptance of her by the right people in Asheville. It was in connection with this line of thinking that I pondered very seriously one long letter Tom wrote Mabel — I am sure you will recognize it — in which he talked to her straight and made a very shrewd analysis of her character and personality and ended by telling her to stop worrying about what other people thought of her.[1] It may hurt Mabel to see this letter in print, exposed for all the world to read. I wondered whether I ought to cut it or cut parts of it anyway, but in the end decided I simply did not have the right. It is one of the finest of Tom's many fine letters, and it contains nothing but the truth. Just the same, that letter still worries me a little and lingers in my mind as something of a problem. When you read your proofs, you might bear this in mind and see whether you think any

190

portions of it are going to cause Mabel serious hurt. If so, cut what you think ought to come out, just for the sake of our common humanity, but don't mutilate the letter. As you see, I am wishing part of my responsibility on you. . . .

Cordially yours,
Ed.

[1] Wolfe's letter to Mabel was written May 10, 1938, and contains the following passage: "You told me one time that it almost killed you to think that people were 'talking about' you. For God's sake, get over it. Get over worrying about what people say. I have been through the whole mill a lot more than any of you ever have, I have read and heard and had brought back to me every kind of lie, myth, fairy tale and legend — some vicious and malicious, some just stupid — it used to burn me up, but it doesn't any more. Why should you care or worry about such lies, as long as you know in yourself what the truth is. Love life and love people, but don't be afraid of foolish little tongues. To be afraid is also defeat.

"And don't apologize for yourself, or for me, or for any of us. We don't need it. . . . Keep your head up, and have faith and courage and belief in yourself and in people and in life, and don't worry about Bingville and what the Women's Club is saying about you, and you're going to be all right" (*Letters*, p. 762).

*

April 4, 1955

Dear Liddy:

I think you will be touched by the enclosed letter from Fred that came last week. Please return it at your convenience.

The same mail also brought a post card from Mabel, saying she was sending me a bushel of Florida fruit and ending with the words "Thanks for fine letter to Fred and me."

Fred and Mabel are both wonderful people, and their individual reactions to that letter of mine are quite characteristic, don't you think? Fred's heart boils over, so he sits down at once and tries as best he can to say what it all means to him. Mabel's heart boils over, too, but she has so much she wants to say which she knows it is impossible to say that she just rushes out and buys the biggest basket of fruit she can find, and then in a post card about that she simply says, "Thanks."

I have been deeply touched.

Cordially yours,
Ed

*

April 30, 1955

Dear Ed: I dont know if you're still away or not. If so, it can wait very easily till you get back. What I have on my mind is this: if Scribners are not going to publish the Letters until Spring, or, preferably, fall of 56, what would you think of trying to sell some parts of them for serialization to the *Atlantic*? Both as advance publicity, and — frankly — because I could use the dough. . . .

Of course I know that Weeks [Edward Weeks, *Atlantic* editor], or any editor, would pounce immediately on (a) the Letters to Perkins and (b) the Letters to Mrs B. I myself have always felt reluctant to have the letters to Perkins serialized for two reasons: it didnt seem fair to sell the letters which CSS made available from their own files (which were, for the most part, not to be found in Tom's files or anywhere else on earth) if the sale of them for serialization was going to impair the sales of the <u>book.</u> Reason two, is the same reason, only selfish. I mean, that if, for a couple of hundred bucks apiece from the Atlantic, we allow them to "scoop" the book, we would be cutting off our own noses on book royalties. I mean, these Letters of Tom's are "For-the-First-Time Revelation of the Truth of Why Wolfe Left Perkins". I would rather save the Great Revelation until the book comes out, because I think it may make quite a stir and I think the Estate and I (and also Scribners) ought to reap the profits, not Ted Weeks and the ghost of your old friend Ellery [Ellery Sedgwick, editor at the *Atlantic*].

That leaves the letters to Mrs B as second choice. I think that from a literary standpoint they are unsurpassed, and I would love to have em published in a magazine as advance publicity, if we could be sure (and I am sure we could) that there was no cheap sensationalism in announcing who Mrs B was, or what she was to Tom. BUT you probably are loth to stir her up or upset her. . . . I guess it would depend on whether she would like a little dough, and would be proud to have those wonderful letters published in a magazine. She might, but you'll know (I dont) whether she is well enough to be disturbed.

Other good series: those to Mabel, ending with the one that worried you till I told you how proud she was of it. Hey, Ed, I think I may have reassured her about the movie sale. I wrote her and quoted the part from the Purdue Speech about Tom's not objecting to being "prostituted" by Hollywood but saying that his attitude was that of the Belgian virgin who said "When do the atrocities begin". . . . Also, she has just written me a Very Swell and unselfish and sympathetic letter about my having to disappoint her because of Mother's cancer.[1] Which is pretty damn swell of her. . . .

Love,

Liddy

[1] Nowell's mother had a mastectomy in May 1955, creating additional financial burdens for the family and preventing Nowell from visiting Mabel.

*

May 4, 1955

Dear Liddy,

Your letter of April 30th took a long time traveling down here, so I am making a special effort to give you a quick answer.

I am definitely not opposed to the serialization of the Letters. On the contrary, I think it may be a good thing to do. But my suggestion is not to pick out just a series of letters to some one person but to let whatever magazine is chosen see the entire lot and make their own choice. There is a problem in connection with this which I will come to in a moment.

But first, I am quite opposed to letting a magazine run the letters to Aline, either alone or as part of a broader serialization. Let me tell you why. Two weeks ago I went to see Aline again, at her request. She is somewhat better now and has recovered the use of the fingers of her right hand a little. She wanted to talk about editing a book containing Tom's letters to her and hers to Tom. She and I have discussed this a dozen times, but now she is feeling rather insistent upon getting it done. For a long while I think she faced some sort of psychological block about doing it, but that seems to be gone now. So I agreed to help her with the job and have drawn a contract for the publication of the book by McGraw-Hill. . . . The thing to do, it seems to me, is to arrange for serialization of selections of the Letters, perhaps in several installments in a magazine, and to have the serialization timed to end to coincide with book publication. If that can be done, the serialization should help the book. As you realize, no magazine can possibly take more than a fraction of it (even if they do run several installments), so such prior use in a magazine should merely serve to give the reader a foretaste of the riches that are in store for him in the book itself. . . .

But is the <u>Atlantic</u> the best place for it? They never published any of Tom's writing while he was alive, and I have always rather resented it. I do not, however, want to make too much of this point. It just occurs to me that we may want to try one of the big-circulation magazines. If they took anything, they would pay more. I do not know exactly where to try: but if you wish it, I could call up Hugh Kahler, of the <u>Ladies</u> <u>Home</u> <u>Journal</u>, whom I know well, and maybe it would not be too farfetched to try <u>Life</u> . . . .

I am terribly sorry about your mother's illness, and I do hope the operation may turn out to have done the job.

Sincerely,
Ed

*

May 10, 1955

Dear Ed: I'm glad Mrs B is so much better, though of course, that awful sense of urgency of hers to edit the letters is terribly tragic, because it undoubtedly comes from a conviction that she isnt going to live much longer. Anyway, I hope she's wrong: she has always been so young and so alive that there may be a lot of resiliency left if she can just get over this first shock and manage to be quiet. You have a damn tough assignment and I certainly agree with you that serialization of the letters to her would not be wise: might upset her. I wouldnt even mention it. . . .

I said the Atlantic because they have always showed great zeal in publishing Tom's letters, and nobody else has. They didnt publish any of his stories, it is true, but I didnt show them more than a few. Mary Lou saw and declined Boom Town and Miss Porters Party (I guess Sedgwick made her — I dont know) but after that I never showed them anything till they bought the 1st 3rd of Story of a Novel, but refused to run the other ⅔ when Wolfe found them and realized he hadnt given them to me, so I recalled the 1st third and sold to Sat Rev of Lit. . . .[1]

I think that your little friend Kahler is a sweetie pie, tho I have never met him in the flesh. I think that LHJ is ever more hopelessly stereotyped nowadays than it was in the old days, which is Stereotyped. I cant imagine what on earth Tom's letters would have to do with the kind of vapid woman for whom the Journal is evidently slanted, but if you want to ask Kahler, go ahead. . . . Life — well, my hunch would be that they might be a better bet than LHJ, simply because they are just trying their wings on fiction, etc. by first class writers and the sky might be the limit on what they'd try.

Love
Liddy

[1] Mary Lou White, later Mary Lou Aswell, had been a junior editor on the *Atlantic* staff, working both for Edward Aswell and Ellery Sedgwick.

*

July 6, 1955

Dear Jack, Dear Ed:

I am rather upset by a hasty pencil note written on yellow paper by Ed and inserted in Box 2 of Volume I of the Letters manuscript. It says: "I am somewhat troubled by the number of letters to A.B. included here. This is contrary to our understanding."

I am upset about this for two reasons. One, because it seems to think that I have taken advantage of Ed or Mrs B or somebody, and taken something that I was not authorized to have. Which is Unfair and Absolutely Untrue. Ed has merely forgotten what the "understanding" was, because we arrived at it five years ago (in January-March, 1950, to be exact). Also, his own attitude may unconsciously have changed since then. In March 1955 [sic], he was only too glad to cooperate with me and CSS and get Mrs B's permission to publish some of Tom's letters to her, but now, in July, 1955, he wants to save them as much as possible for the book of letters between Tom and Mrs B which McGraw Hill is to publish. Well, that, of course, is perfectly understandable, but I know damn well that Ed would never go back on his promise to me and Charlie and to CSS, so I have looked up quotes from the correspondence about this to prove to Ed that I did have and do have and, yea verily, I trust, shall always have permission from both him and Mrs B to use the letters to her that I have included in the manuscript. . . .[1]

So there is the written record of the understanding, and of my permission, and if you dont mind, I'd like to hold fast to it. Having any of the too-few letters to Mrs B omitted from the book would leave an awful weakness in it and would be horribly tragic to me, at least, at this late date. . . .

Guess this is all, except love to both from

Liddy

[1] To support her case, Nowell cited seven letters dating from January 20, 1950, to March 22, 1950, which discussed and/or approved the use of Wolfe-Bernstein correspondence for the collection of Wolfe letters. The final letter Nowell mentioned, undated but probably written on March 22, 1950, was from Aline and said, "I have just finished reading the letters and called Ed just in time to catch him before he went out west. I think they are beautiful, and I am sure will be welcome additions to your book."

*

July 15, 1955

Dear Ed:

It seems perfectly ridiculous, but I am going into the hospital tomorrow for an operation on a growth in my right breast, which may or may not be malignant. If it is only a cyst, I should be out in a few days, I guess. If it is malignant, I would be there for about 2 weeks, or longer, depending on the extent of the malignancy's spread. After going through all this with Mother, it is like "this is where we came in". [1]

Well, for safety's sake, I am sending the good copy of the Letters manuscript to Wallace Meyer by express. I have transferred all the changes to the carbon copy of the Letters, taken out the letters to Mrs B which you dont want shown for serial-sales purposes, etc. I am packing the entire carbon in one box and showing it to Mother, in the hopes that you will tell her to express it to you, to Weeks, or Life, or what-all, in the immediate future.

Ed, I hate to be a nuisance about this but God knows if I dont succeed in selling serial rights I will Never be able to pay for all of this additional hospitalization. I mean mine, on top of Mother's and resulting economic chaos. Well, to hell with it. Got to get a decent night's sleep if I can. Operation isnt until Monday, the 18th. Somebody will no doubt let you know if I do or do not have cancer, and trust you can let us know what to do with the carbon for possible serialization in the meantime. . . .

Nuts!

Love,
Liddy

[1] Nowell did have cancer. A mastectomy was performed immediately, followed by x-ray treatment, which left Nowell feeling weak and sick.

*

Sunday, Aug. 28?

Dear Ed:

I wrote you a couple of days ago — just a horribly messy longhand exclamation of delight about the bare possibility of Life's doing an article about Tom and his letters. Everything I said in that letter to you still goes — very much so — and I'll be hoping that Basso will consent and the thing will go through. [1]

But if Basso should decline, I feel more confident now than when the idea first occurred to me that I could do such an article. I mean, if Basso should decline and you should be faced with the necessity of getting (suggesting) someone else, and not knowing who, exactly. Because we dont want the danger of getting somebody (like Burt, or the NYU people)

196

who would misinterpret Tom or things he wrote or said or did.

Well, why cross that bridge? No reason, except that both mornings, since I wrote you, I have waked up with a feeling that I could do a pretty decent piece, and with a clearer idea of what it could contain. It could be, as I said, along the main theme that he could brook no too-complete or too-long domination. Really no domination at all. Beginning with Mama (and continuing with her all his life), Mrs B, Perkins. And then going into his breach with P and CSS. I know too much has been made of this already, but it has been too much on the hostile side. I think an article could exclaim on the terribly exaggerated reaction to the simple, everyday occurrence of an author leaving his first publisher and making a new start. And could explain why, or try to.

But the value of an article by me would be that I was the chief person who served as an intermediary between Tom and Perkins during the breach, and who (I honestly think) was his confidant as much as anybody during that last part of his life. Of how Tom sent me in to MEP with the story No More Rivers (which is not Old Man Rivers — which was the story about Wallace Meyer, of Perkins reaction, of my telling Tom, of Tom's reaction!! Of the whole mess. Of Tom's (even before that) calling me at night when drunk to announce solemnly "Well, I've done it now" (left Scribners and MEP) so often that when he called me to say he really had, I didnt believe it was really true. Of Perkins calling me. Of Tom's months of doubt till you called me and made him the Harper offer. Of Tom's later letter to me from Seattle (Portland, I forget which) after he had spent a weekend with a bookseller from out there (Ed Miller wrote me the guy's name but the guy is dead) and had evidently heard gossip which he thought had been "spread by Scribners" to defame him. How he wrote me that letter begging me not to tell Perkins anything about him, etc. etc. Of my believing that he really meant it. Of his illness. Of my being summoned to Johns Hopkins, of Perkins phoning me and wanting to go too. Of my discouraging him. Of that tragic glimpse I had of Perkins waiting in the gloom of the tracks of Penn Station when my train from Boston to Baltimore pulled in. Of how he wanted to come with me — how I persuaded him not to, though it damn near broke my heart, but I was trying to do what was best for Tom. Of how he, P, showed up at JH next day anyway, how I got him to agree not to go and talk with Tom. How he acted when Dandy came in and told us it was hopeless.

Well, I guess this is enough. The piece would be sort of tragic last chapter in the Wolfe-Perkins story which no one has told, and which, I guess, no one could tell but me. I am, of course, the villain of the piece, in that I kept Perkins from seeing Tom. I didnt know Tom was going to die — I only wanted him not to get emotionally upset but to go to his big operation as calm and rested as he could be. Also, Perkins had never shown me the last letter of all which Tom had written him. Perkins sensed that I was holding back from him about Tom, which Tom had written me to do.

I guess the piece could end with Tom's coffin being put on board the train, and with the big buck nigger that I noticed (did you?) who put it on, and with you and me standing there as the train began to move, and your suddenly saying "Look" and pointing, and the sign K 19 sliding past as the train picked up speed. [2]

Well, all right, I'll stop. I have always thought I'd try to write down everything I could remember about Tom and MEP, as seen by me personally, so different in tone from the biography. Much more informal and minor, but more intimate and real. . . .

Maybe the stuff I've sketched out (about Tom and Perkins) would be too personal for Life. Maybe they would rather have an impersonal account of Tom in the last 3 years (or thereabouts of his life) which would include leaving MEP and going to you. The more impersonal account is what I have to tackle as the next few chapters of the biography anyway. (I am up to his return from Europe on July 4, 1935). I would want to say that I thought he had "found a way" and was happier, stronger, more adjusted, than ever before. But I think that almost any account of that part of his life has got to center on his leaving CSS and going to Harper, because that was the main thing in his life.

But Basso would be the Grade A Blue Ribbon choice! More than anyone! His slant on Tom and MEP would be about the same, I think, as yours and mine, because founded on the same sources — long talks with (a) Tom and (b) Perkins. And he is a Real Writer, and a Name since Pompey's Head.

To my disgust I find that my x ray treatments run until next Friday, instead of ending tomorrow. But I am slowly getting my strength back anyway, x ray or no x ray sickness, and I think I will really start to get somewhere as soon as they are over with. I couldnt write a piece against an immediate deadline: I would probably take a month to do it, or maybe two. And I MOST CERTAINLY dont want to barge in, or insist on your suggesting me, nor would I feel offended if you can suggest someone else, if Basso couldnt do it. But why cross all these bridges. Pray for Basso to say Yes, and

Love
from
Liddy

[1] Nowell and Aswell hoped that Hamilton Basso would write the article for *Life*. Basso had first known Wolfe through Scribner's and had continued to be friends with both Wolfe and Perkins. As it turned out, however, *Life* chose one of its own writers for the piece.

[2] Wolfe's body was larger than any casket available in Baltimore, so a special one had to be made overnight. The body was put on the train for Asheville. According to both Nowell and Aswell, one of the last cars was number K 19, a Pullman car which Wolfe had frequently written about. However, Aswell's personal papers include a letter from the Pullman Company saying that Pullman cars had names, not numbers. Nevertheless, both Aswell and Nowell always insisted that "K 19" had been inscribed on the washroom window of Wolfe's funeral train.

*

September 14, 1955

Dear Liddy:

The simplest thing is not to write any member of the Bernstein family. Melville Cane tells me that Mr. Bernstein is so far gone himself that he was hardly aware, if he was aware at all, that Aline had died.[1] He was not at the funeral. As for the other members of the family, they seem to resent any further intrusion of Thomas Wolfe, or of anybody connected with Thomas Wolfe, in their lives.

What can be done, if anything can be done, about the Wolfe-Bernstein Letters, I simply do not know at this moment. After a little time has passed, I want to talk to Edla [Aline's daughter] and her husband — just because I do not like to give up until I have tried everything. It seems to me I have one trump card to play. This is the fact that I can publish Tom's letters to Aline and nobody can stop me. I shall try to persuade Edla that it may prove best in the long run — as Aline herself thought — to put Aline's side of the correspondence in the same volume. I shall let you know later what, if anything, comes of this. . . .

My best, as always,
Ed

[1] Aline Bernstein died on September 7, 1955.

*

September 15, 1955

Dear Liddy:

Hold your bonnet, Baby!

Jay Gold, Feature Editor of *Life*, has telephoned me and given a definite commitment on the Letters. They have decided to have the article staff-written by one of their top writers, Robert Coughlin [sic]. He is a Wolfe admirer. *Life* will have the exclusive right to quote anything they wish from the Book of Letters — these quotations to be used in Coughlin's article. The publication of the book will be the explicit reason for the appearance of this article, so the *Life* publicity ought to help sales of the book.[1]

And what do you think? They have upped their price to $2,500, payable now. I am delighted for your sake, and I hope your half of the money will clear up your medical bills and make you feel at ease again. *Life* will send the check to the Estate of Thomas Wolfe, and as soon as it comes, the Estate's check for your half will be mailed to you. . . .

My best, as always,

Ed

[1] Robert Coughlan's two articles in *Life* appeared just prior to the October 2, 1956, printing of Nowell's *Letters*. In the first article, "Tom Wolfe's Surge to Greatness" (*Life*, September 17, 1956), Coughlan called the *Letters* collection a "major literary event," "definitive." His second article, "Wolfe's Grand Vision: A Final Tragedy" (*Life*, September 24, 1956), completed the story of Wolfe's life. The thirty-four pages that *Life* devoted to Wolfe had great publicity value for Nowell's forthcoming book.

*

Sept 16, 1955

Dear Ed:

Your letter with the wonderful news about Life has come, and my first reactions are only inarticulate animal noises: first WHEE and second Whush, or however one spells a great sigh of relief, because I had just about given up hope of anything coming of it. . . . The first day of all that I felt human was after I first got the tentative news about Life from you, and now today. Well, glory be!

But Ed, all animal noises and kidding aside, my almost instantaneous reaction was one of gratitude for you. I dont know what on earth I would have done if I hadnt been able to dump the carbon of the Letters, together with the whole damned problem right into your lap and go off to the hospital knowing that you would cope with it as no one could. You did it with devotion and with courage (I myself might not have had the nerve to try Life but might have just tried Ed Weeks as a safer tho less exciting possibility, sick as I was and in desperation and with no time or courage to expend) and — well — with all the qualities that have always made you such a wonderful executor for Tom. I suppose you realize that you are a far far better executor than Perkins for him: with more youth, more energy, more vision, more devotion to the 9999th degree. I dont mean that Perkins wasnt good, but he was old and tired and discouraged and somewhat limited by nostalgia for the old Scribner-Wolfe days. You know what I mean. Selling the novels to the movies and this sale to Life are both accomplishing the well-nigh impossible, or miracles of faith. [1] They are both due solely to you, or, anyway, to your faith in Tom's own work and power and your zeal to make his "life prevail" as he said somewhere. This is very badly put, but you'll know what I'm driving at, and merely saying "Thank you" for it is an understatement if I ever saw one. When I wrote Mabel the night of Perkins death that I thought Tom had chosen you as the person to trust most after leaving Perkins and that I thought he still would feel that way — well, I have felt surer of it all along all through the almost-ten years since that night. . . .

More power to you, Ed, and thank you loads and

Love from Liddy

[1] Aswell had managed to realize a year-end income for the estate of close to $90,000. Most of the assets were from the sale of movie rights to Gregory-Golman Enterprises, for whichever of three Wolfe novels Gregory-Golman selected (*Of Time and the River, The Web and the Rock, You Can't Go Home Again*). The agreement was initialed by Charles Laughton, according to an interview with Aswell (n.a., "Literary Estate," *The New Yorker* [February 9, 1957]: pp. 24–26). Laughton's interest in Wolfe extended to his doing public readings of some of the long dramatic passages in Wolfe's novels. (Coughlan, "Tom Wolfe's Surge to Greatness.")

*

September 23, 1955

Dear Liddy:

Your wonderful letter of September 16th quite bowled me over. No one ever went quite so all-out in saying I was an all right sort of fellow as you have done in this letter, and I guess I am enough like Perkins to curl up a little bit around the edges when anybody says a kind word about me. I shall take your letter home and keep it and take it out from time to time to reread it when I am feeling low. . . .

My best, as always,
Ed

*

October 4, 1955

Dear Liddy,

I have just learned from Aline Bernstein's daughter Edla that Aline left to her sister, Ethel Frankau, the right to decide what, if anything, was to be done about publishing her letters to Thomas Wolfe. It is the greatest

201

pity in the world that Aline never got around to doing what she told me on innumerable occasions was the dearest wish of her heart: namely, to edit both sides of the correspondence for publication. She, and she alone, had the knowledge to supply the background information wherever it might be needed. There must have been a psychological block that kept Aline from even beginning the task. She first started talking to me about it right after Tom's death, and she kept talking about it for seventeen years.

I have written a letter to Ethel Frankau suggesting a meeting to see what, if anything, can now be done to carry out Aline's wishes. . . . Would you be interested in tackling this assignment? I can mention it only tentatively now, because I have no way of knowing what may come of it; but it might be good to have your answer before I see Miss Frankau, so that I can suggest your name if we get to that point in our discussion.

Of course, I can — as I said before — go ahead and publish Tom's letters to Aline, and there is nothing they can do to stop me. And it is my impression that there are more letters from Tom to Aline than from Aline to Tom. I am also quite sure that Tom probably wrote a hundred words to every one of Aline's, so that there are enough letters of Tom's alone to make a book, if it should come to that in the end. Here again it would be my thought to offer you the job if you want it.

My best, as always,
Ed

*

October 4, 1955

Dear Liddy

. . . .[1] Mabel is a wonderful person. When the *Life* deal was concluded, I wrote her about it and told her what the payment would be, explaining that you would receive half of it. I also mentioned that you had had heavy medical expenses and that this money would come in very handy for you. Mabel wrote back that she was concerned about your "financial status" and suggested the possibility of a loan to me to be passed on to you. Perhaps I am betraying a confidence in telling you this, but the only reason I can think of to explain Mabel's wishing to make the loan through me was perhaps to keep you from knowing the source. Just the same, I think you ought to know of her wish. . . . It restores one's often faltering confidence in the human race when things like this happen.

My best to you, as always,
Ed

---

[1] In the opening paragraphs of this letter, Aswell told Nowell that he was working on

a contract with William Heinemann, Ltd. for the British rights to the *Letters*. Heinemann editor A. S. Frere hoped to bring out the English edition simultaneously with Scribner's, and Aswell, aware of Nowell's medical expenses, planned to ask for a $2,000 advance, payable on signing the contract. He also expected the serial rights payment from *Life* "any day now." These two payments, he wrote Nowell, "ought to help you a lot."

*

October 4, 1955
5 p.m.

Dear Liddy,

Here she is, Baby. Go out and buy yourself a new bonnet.

For the record, this is your half of the $2,500 payment just received from *Life,* covering the first serial rights of Thomas Wolfe's Letters.

My best, as always,
Ed

*

October 5, 1955

Dear Ed:

Thanks about a million-billion times for the $1250, which arrived today. But bonnet, hell: if I buy anything after I finish paying my medical expenses, I'll buy me a falsie, of which there is a bewildering variety of types. I have already informed the denizens of Houghton that I'm going to get a hollow one (there is really no such thing except one kind that you blow up like a balloon, which explodes if you go in airplanes) and use it to smuggle priceless incunabula out past Mister Matthews, the president's English butler who guards the portals.

Ed dearie, of course I would be delighted to edit the Tom-Mrs B letters if Ethel Frankau should consent. I think you could truthfully say that Mrs B had thought of getting me to do it about 5 years ago, before she decided to do it herself. I havent any letter from her saying so, but somewhere I have one from you saying that she and you had considered it, or somesuch. Anyway, you can count on me to edit practically any thing that needs to be done, Tom's alone to Mrs B, or both. Or if it comes out nothing, that is all right too. Whatever is best for you. I agree with you that there are more of Tom's letters to Mrs B in existence that hers to him. Hers are charming and quite personal and slight, whereas his are (as we once agreed) surprising impersonal, for the most part, and some of the most wonderful letters he ever wrote. And of course much longer than hers to him. His alone would make a book — a small book, but God knows a good many times bigger and more important than, for instance, the NYU Wolfe-Watt job. . . .

Ed, Mabel really is a wonderful woman. Here she had every right to be put out with me, getting her all ready for my arrival and then going back on her so completely, but she offers to lend me money instead. I wont say anything to her unless she mentions it to me, but it certainly does make me fonder of her than ever. And I think this, too, is like Tom. They both would deprive themselves of petty comforts for a sense of economy that they got from Mama, but would suddenly turn around with the most wonderful generosity, and in big amounts, and never a thought except affection for the people that they gave it to. It is real magnanimity, and I am so damn touched by her suggesting it that I could sit right down and bawl. . . .

End of page. Thanks for Everything. Everything is OK now, thanks to you and the $1250 bucks!

Love
Liddy

Chapter Eight

"I trust you more than any living editor and want to 'string along with you', as Tom used to say."

NOWELL, JUNE 26, 1956

*

IN SPITE of her illness, which involved several operations, Nowell finally finished the manuscript of Wolfe's letters — her chief occupation since the correspondence with Aswell began. She visited Wheelock and Aswell in New York to go over the typescript with them. Then, in early April, she drove to Chapel Hill and Asheville, where she did further research for her next project, the biography, which McGraw-Hill was to publish.

In June, problems developed. On the night of June 25 Aswell called Nowell to say he had been fired from McGraw-Hill. She reacted with incredulity, terming McGraw-Hill "only a vast trade book dispensary" before Aswell's tenure there and assuring him that she would change publishers along with him. When Aswell found a new job at Doubleday, he arranged for McGraw-Hill to release Nowell's contract, promising her a new agreement from Doubleday. Four months elapsed. Nowell completed almost half of the biography. When in October she still had received no contract from Aswell and Doubleday, she exploded, issuing an ultimatum: either Aswell must deliver on his promise, or she would desert him and return to the original contract with McGraw-Hill.

The October crisis emerged, as before, out of the contrast in Aswell's and Nowell's personalities and the intense personal pressure under which each was now working. Aswell, eager to prove himself, wanted to sell media rights to the Wolfe biography, increasing income for the estate and for Nowell. He was also sidetracked by the details and demands of a new job and by his own literary endeavor — the writing of his sexual autobiography. Nowell, with two children and mounting medical bills, wanted security in the form of a Doubleday contract that would protect her from libel. Once again, she was obsessed with the spectre of being sued and left penniless should CBS or the *Atlantic* or *Life* — in serializing her work — not hold her blameless for Tom's words. She was also pressured by time: she knew that she was dying and wanted desperately to finish her book.

Despite what seemed an impossible situation, the year ended peacefully when Aswell finally responded to Nowell's demands. Nowell accepted the new contract, describing Aswell first as Santa Claus then as Jesus Christ; and they were able to congratulate themselves on being Doubleday author and Doubleday editor.

Dear Ed:

Here, at last, is the introduction for the Letters which Jack says they need soon now. The pencil line after line 8, page 5 marks the way I originally thought of ending it, and the pages thereafter are what I wrote when you answered my question, affirmatively, as to whether you thought I should or should not explain Tom's breaking-away from people. I am not too happy about it: I'm afraid that it may lead reviewers to discuss this one angle of Tom's life which has already been too-much discussed. But maybe something of this sort is needed to prepare for and explain the bitter letters to Baker, Mrs B, + MEP which are in the actual text. God knows.[1]

Well, see what you think, and if you think it is OK, please tell Jack so he can go ahead with getting it set up??

Ed dearie, it was wonderful to see you, and to see you looking so healthy and cheerful and rested! Of course I realize that a lot of your cheer came from the fact that you were going to have four whole days' vacation from the saltmine, but you did look better than those times in Boston when I was so worried about you. Anyway we had a lovely time with you and arrived home Sunday just in time to have Edna get knocked down by a sweet but big and playful boxer [dog] and get a fractured wrist. Was it you, or was it Jack who was playfully reproaching me for writing that we were coming to New York if Edna didnt break anything to prevent it. Well, we made it there and back, but just under the deadline. Anyway, it's only a greenstick crack, so should be OK fine after a couple of weeks in a cast.   Liddy

Ed: I forgot something. If you havent already told Mabel that I hope to come down this year, better not do so. Not that I dont hope to and wont try like hell to, but I dont want to get her all wound up expecting it again so soon for fear I might not be well enough or something might postpone it.[2]

---

[1] Explaining Wolfe's pattern of being attracted to and then rejecting key people in his life, Nowell wrote of Wolfe, "Occasionally he would find a man or woman, such as Professor Baker, Mrs. Bernstein or Maxwell Perkins, who was remarkable enough to withstand this first onslaught of his scrutiny. . . . Then he would be swept up on a great surge of strength and joy and certitude: he would literally idolize his friend, would proclaim his or her excellence to all the world, and would lay the entire conduct of his life into his hands, or hers, repeating, like an incantation: 'If you'll just stand by me, everything will be all right.' However, he could never rest content till he had probed deep into a person's character and decided what the very essence of it was: he seemed always to be searching for a flaw,

although hoping fervently that he would fail to find one. But the men and women whom he worshipped were only human, after all, and when he finally did find fault in them, he felt a bitter disillusionment and a sense of having been betrayed. . . .

"Then would begin the period of his trying to break away which caused so many wounded feelings. Because of his emotional intensity, Wolfe could not drift casually away from an outworn friendship, as an ordinary person does. Instead, he felt a moral compunction to explain the causes of his disillusionment to his defective friend. Sometimes, as with Professor Baker, he merely wrote out his complaint in letters which he never mailed: sometimes, as with Mrs. Bernstein, he delivered it face to face in scenes of violent recrimination: sometimes, as with Maxwell Perkins, he both wrote and talked about it, endlessly, until the latter cried out in exasperation: 'If you have to leave, go ahead and *leave,* but for Heaven's sake, don't talk about it any more!' "(*Letters,* p. xvii).

² In an effort to stop the spread of cancer and extend her life, Nowell underwent several somewhat experimental operations including one in Chicago which she initially thought successful. To her doctor she wrote: "This is just to say that I got home all right, and have been meaning to write and tell you so. When the train got outside Chicago, into open country, there was a thin new layer of snow on everything, like powdered sugar, although the poplars were still covered with gold leaves and the sumachs with crimson. It was perfectly beautiful, and perfectly wonderful to me to be looking at it and so much alive. I dont suppose I can ever thank you for the best imitation of the resurrection invented by man as yet, but — well — I can always try" (undated letter, collection of Clara Stites).

*

January 12, 1956

Dear Liddy:

Last night I read your introduction and think it superb. I am glad you added the part about Tom's breaking away from people, for it was an important part of his character; and you have interpreted it — so I think — just right, making it clear that the thing must be understood on more than one level. (Incidentally, this is the kind of illuminating interpretation that the biography will need at innumerable points).

Several small questions occurred to me as I read the introduction. The carbon goes back to you herewith, so that you can see what my suggestions amount to. I have already mentioned them to Jack on the telephone, and he will wait until he hears from you before doing anything.

First, on page 1, line 5 — Shouldn't the verb be in the past tense and the singular?

Page 4, last line and page 5, first line — The way this is phrased might imply that Aline wanted to suppress Tom's letters to her. As you and I both know, this was not true. The way I have suggested emending this passage will avoid the wrong connotation.¹

Page 6, line 5 — "The separation of his parents." The word "separation" is right enough in one sense but wrong, I think, in a more important sense. It may seem to imply the legal concept of separation as a preliminary to a divorce. So far as I know, there was never anything of that sort in it. As I understand it, when Mrs. Wolfe got too much involved with the boarding house on Spruce Street, Mr. Wolfe preferred to remain in the old family home on Woodfin Street, although we know that he spent a lot of time at the boarding house, too. The place on Woodfin Street was only a few blocks away from the boarding house. It seems to me you ought to explain the circumstances a little bit in order to avoid giving the wrong impression about what the word 'separation' really meant. [2]

Page 9, last sentence — The way this ends does not quite say what you mean, does it? After all, we do know what came in the end, since — alas! — the end happened more than seventeen years ago. My suggested change may perhaps be a more accurate statement of what you had in mind. [3]

Once again, my warmest compliments. You have kept brief what you wanted to say in the introduction and, yet, have contributed something essential to the reader's understanding of the letters and of Wolfe.

My best, as always,

[1] Explaining the basis on which some letters to Wolfe were excluded, Nowell emended the original phrasing to read, ". . . also his more personal letters to Aline Bernstein have been excluded from this volume at her request since it was her intention to edit them herself" (*Letters,* p. xv).

[2] Nowell emended her original phrasing to read, "This quest of his (to find a father) has been attributed to various causes: to a nostalgia for the security of his early childhood which was disrupted by the partial separation of his parents" (*Letters,* p.xvi).

[3] Nowell emended the last sentence to read: "The tragedy, of course, is that the story is unfinished — that his death at the age of thirty-seven has left us only to speculate on what he might have come to, had he lived" (*Letters,* p. xviii).

*

January 14, 1956

Dear Ed:

When I was in New York, I guess it was the night we went to Jack's, I was saying that I thought Jack was the most wonderful critic in the world because whatever I did, he always said that it was "excellent, dear Liddy". But if you think this goddamned introduction is "superb" I guess you win the laurel wreath instead. Or share it with him. I still think you are both nuts, but of course I'm delighted anyway and much relieved.

Ed? I think your few suggestions are fine, and have sent them to Jack to transfer to the copy which he has. I made only two changes to your changes. (1) I omitted the word "longer" in the very end of the very last sentence because I felt that it spoiled the gallumphing iambic pentameter in which I'd written the thing (and incidentally, in which the whole biography is written, partly because that comes naturally to me, and partly because it blends in better with Tom's own, I thought.) In other words, I ended the last sentence with "Had he lived". And let it go at that.

The other thing you may not like, but let me try to persuade you. You explained in detail that Mama and W.O. [Wolfe's father, William Oliver Wolfe] were not actually "separated" but that she just "got too much involved with the boarding house" etc. Well, I think yes and also no to that. I think that in those days one did not leave one's husband because that was not proper, so that one left him but went to great lengths to make it look as if one hadnt, or really didnt mean to, etc. Mother and my father did the same. But you can bet your bottom dollar that Mama didnt sleep with W.O. any more, and that she intended to disrupt their married life. For proof I could quote you quite a lot of places in the Angel such as:

p 48 "her enormous patience was wearing very thin because of the daily cycle of abuse. They slept now in separate rooms upstairs".

p 49 "deep down, between their blind antagonistic souls, an ugly and desperate war was being waged. Yet, had he known to what lengths these daily assaults might drive her, he would have been astounded."

p 51 "Eliza was preparing for a change".

p 129 Eliza moved into Dixieland. "Gant and Eliza, although each felt dumbly that they had come to a decisive boundary in their lives, . . . said nothing clearly. In fact, they felt their approaching separation instinctively: Eliza's life was . . . on the rails. And however vaguely, confusedly, and casually they approached this complete disruption of their life together. . ." etc.

ALSO I couldnt go into the explanation about the boarding house in the middle of the listing for Tom's reasons for feeling he must search for a father, without lousing up the whole paragraph.

SO I wrote in "partial" before "separation" and called it quits. It was certainly a <u>Partial</u> separation, anyway. . . .

Amen, and love from
Liddy

*

Dear Ed:

I was so incredulous last night when we talked on the phone that I couldn't even begin to say the things I really felt.[2] Besides, as Max Perkins once said, "I can't express certain kinds of feelings very comfortably". However, I do want to try to express them now, because I have been thinking about them ever since our phone conversation.

I guess you know that, with the possible exception of Max Perkins, I have always considered you and always will consider you as the editor who is the most fair, the most completely trustworthy, and the most completely sympathetic to a writer. It was because of this conviction about you that I influenced Tom Wolfe to choose you when he had to find a successor to Perkins. And it was because of this conviction that, after eight years during which it was enormously strengthened, I influenced Tom's family to choose you as the Administrator of his estate. I don't mean to pretend that I did it: <u>Tom</u> chose you himself, of his own accord, because you struck a chord of sympathy with him, and then won his complete trust, and at a time when he was inclined to be suspicious of all editors. Moreover, his family came to feel the same way about you shortly afterwards, and has grown more and more convinced with every year, as they (Fred and Mabel) said to me only a few weeks ago. However, this letter is supposed to be a kind of testimonial from <u>me</u>, and so it must be personal.

This same conviction about you led me to take to you at Harper's almost all of my best writers, including two Harper Prize winners, Vardis Fisher and Judith Kelley; David DeJong, who missed the prize by only one vote, and Meindert DeJong, who has just won the Newberry and Caldecott Medals. And, in recent years, when I began writing myself, it led me to leave Scribners (with whom I've had the closest relationship for twenty years) and go to you myself, even though I did not like McGraw Hill except in-so-far as it was you.

I know perfectly well that all the other writers who followed you to McGraw Hill feel the way I do about you. McGraw Hill was only a vast trade book dispensary with no reputation for first-rate creative work, when you went there. The fact that they now have a good list and a good reputation is due solely to your work, and they can't, in any justice, keep it, though I suppose they can coast along on the gravity you gave them for a while. In any case, I certainly have no affection for them, and will be only too delighted if my biography of Wolfe can be taken over by your next publishing associates. If it cannot be taken over, I would hope, as soon as possible, to free myself and renew my publishing relationship with you wherever you might be. This would apply to any books <u>about</u> Wolfe which I may do: the books <u>by</u> Wolfe himself which might be edited by me or by you yourself or someone else would, of course, be yours to place wherever you thought best since you are (rightly!) Tom's Administrator.

Ed, if this sounds formal, it is because I am so deadly in earnest about it all. What it boils down to is that I trust you more than any living editor and want to "string along with you", as Tom used to say. And I know damn well that all those other writers whom you had on your special list at McGraw Hill feel exactly the same way. It is only a question of time and adjustment before we all go blithely on together again, and undoubtedly under a better imprint than the one of McGraw Hill.

Yours as ever,

<u>More</u> than ever,

[1] Five months of correspondence, mid-January to mid-June, are not included here although there are twelve letters from these months in the Houghton files. Most of them, however, are short and many of Aswell's are signed by, apparently, his secretary.

[2] Nowell was reacting to Aswell's news that he had been fired from McGraw-Hill. Hired in 1947 to head Whittlesey House, the trade book division of McGraw-Hill, Aswell had been expected to expand the firm's reputation as a publisher of trade — not just text — books. But the publications of Kay Boyle (*His Human Majesty*, 1949; *The Smoking Mountain: Stories of Post War Germany*, 1951), Catherine Marshall (*A Man Called Peter*, 1951; *God Loves You: Our Families' Favorite Stories and Prayers*, 1953), Cecil Woodham Smith (*Lonely Crusade: The Life of Florence Nightingale*, 1951; *The Reason Why*, 1953), and Taylor Caldwell (*Never Victorious, Never Defeated*, 1954) were not sufficient to sustain the firm's interest. According to Gray Williams, a junior member of the trade book department at the time, Aswell had published some distinguished books, but the line as a whole was not profitable enough to meet McGraw-Hill's requirements. Aswell's other major accomplishment at McGraw-Hill was acquiring publishing rights for the correspondence of James Boswell (1740–95): *Boswell's London Journal* (1950), *Boswell in Holland* (1952), *Boswell on the Grand Tour: Germany and Switzerland* (1953), *Boswell on the Grand Tour: Italy, Corsica, and France* (1955), and *Boswell in Search of a Wife* (1956). Aswell considered these publications to be a coup for McGraw-Hill. But other projects fell through. Neither the Bernstein-Wolfe correspondence nor a follow-up report from Alfred Kinsey's Sex Research Institute was published by McGraw-Hill, despite Aswell's expenditure of time and travel, because both Bernstein and Kinsey died. Undoubtedly, a combination of circumstances contributed to McGraw-Hill's decision to fire Aswell — a dismissal he viewed as a business, not a personal, situation.

*

June 28, 1956

Dear Liddy:

This must be dictated in haste, but I want to let you know that I have discussed with the people here at McGraw-Hill one of the things you and I last talked about on the telephone — namely, what is to happen to your biography of Thomas Wolfe now that I shall no longer be at McGraw-Hill to act as editor of the book. I am glad to report that a friendly agreement has been reached, to the effect that McGraw-Hill will release both you and the Wolfe Estate from the contract on repayment of the advance; and of course this repayment will necessarily have to be made by whatever other publisher I eventually find myself with. I thought it would relieve your mind to know this.

My best, as always,
Ed

*

September 4, 1956

Dear Liddy:

You must have been wondering what has happened to me. The fact is that I've been so busy that I've been unable to keep up with my correspondence.[1] Doubleday does not yet have an office ready for me, so I have been working mostly at home and coming into the city only from time to time. This is the reason why you have not yet received a draft of the Doubleday proposed contract for the biography of Thomas Wolfe. I have the McGraw-Hill contract which you were kind enough to send me and shall use this as a model, including the libel clause, which Doubleday has approved. Just now I am hoping to knock off for several weeks and take a breather. I've wanted to do this before now but was unable to. So unless something unusual occurs I shall be away until the week of September 24th and shall then send you a draft of the Doubleday contract so that you may approve it before the final step is taken of putting through the actual release from McGraw-Hill. We already have Harold McGraw's promise in writing to give that release, so I think everything is pretty much in order.

Cordially yours,
Ed

---

[1] On the basis of recommendations from his neighbor, literary agent Paul Reynolds, and from Lee Barker, who was with the firm, Aswell was hired as senior editor with Doubleday and Company. While his new office at Doubleday was being made ready, he was busy at home writing his sexual autobiography, inspired by his work with the Kinsey Institute.

Aswell's fascination with Alfred Kinsey's reports on male and female sexuality (1948, 1953) had led him to travel frequently to the Kinsey Sex Research Institute at Indiana, where he had persuaded Kinsey to have McGraw-Hill (instead of the medical press of W. B. Saunders) publish his next book.

*

September 16, 1956

Dear Ed:

Well, here is the tenth chapter of the biography which I have been threatening to send down. I guess this is a hell of a time to send you anything to read, but trust that you will get to it eventually at any rate.

. . . I'd like to get it done in time for Fall, 1957, publication. If I only can! I have an awful feeling that there are going to be a lot of people wanting to write about Tom once the Letters have come out, and we cant hold back the crowd forever, nor should we try to. So I guess its up to me to say my two-cents worth and get it over and open up the bottleneck which I make.

Well, OK, Liddy, stop talking about it, and try to get a few sentences written before you go to bed.

Love
Liddy

*

October 17, 1956

Dear Ed:

I am sorry to add to your already-too-great-burden, but you know there are some things that, because of the children, I just can't do. And I'm afraid that this proposed television [program] by CBS of Wolfe's letter to "A Working Girl in New York" is one of those things. You say that Mr Cane and Mr Berner are in favor of consenting to it, with "the stipulation that. . . Thomas Wolfe should not be made a character in the treatment." But that seems to me to have the fascinating illogicality of Alice in Wonderland. You might as well say that it would be all right to televise the crucifixion, but that Jesus Christ "must in no way appear as a character in the treatment." That letter of Tom's, like most of it, is "I, I, I" all the way through. Or to use his own unvarnished speech, the whole point of the letter, and the only thing that it discusses is the fact that he "fucked her because she wanted him to fuck her". I don't see how CBS can televise a fornication anyway, but if they do, there have to be two parties to the deed. The only person who has ever been able to achieve that happy state alone is the Blessed Virgin Mary, and I always suspected the Angel of

214

Annunciation anyway.

In your letter to me of October 11, 1956, you say: "As far as you are concerned, I can't see that you would incur any liability at all, since the only thing CBS will be buying, if they do buy it, will be certain words of Thomas Wolfe's and none of yours". Also, the contract for the Wolfe Letters says in Clause Fifth: "The Publishers and Administrator shall and will and hereby do indemnify and hold harmless from all debts, suits, claims and demands that may be made or brought against her on the grounds that the said work is libelous, scandalous or violates any copyright or civil right or on any other ground whatsoever". I think this would apply to television versions of the book, or the exercise of similar subsidiary rights to it, but before I give my consent to this CBS idea or to any similar exercise of subsidiary rights, I'm afraid that I have to ask you to write me a formal letter saying that it <u>does apply</u>. I know you'll have to take this up with Messrs Cane and Berner, and maybe I will have to ring in a lawyer of my own if there is any difficulty. And if we have to get into a complicated rat-race of this sort, the sooner we can get into it and back <u>out</u> of it, the better. And God knows I'm sorry but I <u>can't</u> expose the children and their money to any half-baked libel suits because of Tom's old indiscretions.

That is the first thing that is on my mind, and has been ever since our phone talk of two nights ago. Before I launch into the second thing, maybe you had better take a coffee break or go out and run round Central Park. The second thing is nothing new: it is the thing that I called you up about two nights ago, and about which you were able, temporarily, to reassure me by your charm and patience and sense of humor and all the other qualities that make you the swell guy you are. But as soon as your personal influence wore off, I went right back to my original conviction.

Ed, do you remember the old story about the child who said: "I want a white rabbit and I want it NAOOOW"? Well, at exactly 2 AM after the evening I talked with you, I suddenly awoke and thought "Goddammit, I <u>still</u> want my contract and I want it NOW." Maybe, after all these years of moaning about "sensitive geniuses" I have picked up the contagion from them, or maybe I have always been a screwball all along. Anyway this seemingly endless delay about the contract drives me wild and wakes me up at night. Moreover when I try to work on the biography and write immortal prose about Tom's reasons for leaving Scribners, all I can think is "Goddamit, what the hell am I batting out my brains to write this stuff for anyway, when I don't know what is going to happen to it!" And the whole thing rises up in a welter of uncertainty and impatience and desperation, and I get nothing done.

Ed, it was on June 25th that you first called me up and told me that you had been "fired" from McGraw Hill, and that I agreed that we should try to transfer the biography from them to whatever publisher you went to next. On June 28, you wrote me that "a friendly agreement had been reached" between you and McGraw to that effect. On August 21st, you asked me to lend you my McGraw Hill contract so that it could be redrawn for signing between me and Doubleday. You kept saying that you wanted to get the biography away from McGraw-Hill as soon as possible, and before any of your other authors tried to leave them. You phoned or wrote me several times and said that the contract had been typed and was being sent to me. But it is now just ten days short of 4 months since I agreed to try to follow you to a new publisher, and it is two months since you borrowed my contract for recopying by Doubleday. But instead of getting any closer to what Tom would call "an end to the devil's business" we are getting farther away!!!

And <u>now</u>, you write me that Mr Berner is "sitting on the contract for the moment because if negotiations are actually entered into looking toward an eventual sale of the movie or television rights of the biography, this will have some bearing on what will actually be said in the contract concerning those rights." To this I protested on the phone, and want to protest again now, in writing. I signed the contract with McGraw Hill and you as their editor, in good faith, and I accepted the advance and wrote the major portion of the book in that good faith, and with the assurance that a contract was a contract. Later, when you got fired, I agreed to stick with you, still in that good faith and with your assurance that "there won't be any trouble about the contract, no matter where I go". As you probably remember, I have always been in a state of extreme anxiety about this, and now it seems as if that anxiety was justified. Certainly if you had told me at that time that Mr Berner was going to "sit on" the contract and dream up new things to say in it, I would have chosen to maintain my contractual status with McGraw Hill. In spite of all your joking on the phone, I have an awful feeling that I may have to maintain it still — in other words, decline the contract which you offer me now for Doubleday, finish the biography and give it to McGraw Hill, for better or for worse, simply for the sake of earning the advance which they have paid me and of washing my hands of the whole unpleasant business. It is my last avenue of escape from an intolerable situation, and I have every legal and contractual right to do it if I have to.

Ed, I know you'll think I am making a mountain out of a molehill, but cant you see that you are under an obligation not to change the terms of the old contract now, since we have got this far into this situation on a basis of mutual trust? Maybe what Mr Berner might cook up after sitting on the contract would be acceptable. But if so, it ought to be embodied in a subsidiary agreement — not introduced in violation of good faith into the contract at this point.

As for the question which he's sitting on, and which I myself raised, I think it is quite simple and has any number of precedents to go on. As you yourself pointed out, the facts of Tom's life are now virtually history, or in the public domain. Like — to use my earlier example — the crucifixion, or like the Civil War, or like the life of Brigham Young which Zanuck bought from me in Vardis Fisher's version, despite the fact that he had all the bearded elders of the Mormon Church and all the histories at his disposal. In other words, it is not a question of buying the historical facts but of buying a certain <u>presentation</u>, a certain <u>version</u>, of them. If NBC wants to base a life of Wolfe upon his novels, then all the rights would be vested in the Estate. (The Estate would be sticking its neck out to admit that the novels are autobiographical, but that is aside from this discussion.) If NBC wants to base a life of Wolfe upon his Letters [sic], then the rights would be vested partly in me and partly in the Estate, in accordance with whatever the McGraw contract says about such rights. That contract is legally binding unless and until I accept another, and I don't believe I <u>will</u> accept another if Mr Berner is going to try to change horses crossing a stream and take advantage of my good faith in you and my everlasting patience in waiting for the contract. If this louses up the possible sale of the biography, all right, it will have to louse it up. Because we cant go on pyramiding possible sales and eventualities: we have got to get a firm foundation of a contract, or things are going to go from bad to worse.

. . . This whole mess has dragged along so long and driven me so wild with exasperation and anxiety and suppression that it has all gone BOOM at once. You said on the phone with touching earnestness that you would not willingly do anything against my interests, and I know damn well that that is true. I know, too, that the only real trouble is delay because of the terrible pressure of your other work but — well — please lets get this whole thing squared away as soon as possible, and meanwhile

Love from Liddy

*

November 28, 1956

Dear Santa Claus:

I got back from Hartford[1] more dead than alive and found so many wonderful letters here from you that I can hardly enumerate them. The letter protecting me against libel, the letter giving me the tentative good news about the deal with CBS, the letter to Ledig [Heinz Ledig-Rowohlt, German publisher], and the one about the letter to Claire which I have sent along to Bond to put the poor boy out of his misery. I seem to have a feeling that I ought to send my answer to all of these by setting it [her answering letter] on fire and letting the flames waft it up the chimney, but I guess I'd better stick to the U.S. mail instead. . . .

I also got a letter from Ted Weeks of the Atlantic saying that he "would like to think" that chapters from the biography would be suitable for the Atlantic and would I please get in touch with him. And before I answer him, I think I'd better get your reaction to that. For one thing, would possible serialization louse things up in any way for Doubleday? Of course I would love the extra money from first serial rights but I would hate to do anything to spoil the standing of the book, or to postpone book publication very long. Also I realize now that I have had a sneaking hope that you might be able to duplicate your miracle of the loaves and fishes with Life Magazine. (First I have you Santa Claus, now Jesus Christ himself!) Well, anyway, IF that miracle could be accomplished it would not hold up publication and help the book instead of hindering it. And would, of course, pay more. But I doubt if it might be possible. They just might be persuaded to do an article on what they muffed before: the chief news value of all these books: the revelation, in detail, of why Wolfe broke away from Perkins. But I think its very doubtful: dont you?

Of course there is also the fact that if the Atlantic serialized the book I would be wide open to libel in their publication, even tho somewhat limited by the contract for the book. And that is my old bugaboo.

Well, I started to write Weeks that, if he wanted, he could skim through the unrevised carbon to get a general idea of the book, but with the understanding that neither he nor I were obligated by his doing so. He is away lecturing so much and so damn slow that that would be the only way, I guess, to sell it to him. But I dont think I want to be that obligated even so. So I guess I will just stall and probably end up by not selling serial rights anywhere: neither to, first wild stab, Life, nor the Atlantic.

As you can see I'm ruminating out loud about this. But if you have any reactions to it all, I'd love to have them.

End of page but thanks loads and loads for everything, past, present, future, world without end, Amen.

Love Liddy

---

[1] Nowell had just returned from Simsbury, Connecticut, where her daughter Clara was a freshman at the Ethel Walker School.

*

December 6, 1956

Dear Ed:

Here are two copies of the release from McGraw Hill, signed by me and for you to keep and send back to McGraw. I guess this winds it up very nicely, and I cant ever thank you enough for "smoothing the way for me" as Tom would say. If anybody had told me six months ago that I was going to be a Doubleday author, I would have laughed in their face: but if anybody had told you that you were going to be a Doubleday editor, you would have too. Which only goes to show that

> Its impossible to tell
> The Depth of a well
> By the length of the handle
> on the Pump, pump, pump.

. . . Well, anyway, thanks loads for everything.

Love, Liddy

Chapter Nine

"You can count on us completely. . . ."

ASWELL, APRIL 11, 1957

*

Nowell's health was deteriorating so rapidly that she began to prepare for her death. Openly, she discussed with Aswell her plans to appoint a guardian for her two children and, as the biography neared completion, authorized him to make any final revisions in the manuscript should her death precede its publication. At the same time, she wrote, "I do not feel like dying yet, at all" and commented on her renewed interest and commitment to Wolfe's notebooks, which, she said, "I am going to be dying to do. . . as long as I can breathe." Her failing health also caused an interesting, new strengthening in the relationship with Aswell. For the first time in their correspondence he signed his letters "Love" or "Yours" and rendered wholehearted support not only for her Wolfe work but also for her girls, whom he generously offered to adopt.

But only a month after Aswell's adoption offer, his life underwent a twist when his wife was killed in a tragic fall. It was now Nowell's turn to console and offer counsel. The only bright spot in this dark year was the phenomenal success of Ketti Frings's adaptation of *Look Homeward, Angel,* which played first to Philadelphia then to New York audiences.

Dear Ed:

I think maybe I am like Tom in some ways after all. After weeks of lying around worrying about my back, I have finally arrived at today which is noteworthy for two occurrences:

1. I have told my doctor to send my medical records to the chief orthopaedic surgeon at Mass General, and to ask for the earliest possible appointment with him. This will be, at first, only for diagnosis. If I have any surgery I will probably have to wait until I can scrape up money enough to pay for hospitalization, nurses, doctors, and what-have-you. Unless it is emergency surgery, in which case Mother would let you know. But I dont think it will be.

Anyway, I'm going to need every red cent I can beg, borrow, or steal, and this therefore is written to say I hope to God that you can also steal — steal enough time somehow to get those German and Italian contracts ready for me to sign, before I vanish in the maw of Mass General (if I do.)

2. I got, finally, a letter from "your friend Charles Ferguson" as Max and Tom used to say, disclaiming any relationship on their part with anyone they were doubtful of. He enclosed a lot of Unforgettable pieces [1] and I regret to say that I think you hit the nail on the head when you told me he was an ex-minister from Texas. Because the ones he chose to send me as examples of what he wants are (a) sentimental and (b) Inspirational enough to make one puke. He also says that "In my view, the whole sordid mess over DeVoto and Scribners and all the rest isn't worth bringing up, unless it needs to come in briefly to show his terrible sensitiveness to criticism." Now what the hell was "sordid" about that? Because "Tom Wolfe Betrayed Perkins" à la Struthers Burt? Or because Tom drank and brooded over it? I am struggling against a horrible temptation to write Ferguson that "Tom Wolfe was a rough, tough, rootin, tootin "sordid" son-of-a-gun from Western North Carolina, and if there was anything he hated it was what he called 'Nice Nellyism'." Maybe I'll be able to restrain myself. Maybe, God help me, I can even manage to be Inspirational for $2500 worth of medical attention. But this piece has got to be about Tom Wolfe, for Christs sake, and not Beatrix Potter. . . .

And so to bed. Now dont start worrying about me. I amnt [am not] going to die and maybe I'm not even going to get carved up, but I am going to Take Steps to Find Out what the hell is wrong with me and try to rectify same. I'll let you know what the doctor says after I have had twenty thousand x rays and a milogram, and until then nothing much will happen anyway. But do please try to get me all the dough that's due me, even tho it will, no doubt, take months to clear from foreign countries. . . .

Love Liddy

¹ Nowell was also working on a Most Unforgettable Character piece about Wolfe for the *Reader's Digest*. She completed at least one draft of the article, but it was never published.

*

April 11, 1957

Dear Liddy,

I have been waiting to write you but hesitated to do so until I knew that you were feeling well enough to receive the letter I wanted to send you. Your letter of April 9th has just come and that gives me the signal to go ahead.

First, the problem of your two girls. Needless to say, I understand your concern. . . . Undoubtedly Jim Casner [Nowell's lawyer and later executor of her estate] is right in advising you to seek court appointment for a permanent co-guardian with you.[1] It is a tedious thing to have to go through, but you should do it. If your cousin, Alice Hedge Brewer, will serve, fine. Someone in your family would be the natural person to select. But let me throw out a thought, something you can tuck in the back of your mind. Had I attempted to write you cold about this, I should hardly have known how to go about it. Your letter makes it possible for me to say what I wanted to say.

As you know, my wife has been in England. I wrote her of your situation. I made no suggestions. She wrote back immediately, warmly, saying that if she could help in any way with your girls she would feel privileged to do so. Last Monday my wife got home. Since then we have talked things over, and I just want to say that my wife's idea has my full concurrence. If the situation should ever make it seem desirable, you can count on us completely, even to the point of taking the girls into our home and into our family. I may add as a postscript to that that my wife is particularly good with horses, dogs, cats, children — and with that most ornery of species, men. As I said, just fold this thought away in your mind as something that is possible, if it should ever seem good or wise.

From what you have told me, I am prepared just as you are to accept what your doctors say as the truth. So let's proceed on the good assumption that you are full of years still to be lived. I'll do anything I can, but you know that already. As for the biography, of course you will finish it. I must get at the remainder of it, which I have not yet sent back to you, and do this without further delay.

As for my serving as your agent — sure. . . .

Mabel was in New York several days last week. She got Cane's office to draw a will which she signed. She was really in fine form, better than I had seen her in recent years. Of course she insisted on telling me all the details about herself. While she was here she submitted herself to another medical examination in the hope of finding someone who would tell her that she did not need an operation. The diagnosis, however, confirmed what she already knew, so she left New York with the intention of entering the hospital in Asheville on April 10th. I have heard nothing further from her, so maybe she did and maybe she didn't.

Keep your chin up, dear Liddy. Yours is a gallant spirit.

Love,
Ed

[1] Nowell was afraid that both she and her mother would die before the girls reached the age of 21.

*

Saturday, April 13 ?

Dearest Ed:

Your letter has just come and I am still sort of swimmy-eyed about it. It is perfectly wonderful of you, and of Mrs A. too. I am trying to remember that sweet little nickname you call her by sometimes, like Bitsy, but that isn't it. [1] Please tell her for me that her character is every bit as lovely as her voice, which has always fascinated me, it is so beautiful. It is very touching to me that you and she should come forward this way so wholeheartedly, when some of my own relatives (not little Alice. . .) are so reluctant. And you, Ed, have been all along the person who grieved most for me except for Mother, and who has come so wholeheartedly to my help in everything that's possible on earth. . . .

Ed, I just can never thank you or your wife. It could mean all the difference to Clara and Edna in the world — the difference from being shunted about from person to person, or having no home, really, at all, and having someone that they could go to and could trust and feel safe with. Of course they'll be in boarding school from now on — I've had a letter from the principal of Miss Walkers saying that Edna is accepted as of year after next, and that if needs be, they can both have scholarships so they "both can have their highschool years here at the Ethel Walker." But they are going to need love and care and good advice and an awful lot of it, especially if Mother should die, too, before they're grown. Clara is a little neurotic but I think she'll be all right: she has, believe it or not, in spite of my trying not to influence her, a good deal of literary ability. Her teacher at EWS is always in an ecstacy about it, and even I think there may be some ability there. But poor old Edna — she's so huge, and young, and such a mess, and I keep bursting into tears at the thought of

225

how she's ever going to get along without me to love her and stand up for her and take her temperature and nurse her through all these horrible emergencies. I told her what you said and she beamed from ear to ear. I am afraid that she is thinking of those dogs you had, and of how you let her smoke the cigarette in fun. Did you know she wrote Clara a postcard from NY saying "Dear Clara: I did two things you didnt do. I went up in the tiniest spire of the Empire State and I smoked a cigarette in the office of the editor on the —th floor of Doubleday and Co." To think that was only a few months ago. It seems as if I've lived through an age of harrowing experiences since. I dont know. I would think that Edna didnt realize I was going to die, except that she has fits of crying about almost un-related things, and cannot stop for a long time. Well, excuse it please. Maybe I can still fool myself and everyone else and live for quite a while. But whether I do or whether I dont, it sure does make things more bearable for me to know that you and Mrs A are so wholeheartedly behind me.

Now I'll stop and go to bed, but thank you more than I can ever say, and

Love to you both
from
Liddy

[1] Aswell's wife's nickname was "Nibs," a nickname for Knyvett, her given Welsh name.

*

June 8, 1957

Dear Ed:

I've been trying to leave you in peace. I called up about a week ago at Chappaqua to see how you all were doing, and to thank you loads for that three thousand bucks (AND THANKS). But Duncan said you were asleep and I thought you might be going through the awful slump when, no matter how brave you have been, your body just couldnt keep up with your heart and mind.[1] If so, I hope its over with, because that is probably the worst stage of the whole thing. But yesterday I got the copy of your letter to Ted Weeks, and gather that, at least in the daily routine of work, you are going on all 8 cylinders. It was a Wonderful letter, and I whooped with joy, just like my aged mother, as I read it.

Well, here is Chapter 13 of the biography, typed by my darling daughter, writ by me. I think I can wind the whole thing up in just one more. Am going to start it now. Ed darling, God knows you cant read the thing now to suggest revisions. I will rewrite the first few chapters that you have already read and returned to me, but if we never get to revisions on

226

the final ones, you can just make any that you think necessary. This is to give you my full consent.

However, I do not feel like dying yet, at all. When I hastily went through the Notebooks ms before I sent it to you, it was all I could do to keep from starting to get that into shape right off. And honestly, Ed, dont feel discouraged. My God, that book is 100000000 times more in shape right now than the Letters ms was for years! I am going to be dying to do it: I always have been and I always will be as long as I can breathe. But I'd better shut up and finish the biography right now.

By the time this gets to you, I may be in New York. Am coming down to see one Dr Frank Adair who supposedly has had "remarkable success" in "arresting" or "retarding" people with malignancies.[2] God knows it may be only a needless ordeal and great expense, but it cant lead to anything worse than <u>not</u> coming, and I never was one for spineless laissez-fairism. If he thinks there is really any fancy treatment worth the gamble, he will probably put me into NY Memorial Hospital for Cancer over on the East River and 68th (?) St. But, Ed, PLEASE dont think you have to come see me, if I do show up there. It may be a pretty depressing kind of place, and you have got to spare yourself right now and get away on your vacation. . . .

Got to stop and send typewriter into town for a new ribbon. Mother jumping up and down like Paul Revere to start driving in. Loads of love, in haste.

[1] Knyvett Lee Aswell died suddenly on May 18, 1957, when she fell from a second-story window of the Aswell Chappaqua home.

[2] By July cancer had spread to Nowell's blood stream, liver, hip, and several vertebrae. As she wrote to a friend, she spent her days "half in bed, half out."

*

July 22, 1957

Dear Liddy:

Here are three copies of the retyped draft of the agreement with Heinemann covering your biography of Thomas Wolfe, in which I have effected the necessary legal separation between you as Author and me as Administrator of the Wolfe Estate. If you find the document in order, please sign all three copies and return them to me. It won't be necessary to have your signature witnessed. I shall then send the three copies to Frere for his signature and eventually we shall each get one fully executed copy returned to us. The advance and all other moneys, as you will see, are to be paid directly by Heinemann to you.

. . . It is just like you to suggest that I take an agent's commission on this Heinemann contract, but in my most polite Southern manner my reply is "Nuts to you, lady." Some things are done for money and some things for love, and if I can imitate Nibs's habit of British understatement, I shall simply remark in a casual tone of voice that I did not do this for money.

All my best.

Yours,
Ed

*

November 12, 1957

Dear Liddy:

Ketti Frings' dramatization of *Look Homeward, Angel* opened in Philadelphia for its tryout last Saturday night. She called me yesterday afternoon from Philadelphia and read me the press notices. They were absolute raves. I have of course read the script, and think she's done a marvelous job, and it begins to look as if the play will be a success.

I was asked to write a brief something about Tom and the theatre to be published in the program notes for the play. This I have done, and a copy is enclosed for your information. [1]

Yours,
Edward C. Aswell
per jr

---

[1] In his program notes, "Thomas Wolfe: The Playwright That Wasn't," Aswell called the play a "final consummation" of Wolfe's failed hopes to write plays. He credited Ketti Frings for adapting Wolfe's "essence" to the theater format. *Look Homeward, Angel,* the play, premiered November 28 at the Ethel Barrymore Theatre on Broadway, starring Anthony Perkins as Eugene, Jo Van Fleet as Eliza, Hugh Griffith as W.O., and Arthur Storch as Luke. It ran for 554 performances and won the New York Drama Critics Circle Award and the Pulitzer Prize for 1958.

Chapter Ten

"I'm working against time and death more
unmistakably than anyone ever did."

NOWELL, JUNE 20, 1958

*

THIS LAST YEAR of a ten-year correspondence epitomizes the personalities
of Aswell and Nowell and shows the degree to which each, in his or her
own way, had been living in the shadow of the giant. Aswell's letters are
uncharacteristically long. Fascinated by the chapters Nowell sent him on
Wolfe's life, he responded in a frenzy of remembrance of times past. He
offered lengthy personal recollections of the events she recorded in the
biography, his sentences taking a rhetorical turn. He corrected Nowell's
phrasing of Wolfe's relationship with Aline, for instance, and suggested
that Wolfe had actually been seeking a mother-substitute, repeating his
idea so that Nowell won't miss its psychological point. Not since 1953,
when he had written ten-page "night thoughts" to Nowell about Perkins
and Terry, had Aswell indulged himself in such a way. Perhaps, in writing
Nowell, Aswell fancied *himself* the writer of Wolfe's life, although he was
unaware of his motives — what Wolfe would call "the buried life."

Aswell was also spurred by the final chapters of Nowell's biography,
those concerning Wolfe's death. Ironically, Nowell sent these chapters to
Aswell between hospital treatments for her own rapidly advancing cancer.
Aswell seemed unaware of this irony. Instead, consumed by memory, he
sought to impress on her his recollection of those final days with Wolfe
at Johns Hopkins Hospital. Her text opened for him an opportunity to
tell his story of Dr. Ruge. But his numerous additions and revisions to
Nowell's chapters — as interesting and informative as they were — missed
the heart of the matter for Nowell: namely, that she was desperate, and
she was dying.

Nowell waited before reminding Aswell of her condition. Then, in
typical plain words, she told him that his responses to her biography

229

chapters were those of a "second type" of editing, which amounted to "virtual collaboration." Were she to live long enough, that second type might do well. But since she knew she was dying, he must allow her to write her book with fewer, rather than more, additions. Aswell quickly agreed to her reproach of his "fine-tooth comb" policy and offered unconditional support.

Nowell then, quite unrealistically, pressed forward onto the next project — the notebooks of Wolfe — and planned to apply for a Guggenheim fellowship. The notebooks project had all along been a favorite for Nowell. She now wanted to firm up a contract for this project as well as to sell serial rights of the biography to *Reader's Digest* or the *Atlantic*. The expenses for medical treatment and hospitalization along with the responsibility to her two children drove Nowell to seek ever more ways to earn money.

Perhaps in response to her failing health, Nowell made a case for the notebooks to Aswell: for why *she* should be its editor. Like Aswell, she had seen herself — surprisingly — all these years as "a ghost of Wolfe himself." She revealed for the first time her own affinity with Wolfe, which enabled her to read not only his nearly indecipherable handwriting, but, she believed, also his mind. So well had she understood the creative material of Wolfe that she now suggested to Aswell that she should be Wolfe's translator. As one who had pored over Wolfe's notebooks and absorbed his consciousness, she — by a process of osmosis — could translate what Wolfe so illegibly wrote.

In this last year of correspondence, Aswell and Nowell emerge as complex figures in a drama of the past. Only at the end, in a year marked by a trilogy of "Wolfe" deaths (hers, his, and Mabel's), do they both show this psychic complicity with Wolfe. Yet how else could it have been? How else could a Yankee woman and a Southern man have maintained a ten-year correspondence from out of the past were it not for some buried life that each of them shared?

Dear Liddy:

You said not to answer your letter of February 5th, but I shall.

I have read the chapter of the biography about the love affair between Tom and Aline Bernstein. As you say, her death makes this less ticklish than it might otherwise have been. As for her daughter Edla, I don't think you need worry. The facts are what they were, and can't be denied. Aline herself wrote about it as well as Tom, so it is already in the record.

My feeling about that chapter in the biography is that you have quoted, I think, too heavily from THE WEB AND THE ROCK in telling the story. You wrote in a note somewhere that Tom could tell it better than you could. But my point is that I think it ignores a very important thing about Tom's writings to assume that what he wrote about this matter, or indeed about anything else, was the literal truth. His imagination played a large role, and rightly so; and he did take liberties with the truth when it suited his artistic purposes.[1]

Still another thing that troubles me about these lengthy quotations is that Tom himself, as he told me repeatedly, was not satisfied with that part of THE WEB AND THE ROCK. He said he had been too close to the event when he wrote it, and he had intended to rewrite that whole love affair rather more objectively. For these reasons I should like to see you rewrite that chapter relating the events in your own words as much as you can. When and if you do quote Tom, it may be well to put in a footnote reminding the reader of the two points I have made here about the role imagination played in Tom's writings and the fact that he was not satisfied with what he wrote about Mrs B. . . .

I have seen LOOK HOMEWARD, ANGEL a third time, and I guess that will just about hold me. It still affected me very deeply. And I was interested to see, as before, that the audience was completely attentive, that there seemed not to be an empty seat in the house, and that the theatre is still packing them in by selling standing room. I shall want awfully to learn your reaction after you have seen the play.[2]

My best as always,

Ed

---

[1] Wolfe was not the only one who took "liberties with the truth." In what has become known as "The Wolfegate Affair," John Halberstadt described Aswell's role in the editing of Wolfe's posthumous material as fraudulent and Aswell as "the dominant contributor" to the later novels of Thomas Wolfe" ("The Making of Thomas Wolfe's Posthumous Novels," *Yale Review*, 1980). *Harvard Magazine* featured a rebuttal by Richard Kennedy ("The Wolfegate Affair," *Harvard Magazine* September-October, 1981). Kennedy described Halberstadt's charges against Aswell as "harmful mischief." "Wolfegate" was a topic in two

subsequent issues of *Harvard Magazine* (January/ February 1982 and March/April 1982), primarily in the Letters section. In his *Look Homeward,* the third biography of Wolfe, David Donald described Aswell's editing of the posthumous works as "unacceptable." Donald conceded of Aswell's role, however, "it is not clear that another editor could have made better, or even considerably different, novels out of Wolfe's manuscripts" (*Homeward,* pp. 483–4). Continuing in Aswell's defense, Leslie Field concluded, after a comparison of four test-case manuscript sections, that Wolfe's posthumous novels were indeed the work of Wolfe, not of Aswell [*Thomas Wolfe and His Editors: Establishing a True Text for the Posthumous Publications:* (Norman: University of Oklahoma Press, 1987)].

  [2] Nowell intended to see the Ketti Frings play when she was in New York but felt too sick to leave her hotel on the evening she had tickets.

*

April 20, 1958

Dear Ed:

You know you say that Mrs B told you that Tom proposed marriage to her and that she refused. Well, if he did, I dont suppose she told you when or where? The truth is, I just dont believe that he did, or not very seriously, but that Mrs B, with the best intentions in the world, romanticized things somewhat after he was dead. If it had been a real honest-to-God serious proposal, one would think there would be some reference to it, or some documentation of it somewhere in all the hundreds of thousands of words that both wrote about their love affair. Or in all the millions of words that Tom poured out verbally on the subject. Or in their letters to each other. For instance, when he was being accused by her so bitterly, for years and years, of having deserted her, wouldnt he have answered, well, you know, I wanted you to marry me once but you refused?

I'm willing to grant that perhaps when he "wanted to possess her utterly" he might have asked her why she insisted on staying with her family, but that if so, it was sort of a left-handed kind of proposal, if you know what I mean. Well, I dont know. I suppose you'll want me to put it into the biography but I just gag at doing it, and if I do, it'll have to be either very briefly, or in just a footnote, saying that "according to what she told you in 1945?, he proposed to her" and let the reader take it or leave it, as they think best. [1] . . .

I am scheduled to come down to New York for my next tests on Sunday, April 26, or is it April 27th. Anyway a week from yesterday. Will bring Edna with me and check into Hotel Gladstone unless my bone-lesions are very bad by that time, in which case I'll go right into Memorial Center. This also applies to whether I will continue to sleep at Gladstone, or go into hospital a few days later — also the question of what tests they want to do and whether I have to be right there, incarcerated on the spot, for some or not. Anyway I'll be having tests like mad, seeing doctors, etc all day Mon and Tuesday. When I get the worst over with I'll give you a buzz but pay no heed until I do. I have myself all prepared to be told that this latest operation isnt holding me, but maybe I am wrong this time. God knows I hope I am.

Love Liddy

[1] Nowell attributed Wolfe's marriage proposal "to what Wolfe told Edward C. Aswell in the spring of 1938 and to what Mrs. Bernstein told Aswell later," and that Mrs. Bernstein "had very sensibly refused to desert her family for him" (*Thomas Wolfe: A Biography*, p. 117). Nowell went on to say that Wolfe, after this, was resentful of Aline's family and pathologically jealous of her activities. David Donald, on the other hand, suggested that Wolfe proposed, knowing that he was certain to be rejected and that Aline's rejection "subtly changed the quality of their relationship" (*Homeward*, p. 143).

*

April 23, 1958

Dear Liddy:

Your letter of April 20th is here, together with the ribbon copy of the final chapter and the new final page of the preceding chapter. As soon as I got this material I dropped everything to read it, not only because this is a very important chapter but because it deals with matters I know firsthand. You have done a marvelous job of presenting the facts and of making understandable the complexities of Tom's final illness. And this chapter moved me to tears, bringing back all the old agonizing memories. Perhaps the general reader will not be affected in the same degree, but he is certainly bound to be affected. It is terrific.

There are some things left out which you may have omitted deliberately, and at a few points I question the accuracy of statements. Let me touch on those things briefly.

Page 11. First sentence at the top. "In a violent access [sic] of fear and anger, Wolfe dismissed Dr. Ruge from his case, and put himself in the care of Dr. Watts, etc." This isn't right, Liddy. Let me go back. I had tried to get Dr. Swift in on the case at the very beginning, not knowing that Swift and Ruge were enemies, had been feuding for years, and were not on speaking terms. Swift therefore never saw Tom while he was in Ruge's care. He did, however, send his assistant, whose name I forget, out to Firlawns to get a report, and Swift wrote me what it was. All of my correspondence with Swift is at Houghton. Now the thing is that from the first I had distrusted Ruge because in his initial telegram to me he betrayed concern over whether his bills would be paid, and because when I checked on him and learned that he was a psychiatrist, I wondered what the hell a psychiatrist was doing treating a pneumonia patient in his little private nut factory, which had no X-ray apparatus. I tried desperately to persuade Fred to have Tom taken out of Ruge's care and put in the Providence Hospital in Seattle, but Fred was so afraid that he would do something wrong that he was incapable of coming to a decision and of doing anything. When it became clear to me from reports received from Swift and Fred that Tom was suffering from serious but still unknown complications at a time when he was supposedly convalescing from pneumonia, I decided to take drastic action. You will remember that Ruge kept brushing me off as if I were a pest who was not entitled to the information I sought, and at one point he wired you to the effect that Tom's friends should stop interfering and that "we are not all wild Indians out here."

I was desperately trying to figure out what to do for Tom. Then I recalled that Henry and Mary Hart had been spending their summer vacation in Spokane, their home town, that they had both met Tom at my house the previous Christmas, and that they had got on famously together. So I put in a long distance call late one night in the early part of August to Henry Hart in Spokane. I explained the situation to him, and urged him, if he could possibly do it, to go to Seattle and talk to Fred and see if he couldn't persuade Fred to take Tom out of Firlawns and into the Providence Hospital. The thing could not be done except through a member of the family, hence an outsider like myself had no standing in the situation. And it was that same night I also put in a long distance call to you in New Bedford and told you this, because I wanted your advice and your sanction for what I proposed to do. Well, the next day Henry and Mary Hart drove to Seattle and talked to Fred, and it was because of their presence and their urging and their moral support of Fred that Fred finally took the necessary action of having Tom removed to Providence Hospital in Seattle. Tom did not do this himself, as you have said.

[Nowell added a handwritten note here: "I said Ruge had him moved there, which he, technically at least, as Tom's doctor, did."]

Page 17. I don't know whether Dr. Swift wrote any books for Harpers or not. Anyhow, that is irrelevant and should come out. The way Swift came into the picture was as follows: When I received Ruge's first telegram about Tom's illness and his financial status, I went to Paul Hoeber, Sr. (now dead), who was head of Harper's medical book department, to get him to help me find out something about Ruge. It was Hoeber who looked up Ruge in a medical directory and discovered the fact that he was a psychiatrist. There was nothing in the record at that time to indicate that Ruge had also previously been in general practice. I asked Hoeber whether he could recommend a doctor in Seattle who could investigate the situation on the spot and report to me. He suggested Dr. Swift. There had recently been a medical convention in Seattle, and Hoeber had attended it and while in the city he had been a guest of Dr. Swift, for the two men were old friends. It was pure accident that Swift was also a brain specialist, and the one man in Seattle who might have been able to detect the seriousness of the condition when the headaches first developed. If it had been possible for Swift to see Tom at that time — but he didn't. Only the physician in charge of a case or a member of the patient's family can call in a consultant. Fred would not have known whom to call in, and Swift would have been the last man Ruge would have called in because of the personal situation between the two doctors. Therefore there is also something wrong in the sentence "He (Swift) had conferred with Dr. Ruge several times." The truth is that he never conferred with Dr. Ruge at all, although Swift's assistant did. That was as close as Swift ever got to the case until Tom had been removed to the Spring Hotel Apartments. And Swift did not see Tom then because of a wire from me. I recall Mabel's telling me that after she got Tom in the apartment and his confused mental state alarmed her so much, she suddenly remembered (because I had informed both Fred and Mabel of my earliest efforts to get Swift in on the case) that Swift was a brain specialist and that he had never seen Tom, and perhaps he was the best man to see him now. So it was Mabel who called Swift in on this occasion. . . .

Page 24. The last two sentences in the last complete paragraph on this page quote Dandy as saying certain things about Tom after the second operation. I was present when he made this report to Mrs. Wolfe, Mabel and Fred, and according to my recollection, what he said was that if Tom survived the shock of the operation by as much as three days, which was doubtful, then he might live six weeks more and be made reasonably comfortable by the administration of drugs — and the rest of it as you have it. The point is that Dr. Dandy emphasized that the second operation, involving as it did taking off the top of Tom's skull, would be a great shock to his system, so that it was doubtful whether he would survive the shock by more than three days. As a matter of fact, Tom died on the morning of the third day, not having survived the shock.

At the bottom of page 24 and the top of page 25 — this is quite moving, the account of Tom's semiconsciousness after the second operation, but I don't know whether it is true. After Tom died, both Mrs. Wolfe and Mabel began to build up what seemed to me to be fantasies about Tom's last hours and what he said to them. For example, Mrs. Wolfe made the statement some time after Tom died that the last time she saw him alive she roused him and he said to her "Momma, I've been a bad boy." Mabel had another version, as you have given it. I am inclined to believe that both were fantasies. I returned to Baltimore after the second operation, and went into Tom's room several times, accompanied by Fred and on Fred's insistence. On each of these occasions Fred tried to arouse Tom, but Tom was completely unconscious. After he died, Dr. Dandy told me he never regained consciousness after the second operation; and I think this may have been the truth of the matter rather than the fantasies that Mrs. Wolfe and Mabel thought up some time after the event.[1]

Page 27. Here you quote what the family had inscribed on Tom's tombstone. It is of no actual importance, but perhaps you would like to know, and perhaps the reader would like to know, why and how the two quotes got there. Well, when the family was preparing the tombstone, either Fred or Mrs. Wolfe wrote to both Perkins and me asking each of us to suggest a suitable quotation from something Tom had written. Perkins suggested the quotation from LOOK HOMEWARD, ANGEL, and I suggested the quotation from THE WEB AND THE ROCK. The original idea had been that there would be only one quotation on the stone. The family could not decide between what Perkins suggested and what I suggested, so they solved the problem by putting both quotations on.[2]

This is all, and it is too long a letter to inflict on you, but I thought I had better give you these reactions while they were fresh.

Cordially,

Ed

---

[1] Nowell's account of Wolfe's last words to Mabel — "All right, Mabel. I'm coming" — was taken from Mabel's interview recorded for the Library of Congress. But according to what Dr. Dandy told Aswell, Wolfe never gained consciousness after the second operation. Nowell handled the discrepancy by saying, in a footnote, "If he (Wolfe) answered Mrs. Wheaton, it was probably almost automatic" (p. 439).

[2] The two inscriptions on Wolfe's gravestone are as follows:

"The last voyage, the longest, the best" (*Look Homeward, Angel*)

"Death bent to touch his chosen son with mercy, love and pity, and put the seal of honor on him when he died" (*The Web and the Rock*)

The second gravestone quotation was actually written by Aswell, although the idea came from Wolfe's manuscript. Mary Louise Aswell, in an undated letter to Pearl Kazin Bell, asked: "Do you think Ed's (and Tom's) spirit will ever be at rest? You realize that Ed convinced himself he was Tom's other *half*. What shocked me was his private satisfaction when words *he had written* [when editing *The Web and the Rock*] were chosen to put on Tom's gravestone. . . . I can't condone his 'editing' but I understand what motivated him."

*

May 7, 1958

Dear Ed:

Just put the ribbon copy of these seven pages in front of Chapter IV, which is where you will start reading when you get to it. They are the new section which endeavors to say in my own words that Tom and Mrs. B had a deep and ever-influencing love. I'll have to do a good deal of revising in the rest of Ch IV too, but you can guess at what that'll be. The main big revision is in these 7 pages.

I just read the Pulitzer news in the local paper, and the thing that flashed into my mind was Tom and Jim Agee sitting talking, talking at your house in Chappaqua one winter Sunday when I was out there.[1] You "sure picked good" as Tom said to Mabel of the Spring Hotel Apartment, and the fact that those two didnt get their awards till 20 years later, and both posthumously, doesnt alter the fact one bit. Au contraire!

ALSO, I suppose you realize that if you hadn't written Ketti Frings that long, frank letter about her first too-happy, too-idyllic ending for the play, it might never have been the success that it has been. Or, if you dont realize it, please <u>do</u>!!

Ed dear, I hope this'll make you so happy that you'll get some reward from all of your exhaustion from it. But that you will also get <u>some</u> <u>rest</u>. I wont write any more now. But I did just want to say what was in my mind and heart. <u>Congratulations</u>.

And love
from
Liddy

[1] Nowell was congratulating Aswell on the news that Ketti Frings's stage adaptation of Wolfe's novel *Look Homeward, Angel* had just won a Pulitzer Prize. Mary Louise Aswell's views of Wolfe and Agee differed from Nowell's. As Mary Lou wrote, "the word *gigantism* seemed to apply (to Wolfe) as well as to his work. I liked him but I wasn't impressed by him. . . . And that had nothing to do with his manner or his out-size sloppiness. James Agee, whom I knew well when he was young, . . . was a premature beatnik in appearance but there was a fire and spirit in him that made me feel, 'Here is a genius.' I never felt that about Tom." (unpublished letter)

*

May 15, 1958

Dear Liddy:

Many thanks for your letter of May 7th, which accompanied seven new pages to be inserted at the beginning of Chapter IV of the biography.

It is remarkable that Pulitzer Prizes this year went to Tom's work and Jim Agee's, and that both of them are dead. I had forgotten that you knew Jim Agee, but it comes back now.

Praise is always sweet, and you say kind things so disarmingly that I almost believe them.

Since the death of Mrs. Lee, I have been up to my neck every night in correspondence with English lawyers, who can be exasperatingly tedious and evasive and slow.[1] It is a sure thing that Dickens did not make up what he wrote about the case of Jarndice vs. Jarndice. The same sort of thing still goes on. In trying to settle Nibs's estate, I now naturally need to know what things belonging to Mrs. Lee will now pass to Nibs's estate. But do you think I can get a simple answer of any kind to this simple question? Not yet.

Recently I made a distribution to Tom's heirs of slightly more than $40,000, this representing the net income of the Estate in the first three months of the year, most of the money, of course, having come from the play. Fred's share of this distribution was around $10,000. Yesterday I had a touching letter from him expressing "humble gratitude" and bemoaning the fact that Tom never had a chance to enjoy the fruits of his own labors. He mentioned the fact that only once in Tom's life had he had as much as $10,000, which had come from me — or rather, through me, from Harpers. Fred is a very fine person who has all the right instincts. Though his grammar may be shaky, his feelings are true.

Charlie Scribner tells me that the first printing of Ketti Frings' dramatization of LOOK HOMEWARD, ANGEL is about exhausted, and that he has gone back on press with a second printing. Strangely enough the book has had almost no reviews, and only one ad that I have seen, so I suppose it is making its way by word of mouth.

Ketti Frings will be in New York soon, and wants to talk to me about her next project. I have been trying to persuade her to do a dramatization of the second half of THE WEB AND THE ROCK, the love story. She has been re-reading the book, and will give me her answer when I see her.

I hope you are feeling better. As you say, I could use a bit of rest just now, but don't see any prospect of getting it. There was Helen's wedding last Saturday, and there are two commencements facing me early in June.[2]

They seem like hurdles to be got over. Maybe I can relax a bit after I have got over them. All my best.

Cordially,

Ed

P.S. Since dictating the above I have read the seven new pages, and think them very fine and true. This is the way Chapter IV should be rewritten. . . .

One important thought occurs to me, and it has probably already occurred to you:

As I told you, I think one thing that was wrong with your original treatment of the Tom-Aline love affair was that you quoted too largely from what Tom wrote about it in THE WEB AND THE ROCK. But there is other source material equally varied and wholly fresh which I think you should draw upon heavily. I am referring, of course, to Tom's letters to Aline. These you had largely to leave out of your book of letters because at that time Aline kept saying that she wanted to edit both sides of that correspondence and make a book of it herself, and God knows I encouraged her to do this right up to her death. After Aline died, I still thought it might be possible for someone, either you or me, to edit those letters, and as I must have told you, I talked a couple of times to Ethel Frankau, who was executor of Aline's estate. She was absolutely cold to the proposal, and refused to permit the publication of Aline's letters. Of course she has no control over the publishing of Tom's letters to Aline, and they are the more important side of the correspondence. So as I say, I think you should now draw very heavily on Tom's letters to Aline. Go just as far as you like, for there is of course no problem of permissions involved. . . .

On page 3A, there are two quotations from letters Aline wrote you. It will be necessary for you to get permission from Ethel Frankau, and I think she may be more likely to answer favorably if you write her than if I do. So why don't you have a try? . . .

At the end of this new section, you speak of Tom's drawing away from his mother, which coincided with the beginning of his relationship with Aline. You link the two things together, and I think correctly. But isn't there still another aspect of this matter which you do not mention? I am thinking particularly of the disparity between Aline's and Tom's ages. It has always seemed to me that just as Tom found a father-substitute in Max Perkins, so, at least in a sense, he also found a mother substitute in Aline. Tom's letters to his mother are one long cry, both for understanding and for financial support. He wanted desperately to make his mother realize that he wasn't wasting his time in trying to write instead of selling real estate. Mrs. Wolfe never did really understand this until after Tom

239

was dead, and then for the first time, being one of the beneficiaries of his will, she realized that Tom's writing was a source of income after all; and from then until her own death, Mrs. Wolfe played a new role she invented for herself of having been the primary one who had encouraged Tom in his career from the start. Of course this was sheer fantasy and self-justification, but she came to believe it firmly. As for Aline, and quite aside from the sexual relationship, she was precisely the kind of dream-mother he had wanted and never had, with her faith in him, her constant encouragement to go on, her knowledge of the world, her cooking for him and picking up after him, her efforts to bring order into his sprawling life, and of course added to all this, her financial support. If you agree with all this, then I think it is a point worth elaborating on, and so far as I know, no one has yet made it, and the point previously stated is this: it was Mrs. Wolfe's rejection of the creative urge in Tom, through lack of understanding, which made it inevitable that when Tom did fall really in love, the woman he chose had to be an older one, one who could have been his mother, and who brought to him all those qualities of understanding and sympathy which his mother had been unable to give him.

ECA

[1] Mrs. Lee was the mother of Aswell's late wife, so Aswell was faced with questions about both estates simultaneously.

[2] That spring in New York City, Helen, the younger of Aswell's two stepdaughters, married Roger Van Ghent, the son of literary critic Dorothy Van Ghent. The two commencements were those of Aswell's son, Duncan, from Harvard, and his daughter, Mary, from the Cambridge School of Weston.

*

June 20, 1958

Dear Ed:

About myself, I might be better and again I might be a good deal worse. At least that was the verdict that I got when I was down for another checkup while you were off on your vacation. The new x-rays showed considerable healing in the lesions of my bones — some bones — and 40% deterioration in some others since May 1st. We suspect the healing took place earlier, and the deterioration is the new trend now. Anyway I'm coming back for another checkup on July 20th, and can tell better then.

I have been fooling around with the biography, making some revisions on my own hook while I waited for you to get a chance to read it, but it isnt very satisfactory because mine may conflict with whatever you may find to ask for yourself. . . . I hope to finish this half-arsed revising of my own on the remaining few chapters in a few more days, but I have some days now when I feel too sick to be able to do any work.

Hint.

Ed darling, there are, I think, two ways to read a manuscript. One, to ask only for revisions which are absolutely necessary: two, to go through the thing with a fine-tooth comb and ask for everything that one can think of that might improve a book, often to the point of virtual collaboration. Well, bless you, I think you did the second kind on the first three chapters but if you can find it within your conscience and sense of rightness to lean more toward the first kind in the future, I think it would be better for your sake and mine. For one thing, I am working against time and death more unmistakably than anyone ever did. For another, you sometimes suggest things which are from your viewpoint, and not mine, and I think that is wrong — that my picture of Tom, right or wrong according to your lights, has got to come through in this simply because it is my picture and my book, and that your picture should be saved to come through your own book or article which you told me you were going to write. You didnt have that so definitely in mind when you made suggestions for the first three chapters but you do have it now. . . .

Guess this is all. Guess it is more than enough. I didnt say that I was glad you got through the two hurdles of commencement anyway: I know that you were sort of dreading them when you were so tired. I hope you arent so tired now. Guess Duncan will be home with you this summer which should be swell for you both, and I hope Mary too. If he wanted, I could write to the few really old good friends that I still have left at CSS — for instance Georgie Schieffelin, Charlie's cousin who owns as much (?) together with his mother, of the joint, but who was the one who asked me to whisper when I went to speak to him, evidently for fear of CS IV, and I said I would be goddamned if I would. Georgie is treasurer, I guess that is his title. But Duncan would probably rather die than have anyone write to anyone about him. I just wish him luck, and I do hope that there is enough of the old Scribners left so that working there will be the wonderful and happy experience that it was 30 years (!) ago for me. [1]

With love to all of you,

---

[1] Duncan, a recipient of a Woodrow Wilson fellowship for two years following his graduation from Harvard, became a reader for Scribner's "slush pile" that summer and the next. The job had considerable prestige, since Alan Paton's work had been part of that pile, and since readers attended weekly editorial meetings. Duncan continued his work in English as a graduate student at University of California, Berkeley.

*

June 26, 1956

Dear Liddy:

In response to your longer letter of June 20th and your telephone call yesterday, I am sending you herewith by first class mail chapters IV through XVI of Tom's biography — that is, the ribbon copy of these chapters. I have read almost all of them in a hurried way, but had meant to go over them again more carefully, taking notes. But I now agree with what you say in your letter, that the microscopic kind of editing which has usually been my way with books I genuinely care about is probably not applicable here, and is certainly not applicable in the present circumstances. So please transfer your corrections to the ribbon copy of the manuscript and send all the chapters back to me when you have done so.

I think there is also merit in your criticism of the questions I have raised and some suggestions I've offered. Certainly it was never my conscious purpose to try to take this book away from you or to impose on you any opinion of my own if it was contrary to your opinion. This book is yours, and the judgments and interpretations in it are also yours.

As you say, if I eventually write a reminiscent something about Tom as I knew him, as I hope to do, I can then say whatever I please, just as you can now.

The one emphatic thing I want to tell you is that this biography of yours represents a terrific achievement, is consistently interesting, will add vastly to what the world knows about Tom, and will make it unnecessary for anyone else to do a job on Tom for years to come. And the circumstances under which you have performed the task you set for yourself make the achievement all the greater and nothing short of miraculous. I am terribly distressed about you, but words fail me now. I shall just hope for a more favorable report when you come down for another checkup in July.

Much love,
Ed

*

June 28, 1958

Dear Ed:

Well, while I'm waiting for you to read the biography, would you be willing for me to take a running start into the Notebooks book? You know, you bought outright my rough-draft manuscript of same, together with all claims that I might have upon it, for three thousand bucks last year. . . .

In earlier discussion of this, you said you were reluctant to make any agreement about paying me royalties for the rough-draft manuscript because it might make it difficult for you to retain some person later to edit the actual book. Well, now that person would be me. Or it would be me as far as I could find the strength and health to go. I dont want to sound conceited, but you would have a tough time finding somebody to do the notebooks right. They need a mind-reader, an expert in illegible calligraphy, an expert on the unconscious, subconscious, creative mind of Thomas Wolfe, and the ghost of Wolfe himself (except that in a letter to Perkins he admitted that even he couldnt read some portions of the notebooks.) I am not pretending to be any of these things, but I <u>have</u> pored over the notebooks so long now that I have got the sense of them by a sort of osmosis. At least, when I have been rereading them lately I have found that I am pretty sure of lots of illegible and cockeyed passages that made no sense to me at first. Dick Kennedy would be the next best bet to me, if he hadnt moved to Wichita, or maybe even if he has. I dont think he would object to dividing royalties with me posthumously, but you might have someone else in mind, God knows who.

. . . . I am sorry that my rough draft manuscript is not final, complete draft. But when I made it I was hewing my way through impenetrable jungle: nobody knew then what the notebooks were, or when they were written, or what they said, or if they were merely worthless scribbling or could be made into a book. If the person you got to edit them lived right at Harvard, he could probably go to Houghton every day and recopy my manuscript with the missing material inserted, but most of it is the almost-illegible stuff which needs poring over carefully in the longhand copy, and I think that anyone, even if he did live at Harvard, could do this more easily at home. I must confess that I am no longer well enough to get up at 5:30, catch the milk train and work at Houghton all day long. If you thought that it would be up to me, because of this, to pay for the photostats, I guess I'd have to give up the whole idea, not that I was angry with you but simply that I have no money to expend. I don't know, I'd have to see.

Well, IF the things mentioned above could be ironed out, I would then apply for a Guggenheim on which to do the Notebooks book, although, between you and me, I'd start work on it long before the Guggenheim decisions were due. As you probably remember, we talked about this last year but we thought that the deadline for applying for Guggenheims was January 1st. It wasnt till December that I found that "the jockeying around for Guggenheims was now done in the summer" and the closing date for applications was in September or October, though the decisions are not made until the following March.

To tell you the truth, I doubt if I'll still be alive, or well enough to work, by March, 1959, but if anyone had told me last year that I'd still be alive now in June, 1958, I'd have told them they were crazy. The only thing to do is to live from day to day and get as much done as rapidly as I can, while I'm still able. If I apply for a Guggenheim, I'm going to tell them that I was found to have cancer in the Spring of 57, that I have had two operations to arrest it (really three, counting the unsuccessful one which had to be redone), and that if I should become too ill to complete my Fellowship Project I would immediately notify them so that they could call it off. I'll have to get Huggins or Adair [Nowell's doctors] to write and explain this to them, clinically.

As regular references, I thought I'd give you, Jack, Frere, and Nancy [Hale] if I need her too. You said last year that you would go and talk to Moe about me but if you're under such an awful strain, I think we'd better spare you on that and just ask you to write a letter. . . .

Ed darling, when you said on the phone: "I'm under terrific pressure all the time" I felt my heart turn over with sympathy for you and with hopelessness for me, and I thought, in one agonized flash, "Oh, I cant say anything to make that pressure worse". I hope this letter isnt going to make it worse, but the trouble is, I'm so <u>dependent</u> on you for all of this, and I really have to explain to you more fully about myself, rather than have it all sprung on you suddenly as an inescapable emergency later on.

What it amounts to is this: I am going to go into what is charmingly described by doctors as my "Agonal Period", sooner or later, when I wont be able to do anything at all except get the heaviest possible medication and the speediest possible oblivion in death. Nobody knows yet when that period will begin: it might start almost any time: it might not for a tear [sic]. But I am in a constant state of apprehension about it, and I am desperate to get the biography corrected and in galleys and read-in-them before I do.

Also, sooner or later, I am going to be desperate for money (a) to pay for any further possible treatments to delay my Agonal Period, and (b) to pay for nursing care and hospitalization when it can no longer be delayed. If I could get the biography into galleys, I was hoping to sell serial rights, preferably to the Reader's Digest, or, as a last resort to the Atlantic. (They both have asked to see it.) Or, if they both declined it, to go ahead with book publication in hopes that it might earn more than the advance before I die. It is all like "Jam yesterday, jam tomorrow, but never jam to-day." In other words, this seems my only hope of getting any money until posthumously, though posthumous money will, of course, help the kids a lot.

Well, forgive me, Ed, and I do want to spare you all I can. I wont say any more now, except Love from Liddy. [1]

[1] Nowell entered Memorial Hospital in New York on July 21, 1958. Shortly afterward, she wrote her daughter Clara an undated, longhand note, "I am sorry to dump so much on you but I am going to be awfully sick if they give me these chemicals & I might even die much faster than we thought. . . . I hope to rewrite the end of Chapter III after chemical treatment if well enough. If I don't make it, send Ch. III as is (ribbon copy) to Aswell together with the rest of book & ask him to get it into the proofs as fast as possible. But wait to see if I can rewrite III. Keep our carbon at home when (if) you send him ribbon copy."

But Nowell died at Memorial Hospital at 3:45 P.M., August 24th. Her daughter Clara finished typing the final manuscript and mailed it to Aswell, who wrote back on September 4th, "the original copy of your mother's biography of Thomas Wolfe is here, so you can rest easy in your mind knowing that it is safe. . . . I have taken a quick glance through the manuscript, and can see that you are right in saying that there is still work for me to do on it. Whatever needs to be done I shall do, with complete devotion to your mother's purposes, and with the expectation of publishing the book next year."

The month after this note was written, Aswell privately mourned the twentieth anniversary of Wolfe's death. One month later, fulfilling his own prophecy and in accordance with his own deeply held conviction that his death would complete a trilogy of deaths, he did indeed become the third "Wolfe" death that year — after Nowell in August and Mabel in September. Aswell died November 5th of a heart attack. At the time, he was editing a biography of Cardinal Spellman by the Reverend Robert Gannon. His ashes were scattered, at his request, by his son in the Lowell House courtyard at Harvard.

Thomas Wolfe: A Biography was offered as a Book-of-the-Month Club selection. The dust jacket on the volume reads, "Elizabeth Nowell, who spent many years compiling the material for this book, was Thomas Wolfe's literary agent and close friend. Her wish was that the attention given to her work be devoted entirely to her subject and not to her. But in simple justice it should be noted that only true heroism in the face of illness and impending death enabled her to complete this book."

Nowell's acknowledgments in the biography include these final thanks: "To . . . Edward C. Aswell, Administrator CTA of the Estate of Thomas Wolfe, for permission to quote freely from the unpublished writings of Wolfe, for his loyalty and devotion, and for his self-sacrificing expenditure of patience, strength, and time" (pp. 8–9).

Epilogue

THE TEDDY BEAR Thomas Wolfe gave my brother sat for years on my brother's window seat. I don't remember my brother playing with it, yet the thing looked remarkably played with, especially around the ears. It was large and tan. Its legs and arms moved easily and made straw noises. It had no name. Literary historians record the fact that the bear — for it *was* a bear, not a dog and not ugly as my father averred — was a Christmas present Wolfe had bought for Ed Aswell's son, age fifteen months. Growing up with the bear, I envied my brother that gift. I knew it was important. I also felt sorry for it and wanted to include it in the tea parties I held next door in my room with Sparkle Plenty, Brownie, and Janey. Somehow the bear, unplayed with and alone, assumed in my mind a mystique connected with the name "Thomas Wolfe."

Now, decades later, the bear becomes a symbol of one concrete object, fact, thing I can use to claim back a portion of my father's past with Wolfe. Other facts and things I remember about my father: his Southern superstition, his seersucker summer bathrobe, his Sunday night suppers of crackers and warm milk, his driving — a maddeningly unathletic affair, hands padding over and over themselves to round a corner carefully at minus three miles an hour. But about the place of Wolfe in my father's life I remember nothing. All those years I was growing up when he was writing Liddy Nowell, some of that writing done in the downstairs study of our home after his playing Mozart's "Turkish Rondo" on the baby grand: nothing. That year 1937–38 before I was born, when my father lived as he had never lived before because of Wolfe; tales around the table, perhaps? Nothing. Stories at Christmas time? Even later, when Mabel Wolfe's baskets of fruit would arrive at our doorstep? Nothing. As girl child, I was not privy to my father's memories of Wolfe. I came after the fact.

My father's curious silence to me about Wolfe, however, was consistent with his personality. He did not reveal the things closest to him. Although others saw him as amazingly cold, he was to me amazingly sentimental. Into a round of rounds I place what I can: a bear, some hunches, a memory.

Opening night of *Look Homeward, Angel* on Broadway, 1957. Thanksgiving time. Gala pre-theater party at someone's apartment in New York. Ladies in long dresses. Black tie. Food canapé style, circulated on trays by maids. William Saroyan over in the corner, surrounded by drunken

247

admirers. Ketti Frings, was she in spangles? Fred Wolfe, very tall, there; but Mabel not there because it was all too painful. My father. Later, after the play, lining up backstage just behind Audrey Hepburn, to shake Tony Perkins's hand. Wolfe and Perkins. A perfect circle.

In college the circle came around again. I was drawn to writing my senior thesis on Thomas Wolfe four years after my father's death. I read all of Wolfe, not so much to read Wolfe as to get a purchase on my father. In reading I found myself developing huge appetites (I, who, upon entering college, had to have appetite pills). I walked with gigantic steps and sought to devour the night. Wolfe opened me up and allowed what was buried to surface: the buried life. And in this new eating and walking I brought back images and sounds. I rediscovered something of my father's Thomas Wolfe, which to this day lives in me like a nighttime Turkish rondo.
Mary Aswell Doll
1987

*

THOMAS WOLFE was always there, even though for years I didn't know his name and didn't understand what he stood for in my mother's life. Later, after we had moved out of my father's house and into my grandmother's, he was still there, and I knew that he wrote books and what he looked like and that he was dead.

Mostly, at night, Wolfe would be there in the sound of my mother's typewriter coming from the back bedroom. She was writing letters, I guess, to people like Mabel Wheaton and Ed Aswell and Dick Kennedy and Nancy Hale and Vardis and hundreds of others whose names are still familiar to me though I never met them. Later, she was working on the Wolfe biography: more letters and the book itself. By now she was very sick, but the typing never stopped. It was the sound I fell asleep to for all the years I was a child, and by then I knew that, mostly, it had to do with Thomas Wolfe.

As I grew older, she took me places with her. We went to New York: John Hall Wheelock, the production of *Look Homeward, Angel,* the woman who'd lived upstairs at 114 East 56 Street and had the piano, Scribner's, Ed Aswell. We stayed at the Hotel Fairfax and looked across the vacant lot where her apartment and garden had been and where Thomas Wolfe must have visited many times.

We even went South, driving through Baltimore and Washington to Chapel Hill, where we stayed several days, but all I remember is a long white porch and walkways through a very green park. And then on to Asheville to see Myra Champion and Mabel and I don't know who else. By now, Thomas Wolfe was more real to me. Bigger than life. But mostly I remember standing at his grave and wondering where the angel was and, later on, standing on the porch outside of Mabel's back door and wondering what to do with the glass of milk that someone — Fred? — had given me. I never liked milk anyway, and this milk had a gray frosting of dust floating on its surface. Finally, I poured it onto the hydrangea by the porch, leaving just enough in the glass to look, I hoped, like the real thing.

So Thomas Wolfe was always there, even though for years I never read anything he'd written. I never read my mother's biography of him either, though I typed many parts of it which she sent me, bit by bit, from the hospitals where she was dying. Looking back, I know she was showing me her life and what she loved.

Clara Stites
1984

Index

Adair, Frank, 227, 244
Agee, James, 237
Albertson, Knyvett Lee. *See* Aswell, Knyvett Lee
Anderson, Sherwood, 92
Aswell, Anna Vera (Vaughn) (first wife), xii
Aswell, Charles (brother), 164, 167n
Aswell, Duncan (son), 90, 226, 240n.2, 241
Aswell, Edward McCoy: as administrator of Wolfe Estate, xi, xviii, 35, 102, 200; Boswell's journals project of, xviii, 28–29n, 88n, 212n.2; character, xi, 79–80n; and Charles Scribner III, 72, 87–88, 100–104, 106–7, 108–11; childhood, xii; death of, xviii, 245n; at Doubleday, xviii, 205, 213; early career, 103; editing of posthumous Wolfe manuscripts, xi, xvii, 44–45, 94, 96, 231–32n, 236–37n.2; first meeting with Wolfe, xv, 47, 91–92, 94; at Harper and Brothers, xiii, xviii, 44; at McGraw-Hill, xviii, 73n.2, 205, 211, 212n.2; marriages, xii-xiii, xviii, 183; Mary Aswell Doll on, 247–48; on Maxwell Perkins, 90, 93n.1, 104n, 143–52, 153n.3, 162, 167; sexual autobiography of, 205, 213–14n; Sir Joshua Reynolds's papers project of, 108; and Terry, 7, 11–16, 21, 38, 129, 132–53, 166–67; and Wolfe, xii, xvi, 5, 23, 93, 95, 97, 162; and Vardis Fisher, 50–51
Aswell, James (brother), 164, 167n
Aswell, Knyvett Lee (third wife), xviii, 224, 225, 226, 227n
Aswell, McCoy Campbell (father), xii
Aswell, Mary (daughter), 90, 204n.2, 241, 247–48
Aswell, Mary Louise (White) (second wife), xii–xiii, xviin.10, 47n, 183, 194, 236, 237n

"Author's Note" to *The Web and the Rock* (Wolfe), 24n.2

Baker, George Pierce, 107, 177–78
Baker, Mrs. George Pierce, 22
Barker, Lee, 213n
Basso, Hamilton, 157, 196, 198, 199n.1
Bell, Pearl Kazin, 236
"Bell Remembered, The" (Wolfe), xv
Berner, Mr. (a Doubleday attorney), 214, 215, 216, 217
Bernstein, Aline, 109, 141; correspondence with Wolfe, 7, 21–22, 23, 32, 33, 34, 40–41, 51, 64, 174, 178, 179, 187–88, 192, 193, 194, 195, 201–2, 203, 208, 209n.1, 212n.2, 239; death of, 188, 199; death of son, 23, 24n.1; as Esther Jack, 107–8, 111–12; suicide attempts, 118–19; and Wolfe, 172, 229, 231, 233n, 237, 239; Wolfe's break with, 169, 177–78, 207–8. Works: *The Journey Down*, 119; *Three Blue Suits*, 174, 175n
Bernstein, Edla, 199, 201, 231
Bernstein, Theo, 24n.1, 107, 111, 172
Bond, William, 17, 179, 180, 218
"Boom Town" (Wolfe), xiv, 194
Boyd, Madeleine, 141, 147–49, 152, 157
Boyle, Kay, xviii, 212n.2
Brewer, Alice Hedge, 224
Bridges, Robert, 62, 63n, 151
Brooks, Paul, 66, 91, 183
Burt, Struthers, 90–91, 93n.1, 96n, 134, 149, 150, 196, 223

Caldwell, Taylor, xviii, 212n.2
Campbell, Carrie, xii
Cane, Melville, 38, 189, 224; advice to Wolfe Estate, 122–23; and libel, 41, 51, 78, 79, 82, 83, 100–101, 108, 185, 214, 215; and Terry, 11, 14, 16, 33, 166
Capote, Truman, xviin.10

251

Cargill, Oscar, 97, 119–23, 173
Carswell, Mrs. Donald, 20
Casner, Jim, 224
Cathcart, Noble, 142
Champion, Myra, 40n, 249
Chase (NYU chancellor), 38
"Chickamauga" (Wolfe), 157
Chickering, Dr. (friend of Nowell), 182
"Child by Tiger, The" (Wolfe), xv
Coates, Albert, 38
Colton, Edward, 25–26, 113, 182, 185
"Company, The" (Wolfe), 15n
Coughlan, Robert, 199–200
Crichton, Kyle, 3

Dandy, Dr. (one of Wolfe's physicians), 68,
    143, 197, 235, 236n.2
Daniels, Jonathan, 142, 149
Darrow, Whitney, 100, 104, 106, 109; as
    characterized in Wolfe's writings, 150–51
Dashiell (head of *Scribner's Magazine*
    before Logan), 106
DeJong, David, 211
DeJong, Meindert, 211
De Voto, Bernard, xv, 223
DeVoy, S. Elizabeth, xiv, 60
Doll, Mary Aswell, 240n.2, 241, 247–48
Dooher, Muredach, 142, 149, 152, 153n.1,
    161n.2, 171
Dorman, Marjorie, 145–46
Dow, Robert Bruce, 121
Dows, Olin, 39, 40n

Ernst, Morris, 117, 146

Fairbanks, Marjorie, 65–66, 107, 111, 170,
    183
Ferguson, Charles, 223
Fisher, Opal, 51
Fisher, Vardis, 12, 92, 121, 211, 217, 249;
    Freudian theories of, about Wolfe, 32,
    48–51, 176; and Nowell, xvii, 48–50, 77
Fitzgerald, F. Scott: Wolfe and, 119, 143
Fleisher, Sidney, 19
Frankau, Ethel, 201–2, 203, 239
Frere, A. S., 20–21, 31, 244; and British
    rights to Nowell's *Letters*, 202–3n, 227
Frere Reeves. *See* Frere, A. S.
Frings, Ketti, 221, 228, 237, 238, 248

From Death to Morning (Wolfe), xiv–xv
Frothingham, Dr. (son-in-law of Maxwell
    Perkins), 119

Gable, Clark, 149
Gannon, Rev. Robert, 245n
Gilman (Scribner's employee), 60
Gold, Jay, 199
Gorsline, Douglas, 146
Gould, Elaine (Westall), 79
Griffith, Hugh, 228n
Grinnell, Sarah. *See* Nowell, Elizabeth
    Howland ("Liddy")

Hale, Nancy, xiv, xvii, 43, 60, 73, 244, 249
Harcourt, Alfred, 151–52, 158, 161n.6
Harding, Helen, 107, 111
Hart, Henry M., 183, 234
Hartman, Lee, 47
Hart, Mary, 183, 234
Helen (one of Aswell's stepdaughters),
    238, 239n.2
Hemingway, Ernest, 146
Henderson, Archie, 38
Hepburn, Audrey, 248
Hilles, Ted, 248
Hills Beyond, The (Wolfe), xvii, 8, 9nn.1, 3,
    63n, 151
Hoagland, Clayton, 12, 134n.1
Hoagland, Kathleen ("Kitty"), 134n.1,
    136, 137–38, 139, 153, 166
Hoeber, Paul, Sr., 234–35
Howland, Clara Earle, xiii, 192, 193–94
Huggins, Dr. (one of Nowell's physicians),
    244
Hurst, Fannie, xviii

"I Have a Thing to Tell You" (Wolfe), xv,
    94, 95
"In the Minute before It Would Strike"
    (Nowell), xviin.9
"I Wish I Was Back in Sugar Loaf"
    (Nowell), xviin.9

Jackson, William, A., 7, 152, 163, 170,
    173, 183
Jassinoff, Gwen, xvi
Jelliffe, Belinda, 59n, 147, 153n.5
Joffee, Eugene, xiv

Johnson, Josephine Winslow, 73n.2
Jones, Dan Burne, 170, 173
Jones, Howard Mumford, 69
Jones, James, 110
Journey Down, The (Bernstein), 119

K 19 (Wolfe), xiv, 198, 199
Kahler, Hugh, 193, 194
Kazin, Alfred, 76
Kelley, Judith, 92, 211
Kennedy, Richard S., xiv, 34n.2, 81, 132,
  155, 243, 249; on Aswell's editing of
  posthumous Wolfe manuscripts,
  231–32n; and Nowell, 70n; research of,
  on Wolfe, 27, 64, 69, 71, 97, 125, 163
Kinsey, Alfred, 214
Knopf, Alfred, 54n
Knopf, Blanche, 54n
Koch, Frederick H., 171

Laughton, Charles, 201n
Leavy, Mr. (consulted regarding libel), 184,
  185
Ledig-Rowohlt, Heinz, 218
Lee, Knyvett. *See* Aswell, Knyvett Lee
Lee, Mrs. (mother of Knyvett Lee Aswell),
  238, 239n.1
Lewis, Sinclair, 136
Lieber, Maxim, xiv, 20, 52; communist
  activities of, 61n.1
Linscott, Robert B., 52, 93n, 95
"Lion at Morning, The" (Wolfe), 64, 141
Logan (last head of *Scribner's Magazine*),
  103, 106
Log of a Voyage (Wolfe), 85n
Look Homeward, Angel (Wolfe), xiv, 50, 53,
  57, 59, 141, 148, 154, 190, 236; dramatic
  adaptation of, 221, 228, 231, 232n.2, 238
"Lost Boy, The" (Wolfe), xv
Luce, Clare, 149

McAffee, Miss (editor at *Yale Review*), 157
McCoy, George W., 15–16n, 97, 113, 115,
  116
McCullers, Carson, xviii.10
McGraw, Harold, 213
MacGregor, Frank, 109–10
Mannerhouse (play) (Wolfe), 37, 74
Marshall, Catherine, xviii, 212n.2

Masters, Edgar Lee, 10–11, 62, 65
Meade, Julian, 19
Meyer, Wallace, 196; as characterized in
  Wolfe's writings, 63n, 150, 161, 197
Miller, Ed, 197
"Miss Porter's Party" (Wolfe), 194
"Mr. Malone" (Wolfe), xv
Moe, Henry Allen, 66, 244
Muller, Herbert J., 8, 9n.1
Munn, James B., 18, 27, 34, 63, 69, 121

"No More Rivers" (Wolfe), xvii, 63n, 64,
  157–58, 161n.5, 197
"Note" to *The Hills Beyond* (Wolfe), xvii, 8,
  9n.3
Nowell, Elizabeth Howland ("Liddy"):
  character of, xiii; and Charles Scribner III,
  60, 97, 99–100, 110–11, 112, 127n.2;
  Clara Stites on, 249; concerns about libel,
  17, 22, 38n.1, 64, 99, 107–8, 170, 171,
  184–86, 206, 214–15, 218; death of,
  xviii, 245n; divorce of, xvii; education of,
  xiii–xiv; failing health of, xviii, 187, 196,
  205, 206, 207, 208n, 221, 222, 227, 240;
  first meeting with Wolfe, xiv, 61n.1; and
  Kennedy, 70n; and Lieber, 20, 60;
  marriage of, xvii; pen names of, xvii; and
  Perkins, 60, 75, 130, 154–58, 160; at
  Scribner's, xiv, 60, 61n.2, 176–77, 178,
  179; at *Scribner's Magazine*, xiv;
  signatures of, 19; and Terry, 11, 13–14,
  19–21, 154, 155–56; and Vardis Fisher,
  xvii, 48–50, 77; and Wheelock, 3, 127n.1;
  and Wolfe, xv, xvi, 34n.2, 97, 120–21,
  160. Works: "In the Minute before It
  Would Strike," xviii.9; "I Wish I Was Back
  in Sugar Loaf," xviii.9; "Standby," xviii.9
Nowell, Joseph Cornell (father), xiii

Of Time and the River (Wolfe), 64, 85n,
  107–8, 112, 141, 149, 154, 161n.3, 174,
  201n
"Old Man Rivers" (Wolfe), 62, 63n, 64, 65,
  151, 153n.6, 197
Oppenheim, E. Philips, 147, 148

Palffy, Countess Eleanor, 142, 153n.2, 155
"Party at Jack's, The" (Wolfe), xvii
Paton, Alan, 241

Pearce, Charles A., 52, 53, 150, 161n.6
Penniman, Joseph. *See* Nowell, Elizabeth Howland ("Liddy")
Perkins, Anthony, 228n
Perkins, Charles Brush (Nowell's former husband), xvii, 156
Perkins, Clara Howland. *See* Stites, Clara Howland (Perkins)
Perkins, Dr. (Nowell's father-in-law), 43
Perkins, Edna Brush (second daughter of Nowell), xvii, 19, 21, 42, 45, 86, 207, 225–26, 232
Perkins, Elizabeth Howland. *See* Nowell, Elizabeth Howland ("Liddy")
Perkins, Liddy. *See* Nowell, Elizabeth Howland ("Liddy")
Perkins, Louise, 75, 91, 146
Perkins, Maxwell E., 51, 103, 211, 236; as administrator of Wolfe Estate, 3, 74, 102, 200; Aswell on, 104n, 143–52, 153n.3, 162, 167; collection of Wolfe letters of, xvii, 7, 16, 33–34, 44, 166; daughters of, as characterized by Wolfe, 146, 153n.4; death of, 101, 105; and Dorman libel suit, 145–46; Nowell on, 75, 91, 106, 154–56, 160; and Terry's planned biography of Wolfe, 5, 11, 129, 133, 136, 137–38, 144–45, 179; Vardis Fisher on, 48–50; and Wolfe, 76n; on Wolfe, 68, 129–30, 136, 139–53, 156, 161n.1; Wolfe's break with, 9, 10n, 63n, 90–91, 93n.1, 141–42, 146, 151–52, 158, 161nn.5, 6, 169, 177–78, 197–98; as Foxhall Edwards, 129, 143, 150
Perkins, Tony, 248
Pinker, Eric, 147, 148
Pollock, Thomas Clark, 18, 122, 123, 173
Powell, Desmond, 121
Preston (Wolfe bibliographer), 69

Raisbeck, Kenneth, 107
Randall, David A., 8, 22, 138, 139n
Rascoe, Burton, 176
Return (Wolfe), 85n, 173, 174n
Reynolds, Paul, 213n
River People, The (Wolfe), 40n, 64
Roberts, Mrs. J. M. (Margaret), 11, 19, 58
Roosevelt, Theodore, 102
Root, Elihu, Jr., 102

Ruge, Dr. (one of Wolfe's physicians), 229 233–34

Saroyan, William, 33, 34, 247
Saxton, Eugene, 92
Sayre, Joel, 39, 40n
Schieffelin, George, 241
Schorer, Mark, 180
Scribner, Charles, III, 4, 43, 52, 57, 77, 81, 99, 100n; and Aswell, 100–104, 106–7, 108–11; character of, 101–7; death of, 97, 99–100, 105, 108–9; and Nowell, 97, 110–11, 112, 127n.2
Scribner, Charles, Jr., 89, 99, 100n, 104, 132, 134; and Aswell, 72, 87–88; and Nowell, 86, 97, 116–17, 124n, 126, 127n.2, 189
Scribner family, 100n
Scribner, Mrs. Charles, III, 105, 116
Sedgwick, Ellery, xii, 192, 194
Smith, Abe, 119
Smith, Cecil Woodham, 212n.2
Smith, Harrison, 90
Stafford, Jean, xviin.10
"Standby" (Nowell), xviin.9
Stanley (Scribner's shipping clerk), 60
"Statement, A" (Wolfe), 35, 44
"Statement of Purpose" (Wolfe), 44–45, 46
Stern, Martha Dodd, 18n
Stites, Clara Howland (Perkins) (first daughter of Nowell), xvii, 45, 245n, 249; education of, 86, 218n, 225–26
Storch, Arthur, 228n
Story of a Novel, The (Wolfe), xv, 57, 141, 194
Swift, Dr. (one of Wolfe's physicians), 233–34, 235

Terry, Harvey, 138
Terry, John S., 16–17, 19–20, 21, 25, 48; death of, 129, 131, 132; as Jerry Alsop, 133, 134n.2, 137, 143, 144, 156; Nowell's distrust of, 116, 154–55; and planned biography of Wolfe, 7, 11, 37–38, 67, 97, 133–34, 140–41, 142, 143–44, 146, 149, 152; selection of, as Wolfe biographer, 5, 8n, 11, 133, 136, 137–38, 156, 160, 166–67; Wolfe and, 156, 161n.2, 171; Wolfe papers of,

(Terry, John S., *continued*)
13–14, 16–17, 33, 131–32, 134–35, 137–39, 144, 153, 179
Tindall, William Y., 121

Van Fleet, Jo, 228n
Van Ghent, Dorothy, 240n.2
Van Ghent, Roger, 240n.2
Vaughn, Anna Vera, xii
Vaughn, Hilda, 96n
Volkening, Henry, 57, 121, 136, 144

Walser, Richard, 71
Walton, Edith Howard, xivn.4
Watt, Homer A., 18, 19n.2, 121
Watts, Dr. (one of Wolfe's physicians), 233
Web and the Rock, The (Wolfe), xvi, xvii, 9n.1, 15–16n, 107–8, 201n, 231, 236, 238, 239
Weeks, Edward, 192, 200, 218, 226
Welcome to Our City (play) (Wolfe), 37, 38, 74, 75, 79
Welty, Eudora, xviin.10
Western Journey, The (Wolfe), xvi–xvii, 85
Wheaton, Mabel (Wolfe) (sister), 39, 115, 126, 175, 178–79, 180, 207, 224–25, 247, 249; character of, 190–91; correspondence with Wolfe, 13–14, 16, 24, 28, 31, 33, 34, 45, 131, 192; death of, 245n; fondness for funerals, 135; offer of financial assistance to Nowell, 202, 204; and Terry's planned biography of Wolfe, 12–14, 38, 97, 172, 173; and Wolfe's last illness, xvi, 235, 236
Wheaton, Ralph: as Randy Shepperton, 15
Wheelock, John Hall, 117, 125, 189, 244; and death of Charles Scribner III, 99, 100; health of and choice of his successor at Scribner's, 103, 104, 107; and Nowell, 3, 60, 127n.1; and Nowell's *Biography*, 112, 114, 169, 175, 176n; and Nowell's *Letters*, 7, 50, 52, 57, 78, 81, 82, 84, 87–88; and Nowell's work on Wolfe notebooks, 88, 89; and Terry's planned biography of Wolfe, 16, 138
White, Mary Louise. *See* Aswell, Mary Louise (White)
Wilcox, Charles, 60
Wilson (Harvard University Press editor), 68, 69, 71
Winter, Ella, 92
Wolfe, Ben (brother), 40
Wolfe, Frederick W. (brother), 126, 150, 172, 173, 180, 234, 235, 238, 248; concerns about family reputation, 24–25, 190–91; as Randy Shepperton, 15n; and Terry's planned biography of Thomas Wolfe, 12, 97; and Wolfe family correspondence, 13–14, 15, 27, 34, 39, 40
Wolfe, Julia E. (mother), 13, 235, 236; separation from William O. Wolfe, 209, 210; and Terry's planned biography of Thomas Wolfe, 12, 139, 156; and Thomas Wolfe, 239–30
Wolfe, Mabel. *See* Wheaton, Mabel (Wolfe)
Wolfe, Thomas: relationship with Aline Bernstein, 21–23, 41n, 107–8, 111–12, 169, 177–78, 197, 207–8, 229, 231, 232, 233n, 237, 239; birth of, xii; Aswell and, xii, xv, xvi, 5, 23, 97, 162; break with Perkins and Scribner's, xv, 9, 10n, 63n, 90–91, 93nn.1, 2, 141–42, 146, 150, 151–52, 158, 160, 161nn.5, 6, 169, 177–78, 197–98, 207; character of, 61, 177–78n, 184, 207–8n.1; and communism, 20, 24, 85n, 155; correspondence with Aline Bernstein, 7, 21–22, 23, 32, 33, 34, 40–41, 51, 64, 174, 179, 187–88, 192, 193, 194, 195, 201–2, 203, 208, 209n.1, 212n.2, 239; death of, xvi, 143, 197–99, 236; and Frere, 20; and Harcourt Brace, 52–53; and Julia Wolfe, 239–40; last illness of, xvi, 99, 233–36; libelous or pornographic writings of, 17–18, 22, 61, 107–8, 171, 214–15; and Maxwell Perkins, 48–49, 76, 153, 197–98; and Nowell, 160; story of, on murder of Budapest antique shop woman, 132, 155; at NYU, 120–21; and Terry, 156, 161n.2, 171; Vardis Fisher on, 32, 48–49, 51; working habits of, xvi, 9n.2, 64. Works: "The Bell Remembered," xv; "Boom Town," xiv, 194; "Chickamauga," 157; "The Child by Tiger," xv; "The Company," 15n; *From Death to Morning*, xiv–xv; *The Hills Beyond*, xvii,

(Wolfe, Thomas, *continued*)
8, 9nn.1, 3, 63n, 151; "I Have a Thing to Tell You," xv, 94, 95; *K 19,* xiv, 198, 199; "The Lion at Morning," 64, 141; *Log of a Voyage,* 85n; *Look Homeward, Angel,* xiv, 50, 53, 57, 59, 141, 148, 154, 190, 236; *Look Homeward, Angel* (dramatic adaptation), 221, 228, 231, 232n.2, 238; "The Lost Boy," xv; *Mannerhouse* (play), 37, 74; "Miss Porter's Party," 194; "Mr. Malone," xv; "No More Rivers," xvii, 63n, 64, 157–58, 161n.5, 197; "Note" to *The Hills Beyond,* xvii, 8, 9n.3; *Of Time and the River,* 64, 85n, 107–8, 112, 141, 149, 154, 161n.3, 174, 201n; "Old Man Rivers," 62, 63n, 64, 65, 151, 153n.6, 197; "The Party at Jack's," xvii; *Return,* 85n, 173, 174n; *The River People,* 40n, 64; "A Statement," 35, 44; "Statement

of Purpose," 44–45, 46; *The Story of a Novel,* xv, 57, 141, 194; *The Web and the Rock,* xvi, xvii, 9n.1, 15–16n, 107–8, 201n, 231, 236, 238, 239; *Welcome to Our City* (play), 37, 38, 74, 75, 79; *The Western Journey [A Western Journal],* xvi–xvii, 85; "A Working Girl in New York," 214; *You Can't Go Home Again,* xvii, 8, 15–16n, 23, 24n.2, 45, 64, 92, 94, 95, 96, 116, 153n.4, 201n
Wolfe, William Oliver (father), 209, 210
Wright, Richard, xviii
Wyckoff, Irma, 24, 28, 46, 140, 141

You Can't Go Home Again (Wolfe), xvii, 8, 15–16n, 23, 24n.2, 45, 64, 92, 94, 95, 96, 116, 153n.4, 201n

Zyve, Claire Turner, 137